READING FOUCAULT
for Social Work

Adrienne S. Chambon

Allan Irving

Laura Epstein

EDITORS

COLUMBIA UNIVERSITY PRESS

NEW YORK

COLUMBIA UNIVERSITY PRESS
Publishers Since 1893
New York   Chichester, West Sussex

Chapter 4 originally appeared in the journal *Esprit* in the special issue "Pourquoi
le Travail Social," April–May 1972 (vol. 4–5, no. 413), pp. 678–703. Reprinted by
permission.

Library of Congress Cataloging-in-Publication Data
Reading Foucault for social work / Adrienne S. Chambon, Allan Irving,
and Laura Epstein, editors.
p.   cm.
Includes bibliographical references and index.
ISBN 0–231–10716–1 (cloth).— ISBN 0–231–10717–x (pbk.)
1. Foucault, Michel—Contributions in social service. 2. Social service—Philosophy.
I. Chambon, Adrienne S., 1949– .   II. Irving, Allan.   III. Epstein, Laura.
HV40.R345   1999
361—dc21   98–30255

∞

Casebound editions of Columbia University Press books are printed on permanent
and durable acid-free paper.
Printed in the United States of America

c 10 9 8 7 6 5 4 3 2 1
p 10 9 8 7 6 5 4

Books are to be returned on or before
the last date below.

**7–DAY
LOAN**

*To Laura Epstein, who opened the doors
and forged the way*

Writing and assembling this book was made especially pleasant by the friendly presence of many individuals who encouraged and supported us along the way. We shared our ideas with them, and they in turn raised intriguing questions that led us to refine and sometimes revise our approach.

We thank our students at the University of Toronto who responded enthusiastically to our early attempts at connecting Foucault with social work practice and research, in particular Adrienne Chambon's class, Epistemology-Methodology, and Allan Irving's class, History and Philosophy of Social Work. Victor Marshall and the Institute for Studies of the Life Course and Aging at the University of Toronto provided an opportunity to present some of this work, as did Monica Heller of CREFO, the Franco-Ontarian teaching and research unit of the Ontario Institute for Studies in Education of the University of Toronto. Participants at the Foucault Symposium of the 1997 Meeting of the Orthopsychiatry Association equally contributed. All these arenas afforded occasions to think through the relevance of Foucault to the times.

We are grateful to a number of colleagues for their thoughtful engagement with the ideas recurrent in the book: the friends and readers of Laura Epstein's work—Peggy Rosenheim of the University of Chicago School of Social Service Administration and Patrick Selmi of the School of Social Work at Syracuse University who shared numerous discussions with Laura Epstein and helped her hone her thinking; at the University of Toronto, Mariana Valverde of the Centre of Criminology, Ann Robertson of Behavioral Sciences, and Pat McKeever of the Faculty of Nursing; and Amy Rossiter at York University's School of Social Work. A friendly acknowledgment to Sylvie Janson of the Canadian Broadcasting Corporation for her warm welcome and absorbing questions about the everydayness of Foucault's thought as it applies to drastically changed work conditions and the spirit of the troubled times.

Particular thanks must go to the Foucault study group, a spontaneous grassroots gathering that met periodically to conduct close readings of Foucault's works and to debate their implications for the transformations of the welfare state. Group members' careful questioning provided a supportive environment for this quest. They identified what was understandable in Foucault and what was not; they shared their immediate responses and explored potential linkages with current social events and broad societal reorganization. Alternating between puzzlement and excitement, they developed a range of opinions and arguments. Group members commented reflectively on early drafts of what later became chapters in the book. These discussions kept our feet on the ground while we explored ideas with caring, respect, and a healthy dose of bantering. In addition to Ken Moffatt, Carol-Anne O'Brien, and Frank Wang, all of whom contributed to the book, we would like to recognize the thoughtful comments of Susan McGrath of the School of Social Work at York University; Jane McMichael of the Department of Social Work at Lakehead University; Ian Morrison, executive director of the Clinic Resource Office of the Ontario Legal Aid Plan; Donna Baines of the School of Social Work at Dalhousie University; and Lea Caragata at Wilfrid Laurier University's Faculty of Social Work. The Social Planning Council of Toronto provided a welcoming space and coffee for some of our discussions in a surrounding that spoke of social commitment when that commitment and the council are under severe pressure.

A number of people left their imprint on this project. Dean Jeanne Marsh of the University of Chicago School of Social Service Administration saw the value of such an enterprise and encouraged the development of this project. A number of lectures and symposia organized by the School of Social Service Administration proved to be fertile ground for our efforts. During these events Laura Epstein presented early versions of her major rethinking about social work. Lester Brown, of the Department of Social Work at California State University at Long Beach and the executor of Laura Epstein's estate, made available to us without hesitation the many drafts of Laura's manuscripts and other archival material from her personal papers. We appreciate the fine eye he demonstrated in sifting through the mass of her papers and knowing which were the right ones to send us. His generosity, warmth, and participation have been most welcome, and the task could

not have been completed without his help. Judith Revel of the University of
Rome III and a member of the Centre Michel Foucault in Paris steered us to
critical materials, including the original French publication of the "Roundtable on Social Work," which appears in the book in translation; Mireille de
Sousa of the journal *Esprit* greatly facilitated the granting of permission to
reprint the original material in translation. The Centre Michel Foucault and
the Bibliothèque du Saulchoir in Paris, former archive for Foucault's papers,
have both been useful resources.

Thanks to José San Pedro, who one summer displayed an astonishing
energy in hunting up hundreds of references to Foucault. Frank Wang
assisted in knitting the project together; at crucial junctures he often came
up with new equilibriums. A meticulous but generous reviewer for Columbia University Press brought to the fore the challenge of making our text
readable. She left no stone unturned as she scrupulously assessed each chapter. Her determined pursuit of coherence and readability improved the initial manuscript tremendously. The book further benefited from the light,
precise, and humane touch of Polly Kummel, the Press's copyeditor. After
she worked her magic, the manuscript seemed to have a newfound elegance.
Centrally, the making of this book and our peace of mind were enhanced
constantly by the unwavering support of John Michel, senior editor at
Columbia University Press. It all seemed possible under his direction and the
way ahead certain. His wonderful humor, enthusiasm, and guiding hand
carried us along as the book lurched its way to completion.

Finally, we thank our partners, Daniel and Dianne, for the many hours
of discussion, sometimes over drinks and dinner, about Foucault and wild
Foucauldian imaginings. Thank you too to Bea and little Dylan who has
stepped on and jumped off many versions of the manuscript, bringing home
to us that Foucault can only be understood through the body.

After these joined efforts the unexplored areas of darkness that remain
are all our own.

Introduction

Adrienne S. Chambon and Allan Irving

The social work profession is being challenged today to adapt to changing sociocultural circumstances and to carve out a new societal niche. This volume is driven by all the changes being wrought in society by new technologies and by the globalization of markets. The cultural and economic effects of those changes are causing the reformulation of the welfare states in the developed countries. Because the modern identity of social work has been tied closely to the various welfare systems, the discipline is bound to respond to all forthcoming changes.

The work of Michel Foucault offers a particularly relevant means for examining such indeterminacies and cultural transformations and for revisiting social work's mission, activities, and objectives. More than any other modern social theorist, Foucault helps us understand the rules that have developed for enabling experts in any field to practice their discipline. His work is enlightening about how the ideas that guide professional practices come into existence and how they acquire power. This book is meant to offer social work such a set of lenses.

An important tribute goes to Laura Epstein, who initiated this journey, lit the first spark as she was known to do, and expected us to carry it through. She was a major architect of this project. Sadly, she passed away in September 1996.

In the last ten years of her life, Laura had embarked on a highly significant program of scholarship, nothing less than a critical reexamination of the field of social work in North America and its underlying assumptions, by one of its major contributors. For her the writings of Michel Foucault had become a major reference because of the historical approach he used to deconstruct the helping professions and the social sciences, and particularly for his pungent analyses of medical and therapeutic conduct. She would often comment on the debt she owed Foucault, the continuous source of inspiration he had been for her over the years, and the influence he had exercised even on her writing style. The work of Foucault had become central in her research, and there were signs that others in social work were starting to pick it up as well.

Michel Foucault has been one of the most influential intellectual figures of the twentieth century, and his vast reach extends across many disciplines. Foucault saw himself primarily as a philosopher, and our intention is for this book to be a signal to begin the move away from the kind of academic carpentry that is all too prevalent in academic social work and toward a much more penetrating and thorough analysis of significant philosophical issues. We envisaged a book that might even take us occasionally to the chill brink of the inconceivable, that would disconcert and agitate. Our view is that the task of the theorist is not always to offer sensible guidance on the conduct of practice but to test and challenge the boundaries of our vision. Theory should be radical, probing, and immoderate. It is when we allow our thinking to be fearless, to encounter philosophical extremities, that we have the best chance of understanding the world at a deep level.

Over the years philosophy had become very important for Laura Epstein, and she more and more came to feel that "philosophical explorations are long overdue in social work, which has historically fitted itself to prevailing views with little if any questioning" (1996:114). New perspectives in the social sciences are introducing alternative bases of knowledge, and we cannot stay at a distance, safely in our cocoon:

> Contemporary debates involve, among other things, issues about the differences between 'modern' and 'postmodern' attitudes toward knowledge and their values and roles in creating progress. Many intellectuals sense the emergence of a postmodern attitude that challenges the received wisdom of traditional science with its expectation of continuous improvement and progress. *(115)*

Debating the scientific orientation of social work practice, she further argued:

> Efficient and effective practice might produce good outcomes. That idea was a product of its time. History is transforming the original aim of this idea, just as it is now transforming social work. We are entering

a new era in social work in which the need has never been greater for excellent thought. What we have gained during the process of developing the idea of scientific practice ought to be capable of being adapted to the emerging scene. We need to develop a different set of themes to help us enter the new era, in which repetition of the old themes no longer will do.   *(117)*

A Critical Perspective

In an earlier collaborative volume, *Essays on Postmodernism and Social Work* (1994), we pointed to new directions and dilemmas for discussing the status of knowledge in social work. This brief collection of papers was the product of a workshop held in 1993 at the University of Toronto, edited by Adrienne S. Chambon and Allan Irving, with the lead paper—"The Therapeutic Idea in Contemporary Society"—written by Laura Epstein (see Epstein 1994). It was a jumping-off place, as it identified certain parameters with which to question established certainties. *Reading Foucault for Social Work* takes up, in part, where the *Essays* left off. Expanding upon one facet, it introduces to a social work audience a key author in critical theory outside social work, for whom there is growing interest in the field, and explores the relevance of his questioning for the discipline.

Self-questioning is not new to the profession. Social work has historically changed directions and periodically revisited its practice orientations and its knowledge base, often with vehement debates to contest and redirect its identity. What follows is a brief review meant to situate the critical Foucauldian approach with regard to existing interrogations in the field.

A major concern often heard is that social work, over time, has relinquished its social justice mission and moved away from social reform and the redress of inequities. Theoretical responses to this question have ranged from radical structural critiques, as exemplified in the earlier work of Bailey and Brake (1975), to the promotion of philosophical notions to sustain practice, such as the principle of "distributive justice" (Wakefield 1988) or, in more ethical terms, the adoption of such notions as "public good," equating the professional stance with that of the "moral citizen" (Manning 1997).

The responsiveness and responsibilities of our field have been greatly enhanced by the development of differentiated knowledge. Extensions have included critical feminist analyses of the meaning of *care* and the place of social work and social welfare (Abramovitz 1988, 1996; Baines, Evans, and Neysmith 1991; Collins 1990), and concepts of "dual perspective" and "empowerment"—introduced by black scholars to address the collective reality of oppression and its counterpart in the professional relationship (Norton 1978; Solomon 1976; Pinderhughes 1989).

Within a historical perspective, Specht and Courtney's recent moral admonishment in *Unfaithful Angels* (1994) challenged social work to reclaim its historical roots and stay committed to work with disenfranchised populations at the grassroots level instead of promoting psychotherapy for middle-class clients. Alternatively, from a classical economic and political viewpoint, Wenocur and Reisch (1989) have argued that the agenda of the profession and its strivings for professionalization can be thought of as an "enterprise" aimed at power and prestige and at keeping control over its domain. By its nature, this enterprise conflicts with its social justice mission.

On yet another front, a questioning of the scientific imperative in professional knowledge has sparked a different debate. As early as 1981 Heineman thus challenged the empiricist and logical positivist model as a unitary norm (see Irving 1992; Peile 1988; Witkin 1991). This resulted in the deployment of alternative epistemologies that are interpretive, hermeneutical, or heuristic (Cohler 1988; Tyson 1995; Weick 1987; "Philosophical issues" 1991). In reviewing the historical shifts in orientation since the days of Mary Richmond, Howard Goldstein (1990) argued that the roots of social work were humanistic and that adopting an interpretive turn would be more consistent with recent developments in the social sciences. This discussion continues today as adamantly as before, as can be seen in the debate about the empirical practice movement in the *Social Service Review* (see Reid 1994 and "Debates with Authors" 1995), and in *Social Work Research*'s issues on qualitative methods ("Book Forum" 1995) and on the scientist-practitioner ("Book Forum" 1996).

Although a Foucauldian approach is concerned with issues of power, exclusion, and marginalization and the nature of knowledge, it also introduces a radical difference by questioning what has become self-evident in knowledge and practice. A recent trend in social work is more clearly affiliated with his project. We can group a number of social work writings dealing with postmodern, poststructuralist theories and the construction of meaning as so many conjoined attempts to deconstruct and reorient some of the professional claims well established in policy and practice.

In this perspective professionals exercise power upon clients by imposing a particular truth. Relevant contributions range from Dorothy Scott's

1989 arguments on the construction of meaning in social work, and its follow-up in Joan Laird's 1993 edited volume on social work education, to Dennis Saleeby's 1994 views that locate social work practice at the intersection of diverse and often divergent cultural meaning systems (or narratives) enacted by worker and client (see also Paré 1995). Because these scholars see expert truth as just one truth among many, their writings encourage workers to relinquish a position of certainty (Pozatek 1994) and to strive to understand the Other, whether in ethnic or racial terms or in other ways (Greene, Jenson, and Jones 1996). These writers redefine the professional task as a reconstruction of meaning (see also Pardeck, Murphy, and Choi 1994) that incorporates previously silenced meaning.

Generally, critical visibility has been given to considering the exercise of power as an integral part of the profession. Drawing from bell hooks's challenge to domination, Ann Hartman's July 1993 editorial in *Social Work* placed power and political considerations as central to all levels of practice.

On the clinical front, psychotherapy has been influenced lately by the field of cultural studies, in which Foucault is a prominent reference (e.g., Flaskas and Humphreys 1993; Madigan 1992; Redekop 1995; White 1993; White and Epston 1990). The family therapy literature now is heavily involved in discussing the discursive power of practitioners in their encounters with clients and the diffuse domination of institutional discourse (e.g., Hare-Mustin 1994), with parallels drawn with the "colonizing of the other" through expert knowledge (Amundson, Stewart, and LaNae 1993).

At the organizational and policy levels, in view of the considerable restructuring and reorganization of human services, McBeath and Webb (1991) point to a postmodern logic of management characterized by decentered rationality, fragmented practices and knowledge, and the dispersal of the individual subject. In a related sense, de Montigny's 1995 study of the discursive practices supporting child protection, published in the same year as the agency-based archival work conducted in England by Cree within a Foucauldian perspective, started to examine how administrative requirements intrinsically shape the daily practice of workers. For his part, through a history of the changing discourse of child protection in England, Parton (1991) analyzed today's location of social work as a response to complex transformations in the management of care and as an outcome of major shifts in political power and in the state (see also Parton 1994a, 1994b).

Consistent theories of knowledge have also appeared, such as the poststructuralist and deconstructionist feminist theories introduced in social work by Sands and Nuccio (1992). Equally inspired by critical feminist theory, Jane Gorman's 1993 article on postmodern social work research transformed the meaning of the research activity to that of a local encounter. From a didactic perspective Rossiter (1996) discusses social work teaching and argues that the "end of innocent knowledge" creates a new responsibility for practitioners and social work educators to produce alternative cultures.

At a metatheoretical level Peter Leonard (1996) has argued that despite their vast differences, the three main social work theories (American casework, British social administration, and Marxist social work) share a number of problematic modernist assumptions about progress, belief in science, control over others, and expert knowledge. Although he positioned himself within a critical postmodern consciousness, Leonard (1994) proposed the reconstruction of the modernist project as an active means of resistance to the current conditions.

Where does this book stand in this constellation of critical studies? In broad terms it stands as a critical reexamination of practices, institutional arrangements, and knowledge in social work through the complex prism of Foucault's writings and various reinterpretations of them. We argue in favor of critical reflexiveness and the examination of unexamined truths, which is consistent with Witkin and Gottschalk's statement that

> Social science and its products are infused with moral and political assumptions. As such, science can be used to provide 'objective truth status' to dominant societal beliefs, or to increase awareness of the processes by which knowledge is created and validated. . . . Critical reflexive theory has a liberating potential because it attempts to expose unquestioned, inherited truth, and proposes alternative conceptualizations. *(1988:218)*

We believe that Foucault's work has the potential to help us step back and reconsider the unexamined rationalities of our profession. Foucault's work is widely referenced, but it is not easy to grasp. To have a fuller understanding of the kind of fundamental questioning it raises, and to be able to draw from it in practice, requires a prolonged exposure.

A Foucauldian Text for Social Work

Writing a Foucauldian text poses a unique set of difficulties. Foucault's work cannot be summarized in unidimensional terms or collapsed into a convenient blueprint. Foucault critiqued facile ways of understanding that turn knowledge in general into slogans. In a 1983 interview he said of his work:

> When I read—and I know it has been attributed to me—the thesis, "knowledge is power" or "power is knowledge" I begin to laugh, since studying their *relation* is precisely my problem. If they were identical, I would not have to study them and I would be spared a lot of fatigue as a result. The very fact that I pose the question of their relation proves clearly that I do not *identify* them.   *(Foucault 1983:210)*

Multiplicity and complexity were central to Foucault's work. Aiming to avoid easy simplifications, we do not provide a recipe that we then apply to various domains. Instead, we propose multiple readings of Foucault's work. The contributors to this volume are not all saying the same thing, but what they say is relevant. Each emphasizes a different set of concepts and highlights a particular slice of Foucault's writings.

The book does not attempt to develop consecutive arguments. It navigates around its topics, adopting different approaches in each chapter. Each arrival or point of destination can in turn become a point of departure. We hope that the work presented here will free us from categorical and teleological thinking, a freeing that is necessary if the field of social work is to survive the torrents of postmodernity.

The book is laid out in two parts. The first part sets the stage in broad strokes, with four complementary chapters. In the second part our goal is to illustrate the wider applicability of Foucauldian thought to specific arenas of knowledge and practice in social work.

In part 1, Laura Epstein's chapter, "The Culture of Social Work," asks us to turn our gaze upon our profession and points the way to a truly Foucauldian project for social work. She sets out to inquire into the origins of the main ideas of the social work profession. Highlighting Foucault's contribution, she defines a framework that retraces some of the historical strands that have made social work what it is today, unencumbered by the many myths that surround it.

This piece of work stems directly from her "Origins" project, the central scholarly work in which she was immersed before she died. In chapter 1 she develops a brilliant exposé of the rationale for such a project and a way of thinking that sustains it. She outlines some of its major building blocks and illustrates the approach in a cogent analysis of the influential work of Charlotte Towle. The chapter as it stands is a reconstruction by Adrienne Chambon of Epstein's work in progress. It is based on her most recent manuscript, and at her request it has been complemented—sparingly—with additional sources from her personal papers.

In chapter 2, "Waiting for Foucault: Social Work and the Multitudinous Truth(s) of Life," Allan Irving explores the influence of the philosopher Friedrich Nietzsche and the playwright and novelist Samuel Beckett on Foucault's thought. All three developed their ideas and interpretations of the world outside the Cartesian/positivist paradigm through a quest that is often tortured and full of struggle. Irving discusses the implications for social work. Foucault's voice as a philosopher comes through, with Irving showing how Foucault overturns two sorts of certainties: an external empirical reality to be perceived and counted and an internal certainty about a solid subjectivity. Through these newfound uncertainties Foucault reorganizes the relationship between the two planes.

Adrienne S. Chambon's chapter, "Foucault's Approach: Making the Familiar Visible," offers directions for a social science reading of Foucault's work. Chapter 3 is a detailed exploration of Foucault's practice of generating knowledge, examining some of the mechanisms and concepts that he developed, including his historical-genealogical analysis and empirical documentation of micropractices, and his explorations of the relation between subjectivity and institution. She stresses how the Foucauldian project is meant to unsettle the foundations of a field and the challenge of importing it into our discipline. She highlights anticipated and unexpected areas of convergence and divergence with social work ways of knowing and suggests new lines of investigation.

Chambon also analyzes Foucault's writing style (drawn largely from the literary) for its contribution to the project of transformation in a research perspective. She presents features of his language and rhetoric in their transgressive efficacy, reminding us that how we use language in our profession is far from neutral—it is a form of action.

Chapter 4, "Social Work, Social Control, and Normalization: Roundtable Discussion With Michel Foucault," is a surprising historical document, a dialogue between Foucault, Donzelot, and some of their contemporaries that was uniquely framed around the nature of the social work profession. Organized at the instigation of the journal *Esprit*, the discussion was first published in French in 1972 in a special issue entirely devoted to social work.

The participants debate the expanded role of the helping professions in the context of historical changes, making references to ideas that are prevalent in Foucault's writings, such as forms of social control and "normalization"; processes of exclusion and marginalization; and the idea of categorization, or what Foucault calls elsewhere "dividing practices." Today, when dramatic transformations are taking place, their arguments appear highly premonitory and of striking relevance.

The version presented here is an original translation by Adrienne S. Chambon. A different version appeared in *Foucault Live* (Foucault 1989), a volume of reprinted interviews with Foucault. Because it was prepared for a different audience, the text omitted sections and arguments of importance to social workers. It was also worded in less accessible language. To our knowledge, this book is the first time that a discussion on social work with Foucault has appeared in a social work text in English.

Particular Foucauldian analyses of social work and related practices make up part 2. All the authors are engaged in such analyses, and their work opens up diverse avenues of inquiry and reflection. We did not seek contributions that proved Foucault's points but rather those that made a heuristic contribution to knowing about practice and about knowledge, how we constitute selves and others. They do so by examining diverse issues, populations, and levels of practice.

This part addresses multiple levels of practice: clinical work (Foote and Frank, chap. 7), direct practice in bureaucratic organizations (Moffatt, chap. 9), service delivery (O'Brien and Devine, chaps. 6 and 10), social movements (Wang, chap. 8), and policy (Parton, chap. 5). Nigel Parton examines the arena of child welfare and child protection. Carol-Anne O'Brien and John Devine discuss, respectively, the professional response to youth sexuality and to minority adolescents in inner-city schools. Catherine Foote and Arthur Frank critically explore therapeutic practice around the issue of grief in families. Frank Wang discusses the changing claims made by the social movements of the elderly. Ken Moffatt examines the microinteraction of low-income clients and workers in welfare offices.

Not only are the chapters substantively distinct, they are different entries into the work of Foucault. Each emphasizes a different set of notions from his writings with overlaps and resonance between the chapters. These can be read in any order. It is up to readers to carve out their own paths of intelligibility. Nigel Parton's "Reconfiguring Child Welfare Practices: Risk, Advanced Liberalism, and the Government of Freedom" invites us to consider child welfare as "an essentially ambiguous, uncertain, and contested arena." The author proposes a historical reading of the changing nature and priorities of the field of child welfare and child protection since the late nineteenth century, from philanthropy and later welfarism to the current state of advanced liberalism. The British example serves as an illustration, while the principles raised are highly relevant to the North American context and more broadly to Western societies.

Parton questions the present situation of indeterminacy in child welfare through a historical review of the field, consistent with Foucault's approach of a "history of the present." Foucauldian notions of "social regulation" and "governmentality" are central to the discussion. The author examines various rationalities of knowledge and practice that govern the conduct of individuals and families, manage populations, and define the role of the professional worker. He analyzes the changing discourses of social work, focusing particularly on the most recent and highly significant discourse of "risk" and "risk management."

In "Contested Territory: Sexualities and Social Work," Carol-Anne O'Brien explores how power relations are constituted in the professional discourse on youth sexuality. To do so, she analyzes shifts in the academic social work literature from the early 1980s to the mid-1990s. These discourses establish constraining identities for youth, which are periodically revised and contested around such diverse issues as childbearing; the co-construction of gender, race, and sexuality; and sexual orientation. She further examines the parallels between knowledge and practice by interviewing clients about their experience with staff in programs for youth.

From Foucault she draws notions that tie knowledge and sexuality to mechanisms of power: the concepts of "bio-power" as the management of populations and of "sexual science" as a field of knowledge and scholarship; the enhancement of parental authority through the "pedagogization" of adolescent sexuality; and the pathologization and psychiatrization of homosexuality. She stresses relations of power among discourses and develops the notion of "subjugated knowledge."

By incorporating "queer theory" into Foucauldian theory, O'Brien highlights the dominant discourse of "heteronormativity" present in social work. Strikingly absent and uninvited is a "discourse of desire," in the words of feminist scholarship.

In "Foucault and Therapy: The Disciplining of Grief," Catherine Foote and Arthur Frank posit that Foucault's work introduces a radical departure from ordinary ways of understanding the conduct of psychotherapy, suggesting that a Foucauldian critique modifies the ways in which we think about the therapeutic task. They explore the ramifications of this idea in the specific case of grief counseling.

Psychotherapy is seen as an institution that masks its own violence.

From the later work of Foucault the authors draw the concepts of "the self" and "technologies of the self" as the means that shape the subjectivity of the bereaved. They argue that "grief work" can be understood as a technology of the self, with therapeutic guidelines laying particular claims to truth. They explore the implications of the Foucauldian concepts of "normalization," "totalization," "individualization," and the "policing of boundaries," paying particular attention to the pathologizing of grief and the establishment of a "grieving self." Positing the existence of a "line of fault" between the dominant discourse on grief and individual experience, Foote and Frank come to redefine the process of "complicated mourning," no longer as pathology but as embodied resistance to the dominant discourse of grieving. In their conclusion they start to formulate a "therapy of resistance" that would cease to be an instrument of dominant discourse.

Frank Wang's "Resistance and Old Age: The Subject Behind the American Seniors Movement" explores the constitution of a collective "subject" through social movements and offers a genealogical reading of the senior citizens movement in the United States. Stressing the "productive" (rather than the oppressive) nature of subjectivities in Foucault's work, Wang examines the dynamic transformation of collective identities and concurrent changes in policy.

Through selective examples Wang shows that discourses are tied to social, economic, and political conditions that enable specific claims to be made. He demonstrates how social movements draw from historically available discourses in diverse spheres—physiology, economics, health, and labor—with one subjectivity developing in response to the next. Resistant discourses equally draw their meaning from local repertoires. A brief discussion of elderly suicide in China functions as a counterpoint to illuminate the cultural nature of forms of opposition. Above all, Wang's chapter helps us to appreciate the strategic and tactical aspects of discourse and to conceive of its results as sets of constraints and possibilities, simultaneously enabling and limiting, inclusive and exclusive, and, in the end, always partial.

Ken Moffatt's "Surveillance and Government of the Welfare Recipient" aims to "unveil the mechanisms of power within the social assistance office." Relying on in-depth interviews of social workers, the author explores the minute acts by which the worker in a welfare office establishes a particular form of knowledge about the client and is in turn enveloped in that logic. At times the workers' words take on a Foucauldian overtone in an uncanny way.

Foucault's concepts of "economy of power" and "governing relations" are key notions in Moffatt's analysis. The author inquires in concrete physical and behavioral terms into the many "disciplinary" mechanisms and "technologies of power" (such as "examination," "surveillance," and "panopticon") and their multiple venues, from the techniques of interview and the bureaucratic forms of documentation to the architectural design of the office. Moffatt questions the veiled nature of professional activities. He alerts us to the consequences of professional judgment, as financially and morally differentiating the poor from the rest of society and the respectable from the deviant; stigmatizing "welfare cheats"; and, in so doing, requiring from the applicants their active participation.

Moffatt discusses the larger societal conditions that serve as the context to such developments. These changing technologies do not affect the client alone but modify the relation between client and worker in important ways. He includes a discussion of the strategies developed by workers to oppose these controlling technologies, with liberatory potential.

John Devine's "Postmodernity, Ethnography, and Foucault" raises questions about the limits of Foucault's theorizing and, more practically, how to use Foucault. Devine argues that Foucault's account of the subtle and pervasive forms of control through disciplinary practices no longer applies to the institution of schools as they exist today in the inner cities. An ethnographic documentation shows that the opposite of Foucault's claims is the reality: schools have not too much structure and discipline but too little. Teachers are not invested in control but do all they can to avoid this, faced as they are with generalized violence.

Foucauldian writings encourage us to conduct close examinations of practices, as ethnography is apt to do. When we do so, we discover that the Foucauldian claims are products of a theory that is severed from daily realities. Devine offers a solution to this dilemma: that we take care to separate the conditions of modernity—which are germane to Foucault's theorizing—from the conditions of postmodernity and its forms of marginalization and vacuity, a point that is often taken up in discussions of Foucault's work (e.g., Hoy 1988).

A cautionary note applies to the style of the contributions. In keeping with his intent to step back from established forms of rationality, Foucault developed a style that does not follow the established norm of writing. Because style is not separate from content, it is not surprising that a number of contributors have written in a way that combines Foucauldian concepts with their analysis, in a manner reminiscent of his work. They tend not to present first the blueprint, then its application. However, they do try to present Foucault's ideas pedagogically. The reader is alerted to this. At times the essays may have an unsettling effect because the writing does not follow a familiar canon.

The glossary at the end of the book is meant to facilitate the readers' task by providing brief overviews of a number of key Foucauldian concepts. Each term is accompanied by a statement and by quote(s) from Foucauldian sources.

What This Book Is Not

This is a book from within the Foucauldian project. We made no attempt to provide a "balanced" view of Foucault. Nor does it include the many critiques of Foucault's project. Providing a critique of Foucault would be coming at his work from the outside. It was our desire to work from the inside out, and we are pleased that the authors have incorporated this approach in their chapters.

We have certainly struggled with this question. We think it is difficult enough to "enter" into Foucault's world. This is nonetheless what we are trying to do. Moreover, the issue of critiques is not as straightforward as it may seem, because a number of those critiques can be countered by Foucauldians and attributed to a misunderstanding of Foucault or to a wish to position oneself "beyond Foucault," which has little relevance to Foucault's work. Such a debate would require another way of approaching this topic than the one we chose.

We have included a counterchapter by John Devine. It presents a critique and breaks with the generally supportive stance of the other chapters. Devine challenges some specific applications of Foucauldian theory and raises the issue of the conditions of its applicability from within a field of practice that is germane to social work—the educational aspect of schooling in lower-income neighborhoods. Another chapter, by Carol-Anne O'Brien, illustrates the possibility of combining Foucauldian concepts with another critical theory framework, that of queer theory.

Some feminists in particular may feel the book is not critical enough. Linda Nicholson's edited volume, *Feminism/Postmodernism* (1990), for example, contains challenging references to Foucault, including Nancy Hartsock's fine essay, "Foucault on Power: A Theory for Women?" in which she claims that Foucault fails to provide a satisfactory theory of power for women. It could be argued that other interpretations would not be quite so ready to dismiss Foucault. Though this book does not deal with those interpretations, the debate needs to be taken up in subsequent work on Foucault and social work.

Feminist strands are, however, included in the chapters by Catherine Foote and Arthur Frank and by Frank Wang. Carol-Anne O'Brien's contribution suggests ways of combining Foucauldian and feminist thought, whereas Adrienne S. Chambon comments on areas of compatibility and difference between the two perspectives.

In all likelihood, feminists and others will find Foucault's use of language jarring (as illustrated by quotations from him in this book), specifically the use of *man*—which is reflective largely of the historical period in which he was writing; translators generally have followed his usage. As editors, we have left it as it was but would hope that this language will be modified in future translations so that it becomes more inclusive.

In some respects it seems obvious that Foucault's work is very Euro-centered. On the other hand, he has had an influence on many non–Euro-centered cultures that have used his work within their cultural contexts, as illustrated by his many exchanges in Tunisia, Brazil, and Japan. Again, although we fully acknowledge that critiques of Foucault can be leveled from this perspective, our view is that his work is important enough for social work not to ignore it and that it remains intellectually viable. The broader issue here is for social work to be in tune with broader intellectual schools of thought, whether Euro-centered or otherwise.

This book does not include a Foucauldian analysis of race and colonialism, an aspect of his work that has been less developed and, overall, less commented upon. In her discussion of the social work discourse on youth and sexuality, O'Brien shows the intersection of sexuality and race in social work discourse. Devine's chapter discusses the exclusionary processes operating in inner-city schools that predominantly affect visible minority groups. Wang illustrates the local and culturally shaped nature of discourses of resistance in the example he gives of suicide among the Chinese elderly.

Indeed, these concerns parallel Foucault's approach in which the concept of race is considered in the context of power relations and articulated with other processes. Here we would like to refer readers to two key sources. Foucault's writings on race have been discussed by Stoler (1995). She points out that the first volume of Foucault's *History of Sexuality* stages the debate on race through the technologies of sexuality and through bio-power—in other words, the management of life and subjugation of self through the body—and through the inscription of difference. Stoler examines the 1976 series of lectures Foucault gave at the Collège de France. In these he tied the notion of race to state racism and to the body politic. He discussed how the discourse on the notion of race became a discourse on the purity of one normative race over another. The "war" between the races was no longer waged on the outside but became internal to a society, with at times extremely destructive consequences. Relations of race are an intrinsic part of nation-states, with bio-power becoming one set of technologies for exercising power over people.

A derivative of Foucault's work, Said's 1979 *Orientalism*, has drawn from Foucault's critical analysis of "discourse" to uncover the making of the Other. In that work Said examined how the "Oriental" person and assumptions about "Orientalness" have been created in Western literature, and he argued that "without examining orientalism as discourse, one cannot possibly understand the enormous systematic discipline by which European culture was able to manage—and even produce—the Orient politically, sociologically, militarily, ideologically, scientifically and imaginatively during the post-Enlightenment period" (1979:3).

However, in a later compendium Said criticized the culture-centeredness of Foucault (Said 1988), a reflection of the complexity of Foucauldian writings and their interpretations.

We view this book as an initial foray into the complex relationships between Foucault and social work. Its purpose is to make a case for social work to incorporate in its theory and practice different dimensions of Foucault's thought. Too often, social work has seemed detached from major intellectual currents. We hope to demonstrate the value of engaging with profound epistemological challenges to social work's body of knowledge and accepted ways of perceiving the world. As the certainties of modernity that we have used to anchor our practice crumble and give way to postmodern flux and wild uncertainty, we need to reinvent the future of our field through, among others, a Foucauldian quest for truths. More work needs to be done. We are inviting other social workers to pursue the enterprise.

REFERENCES

Abramovitz, Mimi. 1988. *Regulating the lives of women: Social welfare policy from colonial times to the present.* Boston: South End Press.

——. 1996. *Under attack, fighting back: Women and welfare in the U.S.* New York: Monthly Review Press.

Amundson, Jon, Kenneth Stewart, and Valentine LaNae. 1993. Temptations of power and certainty. *Journal of Marital and Family Therapy*, 19 (2): 111–23.

Arac, Jonathan, ed. *After Foucault: Humanistic knowledge, postmodern challenge.* New Brunswick, N.J.: Rutgers University Press.

Bailey, Roy and Mike Brake, eds. 1975. *Radical social work.* London: Edward Arnold.

Baines, Carol T., Patricia M. Evans, and Sheila Neysmith, eds. 1991. *Women's caring: Feminist perspectives on social welfare.* Toronto: McClelland & Stewart.

Book forum on qualitative methods. 1995. *Social Work Research* 19, no. 1 (March).

Book forum on the scientist-practitioner. 1996. *Social Work Research* 20, no. 2 (June).

Chambon, Adrienne S. and Allan Irving, eds. 1994. *Essays on postmodernism and social work.* Toronto: Canadian Scholars' Press.

Cohler, Bertram J. 1988. The human studies and the life history: The Social Service Review lecture. *Social Service Review* 62, no. 4 (December): 552–75.

Collins, P. H. 1990. *Black feminist thought: Knowledge, consciousness, and the politics of empowerment.* New York: Routledge.

Cree, V. E. 1995. *From public streets to private lives: The changing task of social work.* Aldershot, U.K.: Avebury.

Debates with authors: Comments on the "empirical practice movement." 1995. *Social Service Review* 69, no. 1 (March):152–69.

de Montigny, Gerald. 1995. *Social working: An ethnography of front-line practice.* Toronto: University of Toronto Press.

Epstein, Laura. 1994. The therapeutic idea in contemporary society. In A. S. Chambon and Allan Irving, eds., *Essays on postmodernism and social work*, pp. 3–18. Toronto: Canadian Scholars' Press.

——. 1996. The trouble with the researcher-practitioner idea. *Social Work Research* 20, no. 2 (June): 113–17.

Flaskas, Carmel and Catherine Humphreys. 1993. Theorizing about power: Intersecting the ideas of Foucault with the "problem" of power in family therapy. *Family Process* 32, no. 1 (March): 35–47.

Foucault, Michel. 1983. Structuralism and poststructuralism: An interview with Gérard Raulet. *Telos: A Quarterly Journal of Critical Thought* 55 (Spring): 195–211.

——. 1989. *Foucault live (Interviews, 1966–84).* Edited by Sylvère Lotringer. New York: Semiotext(e).

Goldstein, Howard. 1990. The knowledge base of social work practice: Theory, wisdom, analogue, or art? *Families in Society: The Journal of Contemporary Human Services* 71 (1): 32–43.

Goldstein, Jan, ed. 1994. *Foucault and the writing of history.* Cambridge, Mass.: Blackwell.

Gorman, Jane. 1993. Postmodernism and the conduct of inquiry in social work. *Affilia* 8 (3): 247–64.

Greene, Gilbert J., Carla Jenson, and Dorothy H. Jones. 1996. A constructivist perspective on clinical social work practice with ethnically diverse clients. *Social Work* 41, no. 2 (March): 172–80.

Hare-Mustin, Rachel T. 1994. Discourses in the mirrored room: A postmodern analysis of therapy. *Family Process* 33, no. 1 (March): 19–35.

Hartman, Ann. 1993. The professional is political. Editorial. *Social Work* 38, no. 4 (July): 365–66, 504.

Heineman, M. B. 1981. The obsolete scientific imperative in social work research. *Social Service Review* 55, no. 3 (September): 371–97.

Hoy, D. C. 1988. Foucault: Modern or postmodern? In Jonathan Arac, ed., *After Foucault: Humanistic knowledge, postmodern challenge*, pp. 12–41. New Brunswick, N.J.: Rutgers University Press.

Irving, Allan. 1992. The scientific imperative in Canadian social work and social welfare research in Canada, 1897–1945. *Canadian Social Work Review* 9 (1): 9–27.

Laird, Joan, ed. 1993. *Revisioning social work education: A social constructionist approach.* New York: Haworth Press.

Leonard, Peter. 1994. Knowledge/power and postmodernism. *Canadian Social Work Review* 11 (1): 11–26.

——. 1996. Three discourses on practice: A postmodern reappraisal. *Journal of Sociology and Social Welfare* 23, no. 2 (June): 7–26.

Madigan, S. P. 1992. The application of Michel Foucault's philosophy in the problem externalizing discourse of Michael White. *Journal of Family Therapy* 14, no. 3 (August): 265–79.

Manning, S. S. 1997. The social worker as moral citizen: Ethics in action. *Social Work* 42, no. 3 (May): 223–30.

McBeath, G. B. and S. A. Webb. 1991. Social work, modernity, and postmodernity. *Sociological Review* 39 (4): 745–62.

Nicholson, L. J., ed. 1990. *Feminism/postmodernism.* New York: Routledge.

Norton, D. G. 1978. *The dual perspective.* New York: Council on Social Work Education.

Pardeck, J. T., J. W. Murphy, and J. M. Choi. 1994. Some implications of postmodernism for social work practice. *Social Work* 39, no. 4 (July): 343–46.

Paré, D. A. 1995. Of families and other cultures: The shifting paradigm of family therapy. *Family Process* 34, no. 1 (March): 1–19.

Parton, Nigel. 1991. *Governing the family: Child care protection and the State.* London: Macmillan.

——. 1994a. "Problematics of government," (post)modernity, and social work. *British Journal of Social Work* 24: 9–32.

——. 1994b. The nature of social work under conditions of (post)modernity. *Social Work and Social Sciences Review* 5 (2): 93–112.

Peile, Colin. 1988. Research paradigms in social work: From stalemate to creative synthesis. *Social Service Review* 62, no. 1 (March): 1–19.

"Philosophical issues in social work." 1991. *Journal of Sociology and Social Welfare* 18, no. 4 (December).

Pinderhughes, Elaine. (1989). *Understanding race, ethnicity, and power: The key to efficacy in clinical practice.* New York: Free Press.

Pozatek, Ellie. 1994. The problem of certainty: Clinical social work in the postmodern era. *Social Work* 39, no. 4 (July): 396–403.

Redekop, Fred. 1995. The "problem" of Michael White and Michel Foucault. *Journal of Marital and Family Therapy* 21 (3): 309–18.

Reid, W. J. 1994. The empirical practice movement. *Social Service Review* 68 (June): 165–84.

Rossiter, Amy B. (1996). A perspective on critical social work. *Journal of Progressive Human Services* 7 (1): 23–41.

Said, E. W. 1979. *Orientalism.* New York: Vintage.

Saleeby, Dennis. 1994. Culture, theory, and narrative: The intersection of meanings in practice. *Social Work* 39, no. 4 (July): 351–59.

Sands, R. G. and Kathleen Nuccio. 1992. Postmodern feminist theory and social work. *Social Work* 37, no. 6 (November): 489–94.

Scott, Dorothy. 1989. Meaning construction and social work practice. *Social Service Review* 63, no. 1 (March): 39–51.

Solomon, Barbara. 1976. *Black empowerment: Social work in oppressed communities.* New York: Columbia University Press.

Specht, Harry and Mark E. Courtney. 1994. *Unfaithful angels: How social work has abandoned its mission.* New York: Free Press.

Stoler, A. L. 1995. *Race and the education of desire: History of sexuality and the colonial order of things.* Durham, N.C.: Duke University Press.

Tyson, Katherine. 1995. *New foundations for scientific social and behavioral research: The heuristic paradigm.* Needham Heights, Mass.: Allyn & Bacon.

Wakefield, J. C. 1988. Psychotherapy, distributive justice, and social work. Parts 1 and 2. *Social Service Review* 62, no. 2 (June): 187–210, and 62, no. 3 (September): 353–82.

Weick, Ann. 1987. Reconceptualizing the philosophical perspective of social work. *Social Service Review* 61, no. 2 (June): 218–29.

Wenocur, Stanley and Michael Reisch. 1989. *From charity to enterprise: The development of American social work in a market economy.* Urbana: University of Illinois Press.

White, Michael. 1993. Deconstruction and therapy. In Stephen Gillian and Reese Price, eds., *Therapeutic conversations,* pp. 22–61. New York: Norton.

White, Michael and David Epston. 1990. *Narrative means to therapeutic ends.* New York: Norton.

Witkin, S. L. 1991. Empirical clinical practice: A critical analysis. *Social Work* 36, no. 2 (March): 158–63.

Witkin, S. L. and Simon Gottschalk. 1988. Alternative criteria for theory evaluation. *Social Service Review* 62, no. 2 (June): 211–24.

READING FOUCAULT FOR SOCIAL WORK

Part One
Social Work in Perspective

CHAPTER I

The Culture of Social Work

Laura Epstein

This chapter is best understood as work in progress, an evolving component of the vast "Origins" project that Laura Epstein started in the late '80s and was to become a book. An abstract of the project presents her intent (1994a):

Aim of the Origins Project

This project is a historical interpretation of the dominant ideas that inform the practices of therapeutic intervention in social work. It will attempt to discern how clinical social work branched out from its early tutelary ways of influencing personal conduct to a technical process based on social science precepts.

Subject Defined

The profession of social work is the generalist among the therapeutic occupations. Its practice invariably includes attributes of *caring, treating,* and *protecting.* Its image is benevolent, its function to administer help to those in need. Through mental healing, social work entrenches in society generalized standards of personal conduct and subjective states. At the same time it honors self-determination and individual autonomy. There is uncertainty about its aims partly because numerous stratagems conceal its power to shape and control thought and behavior. Its practitioners are mainly women whose position among the male-dominated helping professions is problematic in the way they amplify the ambiguity of women's role. The feminization of social work personnel accounts for the fact that although the functions of social work are basic and its powers large, its influence is veiled. Its domain is always endangered, its specialization subsidiary. Perceived as being feminine, it counters this by subscribing to gender-neutral, rational social science. The combination of social science and altruism makes social work into one of the major instrumentalities through which the state governs and provides for the welfare of citizens.

Focus of the Study

Social work today needs to make sense of the changes happening to it, seemingly without agency, in a culture and politics being transformed. Its traditional commitment to helping the poor, alongside its contemporary provision of psychotherapy in both the public and private sectors, arouses complex issues having to do with its worth, the justification for its practices, and its social assignment. This project will study the grounds for these issues by tracing the ancestry and development of dominant clinical social work knowledge. Postmodern social theorists, Michel Foucault and others, provide the main social theory base. This study should produce a picture of controlling ideas in clinical social work and how they relate to the needs of the culture, the state, and life in our times.

This chapter, "The Culture of Social Work," was an intrinsic part of Epstein's larger project. The title reflects one of the numerous ways she characterized her project.

The chapter has three main sections: a discussion of the nature and objectives of the project; a presentation of the approach taken; and an application of the historical reinterpretation of social work to the writings of Charlotte Towle, a key historical figure in the profession whose writings were critical in the constitution of the field's core ideas.

The original scope of the chapter was to broadly trace the development of the social work culture. The manuscript underwent several revisions from June 1995 to the last version, dated March 17, 1996, which is presented here. Work on the manuscript was not completed at the time of her death. The text was twenty pages long. Several sections were written; others were outlined; others were not yet written.

Our approach was to change the manuscript as little as possible to avoid disturbing the voice of the author. We have retained her order of presentation, and we did not touch her wording, except to move a few sentences or a paragraph to improve the flow.

In several places Laura noted which of her documents she intended to draw from, especially the invited lecture she gave on her Origins project on May 10, 1995, at a faculty retreat for the University of Chicago School of Social Service Administration. It was entitled "The Therapeutic Idea: Social Work Influence on the Character of a Century: Introduction to Work in Progress" and was an elaboration of her essay, "The Therapeutic Idea in Contemporary Society" (1994b). She gave the lecture before she wrote the essay.

Laura had outlined how she intended to present her approach and its relation to Foucault, but she had not completed the chapter. She had worked extensively on the writings of Foucault during the late 1980s and early 1990s. Once explicit, Foucault's approach had become more implicit in her work, constituting a central backbone, as she often remarked. By the time she drafted the chapter, she had incorporated his ideas and way of thinking and had become more intrigued with applying these to her research objectives. Following her annotations, the section called "Understanding Social Work" combines her March 1996 draft of the chapter and her May 1995 lecture. We have also included a short section from an earlier document, entitled "April 1993 Lecture," which we found in her personal papers. Inserts are indicated in the text.

There is also considerable overlap between the third section of the manuscript, which traces some of the core ideas of social work to Charlotte Towle, and Epstein's paper, "Charlotte Towle: Theorist of the Golden Age," which she presented on May 31, 1996, at a conference commemorating Towle sponsored by the School of Social Service Administration at the University of Chicago, and for which Epstein was one of the planners. She was working on the two documents simultaneously, and, understandably, one fed into the other. The version presented here is that of the March 1996 manuscript.

Although she developed additional arguments that can be found in other manuscripts, including the May 10, 1995 lecture, they are written in a preliminary way and were not yet honed. Knowing the considerable care and attention with which she reworked her manuscripts until they reached a polished form, we felt that such fragments (although complementary) would not do justice to her sense of rigor and would leave the reader with a frayed sense of her work—the opposite of the tightly constructed and fierce argumentation that characterize her scholarship. However, we have included her outlines for the essay in order to reflect the quality of the work in progress. These outlines provide the reader with an appreciation for the richness and complexity of her endeavor.

Editorial decisions were further informed by the numerous discussions we held with Laura about her work over the years. We thank Lester Brown, her executor and close friend, for generously making available her personal files, texts, and computer disks in the interest of this publication.

The manuscript for "The Culture of Social Work" follows.

Social work is a riddle to some, anathema to others. One of its chief problems is that there are so many different ways to define it, and there is disagreement within its ranks and in the public about what it basically consists of, what the gist of it is. There is an abundance of definitions that explain the way social work is related to other features of society or that show what social work is by comparing it to other activities and institutions. But there does not seem to be a solid definition that is widely accepted inside and outside the profession of social work, that produces immediate recognition so that when you hear it you know *that is social work*, in the same way you know that physicians practice medicine, that lawyers practice law. What is it that social workers practice?

The Nature of Social Work: To Repair, to Control, to Defend

To speak of the culture of social work is a tony way of covering up the difficulty of explaining what social work is. One current statement about the nature of social work (featured in a brochure from the University of Chicago's School of Social Service Administration) is as follows: "The issues that engage [social workers] . . . change over time. . . . The central commitment to helping those in need and working to bring about effective social change, however, remains constant." A problem with this kind of definition is that it does not tell what social work is, it does not specify its characterizations and qualifications. It gives rise to a host of interpretations.

Recently, there seems to have come about a less perplexing definition of social work, simplified in order to make it possible for media people and politicians to put forward beliefs about public matters in which social work is perceived to have some involvement. Thus it has come about that the public discourse will mention social workers in connection with the role of government in safeguarding the public welfare, preventing crime by organizing recreation for poor youth and providing them with "counseling," that is, some technical form of advice, support, and self-understanding. Something new has crept into this discourse lately. Social work seems to be presented as a craft that does many kinds of repairs (social handywomen) to the living conditions and personal attitudes of citizens and has an elite corps that does psychotherapy, figured as minor to major repairs to the soul or consciousness in the mind.

So what is this craft that is practiced by the wives, sisters, mothers, and lovers of middle-class men? What is this craft that gives away taxpayer money to the morally unfit and socially deviant and performs acts of pious healing to the grieving and troubled? That "counsels" the confused and badly informed and, in its role of "mental health professional," treats those who are mentally ill and emotionally disturbed? What is this social institution of modern America that sometimes cannot easily be told apart from the police (who more and more are said to resemble social workers), that cannot be told apart from the various brands of "shrinks" (who fear to resemble social workers), that cannot be readily told apart from friends, neighbors—and the talk show hosts and their guest experts who are pitchmen for therapeutics?

The modern profession of social work is not quite one hundred years old, older than this writer but not by much. I did not know its age or credentials when I first dragged myself into the school of social work at the University of Chicago in 1932. Just going on nineteen, the past was nothing to me. The world began when I was born, and the present was permanent. I figured social work and the Great Depression had always been there and would stay forever. However, there comes a time when one knows that things have histories, constituted by events, by ideas, and according to definitions and rules put out in the midst of a tangle of conflicting stories.

What can one say about the nature of social work that has not already been said? Social work practitioners are said to be intrusive busybodies, bureaucrats, psychotherapists, child minders (Brewer and Lait 1980), society's "response to problems associated with the industrialization and urbanization of the 20th century" (Hopps and Collins 1995). Something much more meaningful needs to be understood about social work because it is a large and impressive social institution that everybody understands vaguely, has spread its influence widely, and has never been seriously inspected. It has been ignored, humiliated, and ridiculed, taken for granted, and sometimes revered; it needs to be studied.

Social Work as Social Science and as Power

Modern social work is perceived by its practitioners and by the public as social science. It has strived to acquire the characteristics of science. Its history and discourse are packed with the language and analytic processes of social science. However, it is not usually recognized that social work is a major social institution that legitimates the power contained in modern democratic capitalist states. Since the English, French, and American revolutions, governments have come to believe that in order to govern, state power must be grounded on broad public support, that it should be democratic (Foucault 1980; Wolin 1988). In democracies public order is achieved by many different means, overt coercion being one—but the last resort. Totalitarianism is outlawed. The modern state must normalize the citizenry and organize large, urban, and diverse populations into workforces that can adequately staff the public and private enterprises that maintain the performance of the economy, preserve civil order and the welfare of the citizens, fend off aggressors, and pursue the political aims of the state in the world order. The state needs the academy, the professions, and the arts to steer the enterprise and mold, guide, and teach the minds. The human or social sciences are the backbone of the technologies that have emerged as instruments by which the state can govern with minimal coercion, or, when coercion is employed—as is the case of young black American men subjected to immense amounts of incarceration—human science offers ways to support, ameliorate, disguise, and justify the state's carceral machinery.

Social work collaborates with other occupations, mainly the "helping disciplines," all of which together manage the population. Social work is the Janus-faced one. To accomplish its purposes social work must dominate its clients, although in theory and in its manner of interpersonal relations with clients it puts forward a democratic egalitarian manner. However, to be effective, to show results, it must influence people, motivate them to adopt the normative views inherent in the intentions of social work practice. It must produce an effect without force, without command, indirectly. It must not be authoritative. It must enable its clients to be transformed, to adopt normative ways and thoughts *voluntarily*. Doublespeak is characteristic of twentieth-century communication in all walks of life, in all corners of social interaction. In social work noninfluential influencing is its communicative art, its specialty. It has evolved complex rationales and methods for appearing to sew together influencing and not influencing, without the seams showing too much. A polished style evolved to conceal this basic dissonance within social work. For example, it is common to state the intentions of social work as helping people to accommodate to the status quo and as challenging the status quo by trying to bring about social change. This dissonance is intrinsic to the nature of social work, to its essence.

The core meaning of "social worker" in the media is one who takes care of and manages "the troubled." That means "troublesome," deviant, afflicted with ill-being. Over years of building up this persona, introducing various pictures of a social worker into news programs, soaps, and documentaries, the media have arrived at a practical appraisal of the function of social work, which is to normalize people. *Normalize* is a funny word. It conveys an idea of manipulation considered not correct with respect to people—as if decent people should not use this word in proper society. Western moral philosophy eschews manipulation of people, even though in many important situations people are clearly manipulated to serve the ends of politicians and advertisers, for example. The meaning of normalize is clear: to make to conform or reduce to a norm or standard, to make normal, by transforming elements in a person or situation. This is certainly what social workers try to do, with the caveat—more observed in the breach—that the persons being transformed should want this, should consent to it, and should do it of their own free will. This is the principle of self-determination.

This normalizing function, even though it occurs in interpersonal space, between people, is not basically an experiential encounter but a technical fix. Early in my career a supervisor of mine tried to calm me when I was immensely anxious because I had not the faintest idea what to do with a client. This supervisor told me: "If you will just relax, take it one step at a time, explore and explore the problem, look at it from all sides, find out what the client can contribute, in time you will know something about the situation, and something will come to mind about possibilities." Over several decades, driven by the necessity of professional social workers to construct "methods," to be a social science, to stay out of the fix I was in with my mysterious client, social work has become a technical fix. This conversion is moving faster under pressure of "managed care," which is overtaking the handling of cases in conventional social agencies. There are large conflicting implications to the appearance of social repair technology, all of which are extremely oversimplified by the media, which constantly disseminate and amplify stories about the deviant and the helpers. The public mind is being filled with erroneous information and false expectations, which become the basis for political decisions about which social welfare programs to fund and which to starve.

Beyond such straightforward questions about concrete social institutions and their life and death are deeper and more worrisome questions. These concern the powerful tendencies in our society to mold all our diverse peoples into American Dream types, a conformity that makes the 1950s look liberal. Social work is one of the chief influences enforcing the moral standards derived from therapy and built into the therapeutic ethos of our time, into the operations of society in the form of the therapeutic state.

Social work is sited in a social space where people address problems in living, their own and other people's problems. It is a major apparatus for enforcing America's ideology of personal responsibility, a view of humanity recently elevated to unique centrality by the political will of conservative elements in the body politic. This view holds that *you can do it, you can have it, it is up to you to pull yourself together to get the skills, to learn the stuff, get on with your life, do it!* This is the contemporary practical essence of individualism, the modern doctrine that asserts that the interests of the individual are or ought to be ethically paramount, that values, rights, and duties originate in individuals. Social work broadly disseminates the ideology of individualism in ways that make it appear believable. The thrust of social work's development of various types of psychotherapy has been to enshrine the values and properties of individualism, disseminating it through a multitude of individual contacts with all citizens, with the millions in all economic classes who experience problems in living, and especially in populations that are impoverished and discriminated against. Social work develops information and theories to pursue the creation of individual initiative and personal autonomy. The psychotherapies that have been derived from psychoanalysis have been especially relevant to concentrating on the innermost mental processes of people so as to indoctrinate them thoroughly with the spirit of individualism.

American society is consumed with moral panic. On all sides are those who have taken it upon themselves to stamp out evil in the form of everything that is fearful and offensive. With the thundering righteousness of Sigmund Freud in the vanguard, the proponents of therapy have evolved a serious belief system that proposes therapy as social theory, as personal salvation, and as technology for the repair of psyches. Social work offers various types of psychotherapy as the vehicle for helping people with their problems and changing society in productive ways. Social work has been instrumental in turning therapy into social policy.

Understanding Social Work

Why We Should Want to Understand the Culture of Social
    Work Now?

The Problems of the Therapeutic State

What Would We Gain from Better Understanding?

What Means Are There for Providing an Understanding?

Foucault vs. Social Science Progress Idea

It is getting very uncomfortable to be at sea about this social institution in a period when the welfare state may be becoming dismantled because social work grew up with the welfare state, is an instrumentality of the welfare state; the women who created and run social work achieved independence from the welfare state.

Social workers have come to appraise social work. What is this social work about in this last part of the twentieth century? The beliefs, the traits, the shape and structure of social work ought to be capable of further clarification if we could unpeel the myths that so encrust our understanding that we simply cannot see the entity for what it is—if we could discern more of the actual elements of the real occurrences that produced the opinions, conclusions, decisions, and viewpoints that collected around the historical acts and movements leading into and out of the acts that made up the nature of the thing: social work.

It has lately come about that analysis of the therapeutic enterprise has attracted interest among historians seeking to get the history straight and straightened out from myths as well as among political scientists interested in analyzing the interaction between the therapy ethos and the polity of the state (Polsky 1991; Epstein 1992, 1994b). Social work's historical commitment to helping the poor and to psychotherapy introduces complex issues concerning its worth, the justification for its practices, and its social assignment. I am attempting in this paper to develop a viewpoint and set out the terms of an argument that might lead to a reinterpretation of the history of social work. Parts of that reinterpretation already exist in current revisionist histories. This project is a historical interpretation of the dominant ideas that inform the practices of therapeutic intervention in social work. My study of the origins of these ideas should help to produce a picture of controlling ideas in clinical social work and how these ideas connect to the needs of the culture, the state, and life in our times.

[From May 10, 1995, lecture] I do not mean to write a chronological narrative that tells events and decisive personalities, inventions, and responses to circumstances, although some of this might have to appear in order for the work to be intelligible. I hope not to repeat work already published recently, tracing the chronological development of clinical practices (such as Ehrenreich 1985; Wenocur and Reisch 1989). I am after the derivation of governing ideas that were implanted in the intellectual mold and the social practices of clinical work. I am interested in unraveling the discourses, that is, the collections of talk, writing, teaching, and meeting that swirl about, invent, develop, remove, and reorganize thought, intentions, plans, disorder, and disjunctions, forming a changing set of practices and rules that establish and reestablish the practices existing and becoming. I am after what social workers thought, where they got their ideas from, to what use they put their ideas, what influence they had. This means finding out and figuring out the origins of fundamental clinical practice ideas, to the extent possible, within my time limits and resources.

The kinds of issues that could be looked into are what social conditions gave rise to the ideas; what crises, disjunctures, influenced them; why and how they became formal standards; how they advanced the status and worth of the women who dominate the profession; how they may have protected or damaged society and the state, the profession of social work; how they may have improved the circumstances of the citizens or failed them; how clinical ideas affected problems that touched on racist, ethnic, gendered, and class tensions.

Michel Foucault

[Continued from May 10, 1995, lecture] In order to do this I had to find out how one thought analytically about the nature of fundamental beliefs, and this led me to philosophy and eventually to the work of Michel Foucault, the social theorist who put the study of the helping disciplines in the center of public affairs. Other writers, such as Rieff (1968), Halmos (1970), and Berger (1977), had studied the special nature of psychologism in modern times, but

it was Foucault who defined the discourse in the broadest and most erudite way, whose work has been immensely influential in changing how the human sciences are understood today. His work has not penetrated social work.

The approach to be taken here in constructing this historical interpretation is influenced by Foucault's analysis of the human sciences and his conception of what questions have to be studied to analyze these disciplines, what methods of historical discovery need to be followed to unravel their origins and influences (Foucault 1972, 1973; Dreyfus and Rabinow 1982; Goldstein 1994).

[From 1993 lecture] Foucault set the agenda for a new wave of historical analysis of the human sciences (dubious sciences)—including social work, psychology, psychiatry, and tangential pastoral counseling (Castel 1988; Donzelot 1979; on social work see Chambon and Irving 1994; Cree 1995; Epstein 1996b; Parton 1994; Sands and Nuccio 1992). The customary way to present history is to describe a development or profession from some chronological point supposed to have been the beginning. Thereafter, the history proceeds to narrate events over time. Intervening events and parallel developments in the society are woven into the story according to prevailing interpretations and the accepted explanations for the directions taken by the history. Foucault is an historian of ideas. He starts his histories with an appraisal of the present condition of the ideas. He then traces backward ("genealogy," "history of the present") the events, beliefs, aims, uses, trajectories taken by these ideas in practice in the world, to see how events shaped ideas and how the ideas shaped the events.

Foucault is of importance to the practice professions because he studies only ideas as they exist in actual practice, and he studies practices as they have been played out and as they created the ideas associated with the practices. By playing around with these ideas, we get hold of a framework for considering the nature of the social sciences, the nature of the helping disciplines, and the nature of their practices.

[From May 1995 Lecture] Foucault's central theme is the study of the processes by which society and the helping professions normalize people (1984a). He studies transgression ("deviance" in American usage). A philosopher by training who ended up holding a chair in social history, Foucault undermined the liberal humanist conviction that technology is intrinsically alien to the study of the human sphere (1980). Foucault's posi-

tion is that the determining feature of modern human sciences and the helping professions is that they are constituted by their technologies of intervention: by observation, measurement, assessment, and administration (1984b). In other words, the human sciences consist of techniques and practices brought into existence in order to discipline, regulate, administer, and arrange all the population of human individuals. The power of the human sciences comes from all the institutions, acts, and discourses occurring in the course of creating and managing these regulatory apparatuses. The knowledge generated in the human sciences is the product of practices developed in the course of and in order to operate these systems. Foucault's work is a study and analysis of the details of practice. He makes no conventional distinctions between the theory and practice of the helping disciplines, rolling the two into one.

The difficulty of Foucault's work is partly style, which is dense and sometimes ornate and literary, especially in his earliest writing. His work is strongly tilted toward French experience. What seems to cause some American readers to become resentful of Foucault is that his work appears counterintuitive, contrary to common sense. It is not in the Enlightenment mainstream position that makes human rights, reason, and the expectation of progress central in one's philosophy (Wolin 1988). Foucault, like Nietzsche from whom he descends, does not believe that reason and science are necessarily progressive, but he is not antiscience. He asks the reader to shift away from a position that makes an individual person's moral autonomy the most important thing in the world, underwriting such rights as self-determination, self-fulfillment, and the like.

The reader has to tolerate the idea that the contemporary social order dominates people, puts them into slots that ordain their lifestyles and characters, conditions them to be ruled and controlled. Their lives and beliefs are organized to accept, internalize, become fully participating in their own domination, not necessarily willingly but as a matter of course. In other words, domination happens. It is one inherent characteristic of our times. Once we put ourselves into this thought framework, the world of human sciences starts to look different, and novel ideas spring up with which to contemplate this scene.

The Foucauldian framework is a sharp critique of customary thinking. It is not a total or all-encompassing set of ideas or viewpoints. It does not stand alone or in a bounded place, as, for example, Freudianism or Marxism. It is a creative means for analyzing problems in the human sciences and has been adapted by numerous scholars who have developed innovative analyses of their own.

The origins of casework are not going to be understood from any linear chronological narration of dates and personalities, books written, organizations started, and cultural influences noted in the margins. That history has to be discovered, narrated, and interpreted. The origins need to be understood because the myths have made important events and thoughts vanish from consideration. Obfuscation has twisted the meanings of events and ideas; thus the standard version of the history of social work treatment will not serve as a foundation from which to build anything that is going to be sturdy in the next century.

The standard history does not deal with the unique practices of borrowing from psychiatry and psychology major chunks of theory, technique, and research findings and weaving some of these borrowings into a special mixture that represents the essence of clinical work in social work. This essence is neither named or celebrated or even noticed particularly, both within and without the profession. What is clinical social work, what is psychotherapy, what is the so-called therapeutic state, and what has it to do with the welfare state of liberal capitalist society? What is the good in social work, and how can it be made to appear?

Left out and distorted from the standard history are the ways in which the dominance of women shaped the character of social work by constructing a mission to protect women's rights and privileges and perpetuating traditional limitations on women (see, for example, Kunzel 1993; Lunbeck 1994; Epstein 1995b; and Muncy 1991). The standard history fails to analyze the effects of embracing social science in such a way that the dominance of men over the epistemology and purposes was given distorted power, the nature of the work "masculinized." The standard history fails to deal with the engrossing question of how it came to be that women found a professional home in clinical social work while they were mostly unwelcome in psychiatry, psychology, sociology, and what the price of admission was. *[Lecture inserts end here]*

Outline of Intended Sections

This outline is provided so that readers can keep in mind the overall picture of the work as they read the historical section that follows and understand how it fitted into the broad spectrum of Epstein's interpretation.

Intended Sections

Origins: Women's Suffrage

Psychotherapy for the Masses

The Talcott Parsons's Spin on Social Work, Ordering into Neat Boxes

The Psychodynamic Spin: Charlotte Towle and Thomas French and
    Franz Alexander; the Hegemony of the Unconscious

The Problem-Solving Spin: Dewey

Individualism

Taking the Side of Women, Blacks, Minorities, etc.

Charlotte Towle: Social Theorist of the "Golden Age"

The theoretical work of Charlotte Towle is important because it is an under-pinning of many present-day beliefs about what clinical social workers ought to think and do. Towle was the first clinician on the faculty of social work at the University of Chicago in 1932. She had been brought in by Edith Abbott to forge a unique treatment practice for social work. This, Towle set out to do over several years.

Hardly known outside the circle of academic women in social work, Charlotte Towle (1896–1996) built a theory of human nature and the social environment attuned to post–World War II American culture. Because she was a professor at a prestigious university, Charlotte Towle's views were thoroughly disseminated among an elite group of opinion makers in social work, especially teachers at graduate schools of social work, and became embedded in the minds of thousands of clinical practitioners, mainly women. They were the ones on or near the "front line": the sites where they were in touch with women for the purpose of improving their behavior and attitudes to enhance their ability to carry out appropriate social roles. In this way, social workers were in a position to be immensely influential in setting up the goals and attitudes that permeated the lives of millions of American working women, their families, and, to a certain extent, poor and underclass people as well.

On its surface Towle's work was a theory of learning and teaching adults. This view was supported by an underlying theory of human nature and conduct that equated learning with "personality growth," that concept educed from the psychoanalytic theory of human nature and conduct. Interwoven with an educational address to teachers of social work was a wide-ranging explanation of ill-being as conceived in America's post–World War II prosperity, what is becoming known in retrospect as America's Golden Age (see Hobsbawm 1994), which prefigured later socioeconomic explosions and impairments.

Towle was a central figure in converting clinical social work into twentieth-century social therapeutics. Towle's major work, *The Learner in Education for the Professions,* appeared in 1954, midway through the Golden Age. This work was a product of that period and reflected its viewpoint. In the twenty-five to thirty years following the end of World War II the United States experienced unprecedented economic expansion and became the dominant superpower. Throughout the entire postwar capitalist world, incomes rose and the well-being of the population increased. In his recent book on the history of the twentieth century, Eric Hobsbawm describes these as years of "extraordinary economic growth and social transformation, which probably changed human society more profoundly than any other period of comparable brevity" (1996:6). The seeds of the decomposition that would take place later were there but muted in the glamor and optimism of postwar prosperity.

The theory of the Golden Age assumed that American society was on the way to providing full employment and an adequate family wage. Thus most individual and family impairments were seen as the result of problems inside the person and within immediate interpersonal relations. It was believed in social work that basic helping theory and technique were adequate to the job of enabling (today's *empowering*) the disadvantaged and despairing to right themselves and fulfill their lives (today's "American Dream" in popular rhetoric).

Clinical social work was optimistic. For example, Grace Marcus, a spokesperson for the field, wrote a panegyric in 1955 celebrating the virtual end of the mystery of what was keeping social work clients from thriving in treatment. She foresaw that a breakthrough was coming—techniques that would do away with impediments to successful treatment. She celebrated the likelihood that because social work was not hampered by traditions, as were unnamed "older professions," social work could forge ahead. This was quite heady stuff (Marcus 1955). What seems important now is that the ideas of the present are not those of the Golden Age. Practitioners and the public today behold doubt and uncertainty about what to think and what to do.

In the fifties, social workers were relatively confident that research and development could eventually increase the power of clinical social work treatment. Alas, the tumultuous experience of several decades has undermined the faith in psychosocial explanations. After the war, social science had turned to the study of psychological and behavioral problems and away from issues of poverty and unemployment, the structural problems of society that had priority after the Great Depression. In this atmosphere the social work profession began revising its theories and practices, taking on traits of modern social science (Diner 1985). In the developing field of clinical social work, not yet renamed but being refashioned from casework, the 1950s saw the development of concepts that, it was hoped, would raise the quality of its intellectual foundations. Academic social workers were pressed to organize ideas in ways that could be communicated to students in an organized way. They developed sophisticated ways to state and explain what practice with individuals and families ought to be. The literature of the time was concerned with identifying a knowledge base and creating a stable framework to enfold and solidify practice knowledge.

The prominent ideas show that suitable selections were made from large bodies of complex and developing theories of social science as debated in the literature of the day. Ideas of *problem solving* came to characterize the goal-driven actions of human beings in society (Dewey 1950). A whole set of related ideas came to be seen as building blocks for systematizing a group of ideas that dealt with social functioning: *person-in-situation*, a complex and uncertainly defined idea, referred to the interrelationships of individuals and society in developing norms, making decisions, conducting actions, and achieving social stability; *role performance* referred to behavioral standards imposed and internalized; *social system* was a metaphor for laying out the idea of an organized and rational world for human beings to exist in satisfactorily (Dewey 1950; Parsons 1951).

Towle's book *The Learner* is a landmark statement of a systematically organized body of knowledge—ideas, theories, observations, and beliefs—about human nature and the social environment. It collected and organized voluminous information for understanding an individual's background, characteristics, and situation—in other words, the detail of the "person-in-situation." It outlined a comprehensive review of what a casework practitioner could do with that knowledge when confronting people in distress. *The Learner* established what constituted the practice of casework (Cockerill 1955; Hamilton 1955).

This book was a remarkable tour de force. Put forward as a book about professional education, its dust jacket announced that it was "a perceptive discussion of education for social work based on the theories of psychoana-

lytic psychiatry, possessing great meaning for all of professional education."
The first half of the book, part 1, is a general discourse on human nature, and
the means by which a human being learns and develops social skills and
capacities in modern industrial society. Included, as a particular example of
human growth and development, is a discourse on the socialization of professional students.

Part 2 sets out a body of principles that explain the phenomena that
constitute social work practice. While delineating what one should teach to
students, the book tells at the same time what one should do with clients.
The business of practice is soldered to the business of teaching students.

The Learner thus has two planes. On the one hand, it figures out and
explains what might be the processes of a teaching-learning encounter. On
the other hand, it states the content of the teaching, which is also the content of casework practice. The book explains the teaching processes according to certain psychoanalytic theories about the characteristics of the growth
and development of personality during various life stages. The work assumes
that learning a subject, casework practice, and learning to live are basically
the same process. It spells out the differences, highlighting how and what to
teach professional students.

The book puts forward a theory of human needs and development
shaped by the social environment. Towle conceives this theory as an explanation of personal growth, of professional education as a version of personal
growth, and of the growth-enhancing therapeutic technology that constitutes social work practice. It is an expansion of an earlier popular work of
Towle's, *Common Human Needs* (1945). In *The Learner* Towle combines the
theories of teaching, learning, and practicing social work into a total system,
into a "grand theory." This is as close as one can get in the social work literature to the valued style of that era, as exemplified in Talcott Parsons's
attempt to create a total theory of society and its relations to the individuals
within it, and in the attempt by David Rapaport and the ego analysts to
build a total theory of general psychology from the disconnected and contradictory parts of Freudianism (Hale 1995).

Wendy Posner, whose 1986 dissertation is a biographical study of Charlotte Towle, has traced the origins of *The Learner*. Towle worked out her
basic ideas about educational practices in numerous articles she published
during the years preceding publication of the book, revising and organizing
those pieces, which would become the text of *The Learner*. The basic educational philosophy followed the ideas developed by Ralph Tyler, a leading
scholar in the University of Chicago's Department of Education who wrote

the foreword to the book. The observations, conclusions, and recommendations for the uniquely social work education aspects of the book are derived from Towle's reflections on years of experience as a social work educator and from collegial work with faculty in curriculum development, a project taken with the utmost seriousness at a time when the field was deeply committed to constructing a solid generic approach to casework.

Thomas French was an important collaborator in developing the theory of human development explicated by Towle. He was a psychoanalyst at the Chicago Institute for Psychoanalysis and a colleague of Franz Alexander, a leading psychoanalytic theorist of the period. Alexander, in collaboration with French, gave us the idea of the "corrective emotional experience" as a major therapeutic modality. Alexander and French also produced many ideas that became the vogue for psychosomatic medicine, now virtually extinct as a viable idea (Alexander and Ross 1952; French 1952). French taught a course in psychopathology at the School of Social Service Administration, consulted widely with elite social agencies in Chicago, psychoanalyzed elite social workers, and was well connected to the social work community as a psychoanalytic mentor. His was a straightforward and no-nonsense type of psychoanalysis that valued what he called "problem-solving insight" and other rather straightforward types of practical ideas attached to the psychoanalytic core. His views, as shown in his important work on the integration of behavior, were a good match with the equally no-nonsense approach of Towle. By no-nonsense we mean the attempt to use a rhetoric of psychoanalysis that avoided making therapy seem mysterious or glamorous or strange and instead made it appear matter of fact.

Intended Sections

Alexander's influence in Towle's work–the discussion of the
    irrational underlay

Alexander–provides the main rationale for putting unreason, unconscious, underlying processes foremost, and reason only a bit.

Psy-complex needed to establish its scientific respectability.

Social work also

Chicago subculture: social work, psy., agencies

Social theorists: Rieff, Halmos, London

Era of individualism: body snatchers movie etc.

Destruction of the collective

Rampant laissez faire

Stage of capitalist society

Before the welfare state took hold

Common Human Needs: set the wide stage, including social policy

Provided rationale

Theory of the Golden Age

Charlotte Towle's earlier work and better-known work, *Common Human Needs*, is fifty years old, having appeared first in 1945. Its publishing history is dramatic because it is the only social work book ever destroyed by the government. Actually, the story is in some ways more mundane. The book became accidentally enmeshed in a political contest played out by liberals and reactionaries over a Truman proposal to introduce universal health care into the United States, a program attacked by the American Medical Association as "socialized" medicine. That kind of name calling was carried out in an endeavor to demonize the health care proposals and cause the public to react against them. The ploy succeeded, and in the process it was discovered that Towle's text, which was being used for in-service training in the newly formed public assistance programs, contained a sentence that hoped for an ideal society without want or oppression and called that a "social society," meaning humane. A recent article by Wendy Posner (1995) has gone into detail about this incident. For purposes of this essay, it is enough to say that Charlotte Towle was an inadvertent victim of a campaign to turn the American public against humane public provisions for health care and social services, and she was in the way when a steamroller came along. Like other brave women, Towle—and social work—recovered, and since then her book has been republished many times.

Common Human Needs has long been recognized as a milestone in clinical social work history. Its significance marked the end of the era of patronizing the poor, sequestering the deviant, and pursuing Victorian moral uplift as the prevailing method. *Common Human Needs* ushered in the twentieth-century modern social work that had been emerging since the 1920s.

1917	Richmond
1930	Virginia Robinson
1937	Taft
1940	Hamilton 1st ed.
1945	Towle—*CHN*
1951	Hamilton 2d ed.

1954	Towle—*Learner*
1957	Perlman
1964	Hollis—1st ed.
1965/67	Parad/Rapaport
1967	Ed Thomas
1972	Reid-Epstein

In the twentieth century, clinical social work put priority on particular beliefs and methods that were basic to modern thought everywhere. These were

- Basic human rights—in social work: Common human needs
- Basic individual rights—in social work: Self-determination
- Adherence to science—social science theories justified social work's goals, concepts, and methods.

The basic human rights addressed were

- Equality, meaning to be respected, whether of high or low status
- Opportunity, or to enjoy equal opportunity
- Freedom from oppression, to be entitled to social provisions that mitigate the most severe deprivations arising from unregulated free enterprise. (Keynes, welfare state)

The basic social science theory was an amalgamation of the then-prominent theory that social order came from a balanced person-environment equilibrium (Parsons 1951; see Johnson 1981). The developing consensus of the time was that psychodynamic personality theory (Freudianism) provided the basis for a universal set of standards and processes, establishing appropriate norms of individual development and necessary building blocks toward a good life. From these underpinnings of *Common Human Needs* came the famous viewpoint that

> the social work profession has the broad purpose of trying to make it possible for every individual to have the most productive life of which he is capable. In achieving this purpose it works within a framework of institutions in two ways: efforts that aim to reshape institutions that are failing to fulfill their function and creation of special services for groups whose needs are not met. Traditionally this second area of activity has been more peculiarly and especially the province of social work.
>
> (*Towle 1945:13*)

It is this vision of a just and compassionate humanitarian mission which is now—after fifty years—being revised in Congress and elsewhere. But Towle's legacy as the conceptualizer of this view retains a powerful pull that liberals can call upon.

Charlotte Towle was an innovator. She had no model or text, except *The Learner*. Charlotte Towle was a theoretician. She set up the rationale and framework for the technologists to work with. She was working on the creation of a clinical practice uniquely oriented to social work and that was to do something different from making remedies for disease entities. It was to affect the quality of life. It aimed to restore, rehabilitate, reconstruct, and enhance.

This aim became operationalized as a triad of social products, namely, *care-protection-treatment*. So what came to represent the distinguishing feature of clinical social work was psychotherapy with a difference; the treatment of clinical social work took into consideration treatment of a particular condition, but also and equally important were social responsibility (care) and defense against loss, insult, and danger (protection). Those are the unique elements that distinguish clinical social work and that also are sources of difficulty because they thrust this field into social domains beyond technology.

Towle did her share to put women on a plane of intellectual respectability and theory building: numerous articles on conceptualizing casework practice, curriculum building, the first course in human development, *The Learner in Education for the Professions*. Towle was of the pre-1960s generation of intellectual women who were silent on the subject of gender. Those women made no issue of being leaders in a profession started by male philanthropists, doctors, and politicians and operated by women. These women tried to carry on in a nongendered atmosphere, but that could not be. They had no choice because society in general was keeping gender issues a secret. Secret or no, the hidden dynamic of gender distorted social work.

Beyond Technology

Many people—in and out of social work—are interested in these questions: What is the role of social work in this complicated American present? What should its role be? And how has the feminine caste system shaped its history and mission? These are our issues today. They were not Towle's. She knew nothing of them. Her work is foundational. But social work today needs to make sense of changes happening to it—seemingly without agency—in a culture and politics being transformed.

Social work today is a different entity than in Towle's day. It is the generalist among the therapeutic professions. Its image is distinctly benevolent. But its function has become more and more to regulate conduct and attitudes or beliefs. Through processes of mental healing it entrenches a standard of conduct and subjective states. At the same time its adherence to belief in self-determination and individual autonomy creates inevitable tension within its processes. Combining social science, altruism, and women's conventional roles, social work's influence today is everywhere in America and has become a major instrumentality through which the state governs and provides for its citizens. I don't think all this would be too surprising to Charlotte Towle, but it surprises some of us going through these changes.

REFERENCES

Alexander, Franz and Helen Ross. 1952. *The impact of Freudian psychiatry*. Chicago: University of Chicago Press.

Berger, P. L. 1977. Toward a sociological understanding of psychoanalysis. In P. L. Berger, *Facing up to modernity: Excursions in society, politics, and religion*, pp. 23–35. New York: Basic Books.

Brewer, Colin and June Lait. 1980. *Can social work survive?* London: Temple Smith.

Castel, Robert. 1988. *The regulation of madness*. Berkeley: University of California Press.

Chambon, Adrienne S. and Allan Irving, eds. 1994. *Essays on postmodernism and social work*. Toronto: Canadian Scholars' Press.

Cockerill, Eleanor. 1955. *The Learner in Education for the Professions as Seen in Education for Social Work*, by Charlotte Towle. *Social Casework* 36, no. 4 (May): 222–23.

Cree, V. E. 1995. *From public streets to private lives: The changing task of social work*. Aldershot, U.K.: Avebury.

Dewey, John. 1950. *Human nature and conduct: An introduction to social psychology*. New York: Modern Library. .

Diner, H. R. 1985. *Service and scholarship: Seventy-five years of the School of Social Service Administration of the University of Chicago, 1908–83*. Chicago: University of Chicago, School of Social Service Administration.

Donzelot, Jacques. 1979. *The policing of families*. New York: Pantheon.

Dreyfus, H. L. and Paul Rabinow. 1982. *Michel Foucault: Beyond structuralism and hermeneutics*. Chicago: University of Chicago Press.

Ehrenreich, J. H. 1985. *The altruistic imagination: A history of social work and social policy in the United States*. Ithaca, N.Y.: Cornell University Press.

Epstein, Laura. 1992. Book review of *The rise of the therapeutic state* by A. J. Polsky. *Social Service Review* 66, no. 3 (December): 655–58.

——. 1993. April 1993 lecture. Personal papers. Estate of Laura Epstein.

——. 1994a. Origins project. Personal papers. Estate of Laura Epstein.

——. 1994b. The therapeutic idea in contemporary society. In Adrienne S. Chambon and Allan Irving, eds., *Essays on postmodernism and social work*, pp. 3–18. Toronto: Canadian Scholars' Press.

——. 1995a. The therapeutic idea: Social work influence on the character of a century: Introduction to work in progress. Invited lecture for faculty symposium. University of Chicago, School of Social Service Administration, May 10.

——. 1995b. Book review of *Fallen women, problem girls: Unmarried mothers and the professionalization of social work, 1890–1945* by R. G. Kunzel. *Social Service Review* 69, no. 3 (September): 528–30.

——. 1996a. Charlotte Towle: Theorist of the Golden Age. Invited paper presented at the conference "Exploring the Development of Social Work Practice in the Early Twentieth Century," organized in commemoration of the fiftieth anniversary of the publication of Charlotte Towle's *Common Human Needs*. University of Chicago, School of Social Service Administration, May 30–31, 1996.

——. 1996b. Book review of *From public streets to private lives: The changing task of social work* by V. E. Gree. *Social Service Review* 70, no. 2 (June): 338–41.

Foucault, Michel. 1972. *The archaeology of knowledge*. Translated by A. M. Sheridan Smith. New York: Pantheon.

——. 1973. *The order of things: An archaeology of the human sciences*. New York: Vintage/Random House.

——. 1980. *Power/knowledge: Selected interviews and other writings, 1972–77*. Edited and translated by Colin Gordon. New York: Pantheon.

——. 1984a. *The birth of the asylum*. In Paul Rabinow, ed., *The Foucault reader*, pp. 141–67. 1965. Reprint, New York: Pantheon.

——. 1984b. *The politics of health in the eighteenth century*. In Paul Rabinow, ed., *The Foucault reader*, pp. 273–89. 1977. Reprint, New York: Pantheon.

French, T. M. 1952. *The integration of behavior, vol. 1: Basic postulates*. Chicago: University of Chicago Press.

Goldstein, Jan, ed. 1994. *Foucault and the writing of history*. Cambridge, Mass.: Blackwell.

Hale, N. G. Jr. 1995. Psychoanalysis and science: American ego psychology. In N. G. Hale Jr., *The rise and crisis of psychoanalysis in the United States: Freud and the Americans, 1917–85*, pp. 232–44. New York: Oxford University Press.

Halmos, Paul. 1970. *The faith of the counsellors: A study in the theory and practice of social case work and psychotherapy*. New York: Shocken Books.

Hamilton, Gordon. 1955. *The Learner in Education for the Professions as Seen in Education for Social Work*, by Charlotte Towle. *Social Service Review* 29 (2): 207–209

Hobsbawm, Eric. 1994. *The age of extremes: A history of the world, 1914–91*. New York: Pantheon.

Hopps, J. G. and P. M. Collins. 1995. Social work profession overview. In *Encyclopedia of Social Work*, 19th ed., p. 2266. Washington, D.C.: National Association of Social Workers Press.

Johnson, H. M. 1981. Foreword. In François Bourricaud, *The sociology of Talcott Parsons.* Translated by Arthur Goldhammer. Chicago: University of Chicago Press.

Kunzel, R. G. 1993. *Fallen women, problem girls: Unmarried mothers and the professionalization of social work, 1890–1945.* New Haven, Conn.: Yale University Press.

Lunbeck, Elizabeth. 1994. *The psychiatric persuasion: Knowledge, gender, and power in modern America.* Princeton, N.J.: Princeton University Press.

Marcus, Grace. 1955. The advance of social casework in its distinctive social usefulness. *Social Casework* 36, no. 9 (November): 391–98.

Muncy, Robyn. 1991. *Creating a female dominion in American reform, 1890–1935.* New York: Oxford University Press.

Parsons, Talcott. 1951. *The social system.* New York: Free Press.

Parton, Nigel. 1994. The nature of social work under conditions of (post)modernity. *Social Work and Social Sciences Review* 5 (2): 93–112.

Polsky, A. J. 1991. *The rise of the therapeutic state.* Princeton, N.J.: Princeton University Press.

Posner, W. B. 1986. Charlotte Towle: A biography. Unpublished doctoral dissertation, School of Social Service Administration, University of Chicago.

——. 1995. *Common Human Needs:* A story from the prehistory of government by special interest. *Social Service Review* 69, no. 2 (June): 188–225.

Rieff, Philip. 1968. *The triumph of the therapeutic: Uses of faith after Freud.* New York: Harper and Row.

Sands, R. G. and Kathleen Nuccio. 1992. Postmodern feminist theory and social work. *Social Work* 37 (6): 489–94.

Towle, Charlotte. 1945. *Common human needs: An interpretation for staff in public assistance agencies.* Public Assistance report no. 8. Washington, D.C.: Government Printing Office. Rev. eds., Washington, D.C.: American Association of Social Workers, 1952; National Association of Social Workers, 1957 and 1965.

——. 1954. *The Learner in education for the professions, as seen in education for social work.* Chicago: University of Chicago Press.

Wenocur, Stanley and Michael Reisch. 1989. *From charity to enterprise: The development of American social work in a market economy.* Urbana: University of Illinois Press.

Wolin, Sheldon S. 1988. On the theory and practice of power. In Jonathan Arac, ed., *After Foucault: Humanistic knowledge, postmodern challenge,* pp. 179–201. New Brunswick, N.J.: Rutgers University Press.

CHAPTER 2

Waiting for Foucault: Social Work and the Multitudinous Truth(s) of Life

Allan Irving

Moments for nothing, now as always.

In reality I said nothing at all, but I heard a murmur, something gone wrong with the silence.

Where obscurity and light meet, there we find the inexplicable.

—Samuel Beckett

Can a play change your life? That's what happened to twenty-six-year-old Michel Foucault (1926–1984) when he went with friends to the Théâtre de Babylone in Paris in the early winter of 1953. Samuel Beckett's *Waiting for Godot* had become the theatrical talk of the town, the play everyone wanted to see (Knowlson 1996:350). A searing tragicomedy of endless waiting in a world stripped of meaning, suffused with loss and despair, *Godot* was something of an epiphany and a key formative influence for Foucault. Foucault often mentioned that in the 1950s Beckett (1906–1989) was a radical departure from the prevailing philosophical schools of thought. Shortly before Foucault's death in 1984, he remarked that

> I belong to that generation who, as students, had before their eyes, and were limited by, a horizon consisting of Marxism, phenomenology, and existentialism. Interesting and stimulating as these might be, naturally they produced in the students completely immersed in them a feeling of being stifled, and the urge to look elsewhere. I was like all

other students of philosophy at that time, and for me the break was first Beckett's Waiting for Godot.   *(Begam 1996:185)*

Beckett often claimed that he worked out of impotence and ignorance, failure, and intuitive despair and once described his characters "as falling to bits" as they try to fend off the silence of an impending and foreboding nothingness (Gontarski 1985:6, 14). Beckett was drawn to pure incoherence and had a deep distrust of rational efforts to shape, explain, and dispel the chaos of human affairs. Shortly after he saw Beckett's play, Foucault began reading the nineteenth-century philosopher Friedrich Nietzsche (1844–1900). The central questions I explore in this chapter are why Beckett and Nietzsche were so important to Foucault, how all three thought about the multitudinous truth(s) of life, and, most important, what social work might look like filtered through the lens of Nietzsche, Beckett, and Foucault.

All three developed their ideas and interpretations of the world outside the Cartesian/positivist paradigm, through a quest that was tortured and full of struggle. I explore Foucault's work as a philosopher and suggest that Foucault overturns two sorts of certainties: an external empirical reality to be perceived and counted, and an internal certainty about a solid subjectivity. Through these decentering uncertainties Foucault reorganizes the relationship between the two planes. Beckett remarked that "anyone nowadays, anybody who pays the slightest attention to his own experience, finds it the experience of a non-knower" (Shenker 1974:198), and in 1946 he spoke of "an inkling of the terms in which our condition is to be thought again" (Gordon 1996:202). As modernity moves relentlessly toward the threshold of its dissolution, we need to consider how our social work condition is to be thought again, of how—from a postmodern perspective informed by Nietzsche, Beckett, and Foucault—social work's intellectual heritage of the Enlightenment—humanism, rationalism, and science—needs to be subjected to an extended critique and ultimately transformed.

At the end of her provocative 1997 book, *Under the Cover of Kindness: The Invention of Social Work*, Leslie Margolin observes that social workers often offend "against discourse, complexity, difference." Social work steers away, she argues, from making deep criticisms of itself "for fear of destroying an illusion of unanimity." Social work constantly invents favorable stories about itself and "condemns reformulation to silence and bad conscience." As did Beckett, she entreats us to explore "new, radically different understandings . . . if we are to find a way out" (1997:179, 180). Resident on this chapter's tongue is the wish to avoid safe thoughts and to try to open up intellectual horizons. It does not offer immediate and practical guidance on the conduct of social work but moves toward testing our boundaries and visions of social life. I have written in the belief that radical questioning and fearless thinking at the extremities can lead to an understanding of the world at a deeper level. Like the characters in Don DeLillo's novel *Underworld* (1997), we can try to grasp the world in all its lyric discontinuity. In this process the reader has an active role to assign meaning to the words, to be a mediator of the meaning.

Beckett's idiom certainly found its way into Foucault's work on the "cogito and madness," the "death of the author," and the "end of man," and Foucault describes his own work as his "great Nietzschean quest" (J. Miller 1993:68). Undoubtedly, Foucault's quest was inspired too by the example of Beckett's characters, who struggle heroically toward identity and meaning in a world that is ultimately unfathomable (Gordon 1996:82). All Beckett's work shimmers with the impossibility of communication because "there is *nothing* to express, nothing with which to express, nothing from which to express, no power to express, no desire to express, together with the obligation to express." When Beckett says there is "nothing from which to express" he means that the self is not a unity, not a fully coherent being, but rather an interplay of presence and absence. Describing the world as "the mess," Beckett suggests that our only hope for redemption is "to open our eyes and see the mess. It is not a mess you can make sense of" (Gontarski 1985:10, 20).

Beckett was something of a Nietzschean, who, in his novels and plays—to use Nietzsche's words from his 1873 essay "On Truth and Lies in a Non-moral Sense"—takes the "immense framework and planking of concepts" (1979:90) that is Western metaphysics and "smashes it to pieces, throws it into confusion, and puts it back together in an ironic fashion" (Begam 1996:9). Irony here means a recognition that the world in essence is paradoxical and only an ambivalent approach and attitude can grasp its contradictions; irony releases the possibility for holding widely divergent interpretations, including that of not knowing. This too was the landscape that Foucault sifted through and tore apart, endlessly reworking the way we saw the world, society, and the self.

A brief comment about the transition from modernity to postmodernity may help to provide some explanatory scaffolding and a broad context for what follows. Scholars now widely accept that postmodernism is the best concept for understanding our present historical condition (Harvey 1989; Jameson 1991; Lyotard 1991; Chambon and Irving 1994). As historian Keith Jenkins has intimated, our postmodern condition has developed from the failure of the "experiment" in social living known as modernity. This has revolved around the failure of the eighteenth-century Enlightenment to create through reason, science, and technology social and economic well-being. The Enlightenment established a metanarrative claim that history has meaningful trajectories, purposes, and teleologies (definite ends) such as the Enlightenment story of the steady progress of reason and freedom or Marx's inevitable path to a communist utopia. Within the context of modernity, history was seen as operating according to specific laws of development that were inevitably progressive. Postmodernism challenges this view and suggests that no "real foundations" or essences ever have undergirded the modernist experiment. Postmodernism posits uncertainty, dispenses with objectivity and disinterest and notions of stable truths. In place of modernist certainty, postmodernism calls us to various positionings, perspectives, and creations (Jenkins 1997:4, 20–24).

The period from the 1870s through the 1950s can be viewed as a solid era of scientific positivism in intellectual life, including academic social work. Reliance on scientific method, regardless of field of inquiry, was seen as the only sure guide to progress and provided reliable standards for truth, because empirical methods lead inexorably to conclusions on which everyone can agree. A good example is the pragmatism of philosopher John Dewey, who, in works such as *Reconstruction in Philosophy* (1920), regarded human history as advancing in an evolutionary way from more "primitive" periods, when the irrationalism of religion was supreme, to our more "advanced" modern period, when scientific method created "higher" stages of fulfillment. The quest and desire for objective truth meant, *inter alia*, the replacement of religious authority with scientific governance (Marsden 1997:26–27).

Until the 1960s the rule of science was a characteristic of modernity in academic life; however, since then there has been a trend, gradually establishing a region of postmodernism, that runs counter to a faith in a universal and objective scientific methodology. Since the publication of Thomas Kuhn's *The Structure of Scientific Revolutions* (1962), most scholars have come to agree that science itself rests on assumptions that lie beyond scientific proof. "In the humanities in recent years," writes historian George Marsden, "much of the most heralded scholarship has been directed toward attacking the assumption that there should be one objective, scientifically based outlook on which all fair-minded people should agree" (1997:27).

Nietzsche, Beckett, and Foucault call into question and hurl into doubt the foundations of modernity and its assumptions about truth and knowledge that underpin a field such as social work. All three split open the ground under the present, revealing a cruel vein of awareness that the Enlightenment certainties, which we built and relied on, have crumbled into dust. They all challenged and worked outside the modern tradition of truth and knowledge established by one of modernity's key intellectual founders, the seventeenth-century French philosopher and mathematician René Descartes. In works such as *Discourse on the Method of Rightly Conducting One's Reason and Reaching the Truth in the Sciences* (1637) and *Principles of Philosophy* (1641), Descartes lays out the essentials of the Cartesian system. He describes philosophy as being like a tree: the roots are metaphysics, the trunk physics, and the branches the different sciences. This famous simile illuminates three central characteristics of the Cartesian system.

First, Descartes insists that all knowledge has an essential unity, a striking contrast to Aristotle's notion of the sciences as a string of separate disciplines with their own methods and ways of measuring the truth. Second is Descartes's view that philosophy raises a canopy of useful postulates, namely, that philosophy has utility for ordinary living. Sticking with his figurative tree, he suggests that its fruits can be gathered "not from the roots or the trunk but from the ends of the branches" representing the practical sciences. We should, he avers, acquire knowledge that is "useful in life" and would ultimately make us "masters and possessors of nature" (Cottingham 1995:194). Third, comparing metaphysics, or "first philosophy," to the roots of the tree established Cartesian foundationalism: the position that knowledge must be constructed from the bottom up and based on first principles (194). Social work from its origins to the present has located its center of gravity in these Cartesian foundations of modernism. The nature of knowledge, research, and truth for social work has largely relied on the methods of Descartes.

Nietzsche, Beckett, and Foucault all advance forms of anti-Cartesianism and offer extended critiques of the intellectual heritage of the Enlightenment and hence of social work. It is important to keep in mind that the word *Enlightenment* was and is a highly gendered term, for, as Sandra Harding informs us,

> The Enlightenment vision explicitly denied that women possess the reason and powers of dispassionate, objective observation [and stated that] . . . women could be objects of masculine reason and observation but never the subjects, never the reflecting and universalizing human minds. Only men were in fact envisioned as ideal knowers, for only

men (of appropriate class, race and culture) possessed the innate capacities for socially transcendent observation and reason.   *(1992:345)*

Nietzsche, Beckett, and Foucault subject two features of the Cartesian legacy in particular to the intense glare of criticism: philosophical foundationalism and intuitional normativism. Philosophical foundationalism, known as Descartes's famous Method, is premised on the view that all genuine knowledge is constructed on the foundation or ground of an indisputable first truth such as the cogito—Descartes's cogito, ergo sum—the starting point of his system of knowledge. All knowledge that flows from this first indisputable principle will be valid as long as it is correctly reasoned. Intuitional normativism refers to Descartes's notion of empiricism, that the truth lies "out there" in some objective sense, waiting to be discovered or found. Nietzsche, Beckett, and Foucault all depart from these Cartesian principles on which modernity has been constructed, seeing reality instead as contingent and historical, constructed out of language and cultural codes. There is no knowledge that is true in itself, that is independent of the languages and institutions that we create and invent. Empirical reality does not exist as a universal truth but as an unending collection of "stories" that we tell. The truth is made, not found (Begam 1996:15). Meaning is acquired through culturally conditioned paradigms. In the preface to *The Order of Things: An Archaeology of the Human Sciences* (1970) Foucault draws this picture: "The fundamental codes of a culture—those governing its language, its schemas of perception, its exchanges, its techniques, its values, the hierarchy of its practices—establish for every man, from the very first, the empirical orders with which he will be dealing and within which he will be at home" (1973:xx).

Nietzsche

Nietzsche was among the first to offer a sustained critique of the Cartesian worldview, and his influence on Foucault was early and profound. "Nietzsche was a revelation," Foucault said years later. "I read him with a great passion and broke with my life. . . . I had the feeling I had been trapped" (J. Miller 1993:67). In his preface to the original French text of *Madness and Civilization: A History of Insanity in the Age of Reason* (1961) Foucault alludes to the deep influence of Nietzsche. His own work, Foucault suggested, would be "to confront the dialectics of history with the unchanging structure of the tragic" (quoted in J. Miller 1993:67). All his intellectual inquiries would be carried out, Foucault declared, *"sous le soleil de la grande recherche Nietzschéene"* (under the sun of the great Nietzschean quest).

It was Nietzsche's *Untimely Meditations* (1876), a collection of four essays, that in the summer of 1953 first laid siege to Foucault's imagination. In an earlier work, *The Birth of Tragedy* (1872), Nietzsche had unveiled a striking theory of tragedy. The tragic for Nietzsche and for Foucault consists of two contested fundamental drives: the Apollonian desire to shape the world according to logic and order and pleasing proportions, and the Dionysian compulsion to shatter all forms of order and to endlessly transgress all boundaries between the conscious and unconscious, reason and unreason (J. Miller 1993:67).

Untimely Meditations was Nietzsche's attempt to sort out for himself some purpose and direction. His search, and it became Foucault's too, was for some realization of "how one becomes what one is" (Nietzsche 1983:155). Foucault was especially taken with one of Nietzsche's aphorisms: "The enigma which man is to resolve he can resolve only in being, in being thus and not otherwise, in the imperishable. . . . Be yourself! All you are now doing, thinking, desiring, is not you yourself" (127). Both Nietzsche and Foucault dismiss the notion that the self is simply given. Truth for both, and this includes the truth about one's self, "is not something there, that might be found or discovered . . . but that must be created" (Nietzsche 1966a:26). As Nietzsche puts it, "Our body is but a social structure and our self is but the contingent and changing product of a shifting deployment of cultural and corporeal forces" (1967:298). Reading Nietzsche convinced Foucault that to even begin to approach the truth means tearing oneself out of the routines and habits of everyday life. People concerned with finding their own truth must descend, Nietzsche writes in *Untimely Meditations,* "into the depths of existence with a string of curious questions . . . : why do I live? what lesson have I to learn from life? how have I become what I am and why do I suffer from being what I am?" (1983:154).

In his 1873 essay "On Truth and Lies in a Nonmoral Sense" (in *Philosophy and Truth)* Nietzsche launched what was to become a central theme that threaded its way through all his philosophy: a critique of the intellectual heritage of the Enlightenment. The essay was a complete repudiation of the empirical paradigm. Nietzsche rejected the Enlightenment-Cartesian assumption that the cogito provides the ground for all knowledge. In an often cited passage from his essay, Nietzsche suggests that truth is only and always a "movable host of metaphors . . . a sum of human relations"

(1979:84). Ultimately, Nietzsche pinpoints two fundamental problems in the empirical tradition. First, it disregards the role that language has in creating and constructing the world, and, second, it assumes that everyone perceives the world in the same way. This second observation is Nietzsche's celebrated notion of perspectivism—that every view is only one among the many interpretations possible. Alexander Nehamas in *Nietzsche: Life as Literature* suggests that Nietzsche regarded the world as an artwork, a kind of literary text (1985:1, 3). Just as literary texts can be interpreted in quite different and often incompatible ways, Nietzsche argues that the world is open to similar kinds of interpretation.

It is not possible, Nietzsche argues, to claim that one framework is true and another false. No universal criteria or higher authority (once a belief in God had been dispatched) can be invoked to assert that one perspective is true and another not. Nietzsche also tore ruthlessly into the rationalism and scientism that underlay the empiricist paradigm. Within the confines and restrictions of this paradigm, individuals were constantly trying to demonstrate that they were rational beings by putting "their behaviour under the control of abstractions" and by "universalizing all these impressions into less colourful, cooler concepts, so that they can entrust the guidance of their life and conduct to them." Science and empiricism imposed more rigid ways of thinking and stripped away the role of language in constructing the world in a multitude of ways. But Nietzsche was adamant that science and empiricism offer no more an "objective" explanation of the world and reality than, for example, ancient myths (1979:84–88). Throughout his writing Nietzsche casts adrift the most fundamental ideas of Western culture: disinterested thought and objective truth. For Nietzsche, the search for disinterested truth is nonsense, because all the search can ever amount to is a setting forth of one's own "truth." Philosophers in the future, Nietzsche argued, would not make extravagant claims that they were seeking the truth. They would say with Nietzsche, "My judgement is my judgement: no one else is easily entitled to it. . . . What the philosophers of the future say will be their truth; it will not be a truth for everyman" (S. Miller 1997:31–32).

In *The Will to Power* Nietzsche boldly asserts that "facts are precisely what there is not, only interpretations" (1968:481). Universal notions of the truth lead inevitably toward dogmatism. It is crucial to recognize that one's beliefs may not be true for everyone. The "new philosophers" (could we say new social workers?) that Nietzsche envisaged would be encouraged to speak their beliefs in this nondogmatic sense:

Are these coming philosophers new friends of truth? That is probable enough, for all philosophers so far have loved their truths. But they will certainly not be dogmatists. It must offend their pride, also their taste, if their truth is supposed to be a truth for everyman—which has so far been the secret wish and hidden meaning of all dogmatic aspirations. "My Judgement is my judgement": no one else is easily entitled to it—that is what such a philosopher of the future may perhaps say of himself. (Nietzsche 1966:53)

Accepting these sentiments means going beyond simply assenting to sets of propositions. It also involves accepting the values that are preconditions for and undergird those views that are different and understanding and accepting the modes of life that arise from those values. Nietzsche believed that no one mode of life is proper, desirable, or even possible for everyone; therefore, no set of views can command universal assent (Nehamas 1985:34).

Social work has not yet fully absorbed this Nietzschean news and the implications for a truly diverse multicultural practice. It would mean, among other things, consigning empiricist/positivist explanations to one of many stories or interpretations with no particular privilege over any other. To transform social work from a modernist practice to one that truly is diverse and postmodern would be to draw on styles other than just science: the arts, the humanities—literature, poetry, philosophy, theology.

Nietzschean perspectivism certainly implies that no particular point of view is privileged so that those who hold it can claim a better or truer picture of the world than any other. Science, for Nietzsche, is an interpretation and provides neither an ultimate interpretation of the world nor a description of the world as it actually is. Science is not a practice that is superior to other ways of knowing—other ways that are, at least in social work, all too often deemed secondary and inferior. In social work the methods of science, at least since Abraham Flexner's famous speech in 1915 when he declared that social work could not be a profession because it was not scientific enough, have been assumed to be better than any others. The humanities, for example, are viewed as not offering the same kind of certain foundation for knowledge (Austin 1983; Nehamas 1985:65). Nietzsche flays the privileging of the methods of science and its exclusive claims to truth, and in *The Gay Science* he excoriates the elevation of empiricism:

That the only justifiable interpretation of the world should be one in which *you* are justified because one can continue to work and do research scientifically in *your* sense (you really mean, mechanistically?)—an interpretation that permits counting, calculating, weighing, seeing, and touching, and nothing more—that is a crudity and naivete, assuming that it is not a mental illness, and idiocy.   *(1974:373)*

Foucault is the most iconoclastic of postwar Nietzscheans. He extended Nietzsche's critique of disinterested, objective truth, arguing that we all are captive of what he calls "regimes of truth" or the prevailing norms of a particular society at a particular historical time. Nietzsche's notion of genealogy, a practice that exposes the particular, interested origins of particular views when they first emerge, origins that we subsequently forget are views only and begin to regard as facts, is crucial for Foucault, because it becomes for him the way for putting truth in its place, that is, in its historical context. Foucault acknowledges that we cannot think other than as we do, within the contexts and confines of a specific era, but realizing this limitation offers a bright promise: we might be able to call certain truths into question and to challenge accepted beliefs (S. Miller 1997:32–33; Hutchings 1996:104). All Foucault's work is shot through with a concern for limits and the possibilities for transcending all limits. These themes are a central preoccupation of *The Order of Things*. Foucault is much less interested in tracing ideas as they develop historically than in excavating the conditions of their possibility, what he calls an epistemological field, or "episteme." By the episteme of an age Foucault means not a worldview or ideology but instead a potential system of discourse that underlies bodies of knowledge and allows some statements to be seen as true and others false (1980:112–13). This discourse is what Foucault designates as the historical a priori: "This *a priori* is what, in a given period, delimits in the totality of experience a field of knowledge, defines the mode of being of the objects that appear in that field, provides man's everyday perception with theoretical powers and defines the conditions in which he can sustain a discourse about things that is recognized to be true" (1973:158).

In *The Order of Things* the concept of the episteme defines the conditions of possibility of thought in a given historical period, legislating and establishing the limits of understanding: "In any given culture and at any given moment, there is always only one *episteme* that defines the conditions of possibility of all knowledge, whether expressed in a theory or silently invested in a practice" (1973:168).

Nietzsche was the originator of the agenda that reappears in Beckett and Foucault for what is known as the "end of modernity" discourse—a piercing critique of those customs, practices, and vestments of the Enlightenment.

Foucault's startling and famous claim in *The Order of Things*, that the "end of man" is very close to arriving, has become a touchstone in the larger colloquy about the end of modernity. The concluding few sentences of *The Order of Things* are chillingly apocalyptic:

> The archaeology of our thought easily shows man is an invention of recent date. And one perhaps nearing its end. . . . If those arrangements [which define man] were to disappear as they appeared, if some event . . . were to cause them to crumble, as the ground of Classical thought did, at the end of the eighteenth century, then one can certainly wager that man would be erased, like a face drawn in the sand at the edge of the sea. *(1973:387)*

In relentlessly pressing for what was philosophically new, for possibilities of thought that lay beyond Enlightenment empiricism, Foucault in *The Order of Things* recognizes his deep debt to Nietzsche and his critique of the foundational grand narratives (science, empiricism/positivism, reason, the nature of man, universal morality, progress) of the Enlightenment:

> Nietzsche rediscovered the point at which man and God belong to one another, at which the death of the second is synonymous with the disappearance of the first. . . . In this, Nietzsche, offering this future to us as both promise and task, marks the threshold beyond which contemporary philosophy can begin thinking again. . . . Then the end of man . . . is the return of the beginning of philosophy. It is no longer possible to think in our day than in the void left by man's disappearance. For this void does not create a deficiency; it does not constitute a lacuna that must be filled. It is nothing more, and nothing less, than the unfolding of a space in which it is once more possible to think.
>
> *(1973:342)*

Nietzsche was the first to offer a sustained offensive against modernity's fixation with "knowing the truth." We should, he maintains, abandon the desire to find a single context for all human lives. In achieving self-knowledge, we are not discovering a truth out there; instead, self-knowledge is only and always self-creation. Nietzsche's profound message is that there are no enduring truths beyond time and chance. Rather than a futile search for eternal unchanging truth and meaning, Nietzsche urges the creation of new meaning out of the contingencies of one's existence. Life is something to be fashioned in the process of becoming who one is. (Rorty 1989:27, 29; Nehamas 1985:7).

Throughout his life Foucault drew sustenance and courage from Nietzsche's thought, and tucked away in the crevices of Foucault's mind were the insights gleaned from a deep immersion in the philosopher's works. Foucault's intellectual indebtedness to Nietzsche was brilliantly on display in 1971 when he delivered a series of lectures on Aristotle and Nietzsche that offer a pellucid guide through the tangles of Nietzsche's convictions about the nature of knowledge and truth. Foucault also used the occasion to set out his own beliefs:

- Knowledge is an "invention" behind which lies something completely different from itself: a play of instincts, impulses, desires, fear, a will to appropriate. It is on the stage where these elements battle one another that knowledge is produced.

- It is produced not as a result of the harmony or happy equilibrium of these elements, but rather as the result of their antagonism, of their dubious and provisional compromise, of a fragile truce that they are always prepared to betray. Knowledge is not a permanent faculty, it is an event, or perhaps a series of events.

- It is always enslaved, dependent, and enthralled (not to itself but to whatever can enthrall an instinct, or the instincts that dominate it).

- And if it presents itself as knowledge of the truth, it is because it produces the truth, through the play of a primary and always reconstituted falsification, which establishes the distinction between the true and the false.

    (J. Miller 1993:214)

These perspectives on knowledge and truth were decidedly anti-Enlightenment, and in *The Order of Things* Foucault drove his thought to the extreme position where he describes a modernist/postmodernist culture where there is no "nature of man," science is no longer autonomous or universal, no morality is possible at all, and the question of the "limits" of experience is taken up by avant-garde artists. Scientific, aesthetic, and moral problems become problems of language, which have no foundation beyond themselves. Thought through language tries to uncover the structures of our society and experience, and it goes further in trying "to think the unthought" (Foucault 1973:322–27). The unthought! This is Beckett territory, and Hill has observed that "the crux of Beckett's writing [is what] . . . cannot be named . . . that which is in-between positions of meaning, neither positive or negative, constantly shifting and irreducible to either object or subject" (1990:8–9). In the early 1930s Beckett spoke of a radical new kind of literature, what he calls the "literature of the unword" (1984:173). In Foucault's singular efforts to undermine the metaphysical and humanist/rationalist traditions of the Enlightenment, his writings contain many Beckettian resonances, and the notion of the unword is one of the most striking. In a section of *The Order of Things* called "The 'Cogito' and the Unthought," Foucault writes of trying to think beyond the outer limits of Cartesian dualism in a way that noticeably recalls Beckett's novel *The Unnamable* (1958): "The question is no longer: How can experience of nature give rise to necessary judgements? But rather: How can man think what he does not think, inhabit as though by a mute occupation something that eludes him, animate with a kind of frozen movement that figure of himself that takes the form of a stubborn exteriority?" (1973:323).

Beckett

At the center of Beckett's art is a profound yet heroic pessimism. Mired in despair, one searches for hope and goes on in the profound stoicism contained in the final words of *The Unnamable*: "You must go on, I can't go on, I'll go on" (1965:414). In *Worstward Ho* a character says, "Try again. Fail again. Fail better" (Gussow 1996:68). In novels and plays that are as lilting and mournful as the sea, Beckett unsparingly examines the abyss, although the struggles and endurance of his characters are arrows aimed straight at the heart and their monologues tend "towards the condition of unanswered prayers" (Higgins 1996:7–8). Asked what he valued most in his own work, Beckett replied, "What I don't understand" (19).

Beckett speaks of throwing away all intellectual solutions and moving away from the destructive need to dominate life; "It is not even possible to talk about truth," Beckett remarked, "that's part of the anguish" (Juliet 1989:17). He had great admiration for the mystics, for those who viewed the world and the self outside Cartesian logic: "I admire their disregard for logic, their burning illogicality—the flame that consumes the rubbish heap of logic" (27). All Beckett's work takes us beyond the severe limitations of Cartesian dualism, away from the blinding glare of rationalism and empiricism into the night where things, in the process of decomposition, also reawaken our senses, as described in his 1958 novel *Molloy*: "And that night there was no question of moon, nor any other light, but it was a night of listening, a night given to the faint soughing and sighing stirring at night in little pleasure gardens. . . . where there is less constraint. . . . Yes, there were

times when I forgot not only who I was, but that I was, forgot to be"
(1965:48, 49).

For Beckett, Descartes's dualism contains a kind of madness that radically splits mind and body and presents experience in distinct realms—the
necessary precondition for rationalism, empiricism, and science. Beckett's
deconstruction of the Cartesian paradigm and his continual exploration of
Nietzschean themes of indeterminacy, contingency, and unfixed and unpredictable forms takes on a new intensity in a sudden revelation in 1946. This
revelation shattered Beckett's trust in empirical knowledge, when the need
to know things intellectually collapsed for him (Juliet 1989:18). This vision
is given life in his play *Krapp's Last Tape.*

> Spiritually a year of profound gloom and indigence until that memo-
> rable night in March, at the end of the jetty, in the howling wind,
> never to be forgotten, when suddenly I saw the whole thing. The vision
> at last. This I fancy is what I have chiefly to record this evening, against
> the day when my work will be done and perhaps no place left in my
> memory, warm or cold, for the miracle that . . . for the fire that set it
> alight. What I suddenly saw then was this, that the belief I had been
> going on all my life, namely—great granite rocks the foam flying up in
> the light of the lighthouse and the wind-gauge spinning like a pro-
> peller, clear to me at last that the dark I have always struggled to keep
> under is in reality my most-unshatterable association until my dissolu-
> tion of storm and night with the light of the understanding and the
> fire.   *(1958:20–21)*

This passage represents one of Beckett's intuitive flashes of a non-Cartesian
beyond, a disruption of the wilderness of Cartesian dualism of distinct
minds and bodies. In Cartesian epistemology the way to knowledge is
through an observer standing in relation to the world, a subject (mind) in
relation to an object. The Cartesian mind sorts data, organizes material, and
scrutinizes validity. Beckett's literary works undermine Cartesian dialectics
and all apodeictic (absolutely certain) knowledge. In his novel *Watt* ([1953]
1959) Beckett gives us a vision of the cogito, the knowing mind come to
nothing. Subjectivity is so enfeebled that it is an absence, a departed presence, where even the certitude of inner existence collapses into nonbeing.
The Cartesian self as self-presence, existing beyond all doubt as the foundational starting point for all certain knowledge, in Beckett becomes a nullity
(Begam 1996:66, 86, 87).

Both Beckett and Foucault reject—as Nietzsche did before them—the postmedieval tradition of humanism, which developed through the Renaissance into the full-blown rationality of the Enlightenment. Associated with this tradition is the belief in the ability of humanity to know the universe and to understand our place in it. This is the empirical world of the schoolroom, the laboratory, science, mathematics, proportion, the world of the *pensum* (the mind, cogito). For Beckett's characters and narrators the *punctum* (the body), the lived, feeling experience of existence, punctures the known world of the mind. Offsetting the certain world of the mind is the dark, mysterious, inexplicable chthonic (the underworld) of the punctum (Gontarski 1995:xxv). Beckett's novel *Murphy* (1938) finds at the heart of the cogito not the rationalism and certainty and stability of the Enlightenment but the insanity of the lunatic asylum; all through Beckett's novels, images of the madhouse recur where chaos and unmeaning prevail (Begam 1996:38, 40).

In *Murphy* Beckett explores the space that separates reason from unreason and the cogito from madness. Subsequently, Foucault explores this region in *Madness and Civilization* (1961). Foucault's central argument is that during the Middle Ages and the Renaissance madness was considered more a part of everyday life and not excluded from society. Earlier historical periods saw a relatively free exchange between the "sane" and the "mad," with the mad having a culturally significant role to play in society. Madness itself was a form of knowledge, pointing to "the secret powers of the world," and madness was "the truth of knowledge" (Foucault 1965:xii, 21, 25). With the Enlightenment and modernity, this reality shifted to what Foucault calls the Great Confinement; the mad were no longer seen as citizens, and they were placed in asylums away from the society that now tried to deny their very existence. Madness was now clearly marked as the negation of reason, its antithetical Other, a condition of nonbeing:

> Joining vision and blindness, image and judgement, hallucination and language, sleep and waking, day and night, madness is ultimately nothing, for it unites in them all that is negative. . . . There is only one word which summarizes this experience, *Unreason:* all that, for reason, is closest and most remote, emptiest and most complete; all that presents itself to reason in familiar structures—authorizing a knowledge, and then a science, which seeks to be positive—and all that is constantly in retreat from reason, in the inaccessible domain of nothingness.
>
> *(Foucault 1965:107)*

Foucault contends that a direct parallel exists between the way the Enlightenment tried to eliminate madness from society and the way

Descartes tried to expunge Unreason from philosophy. As Foucault suggests, Descartes places madness outside the structures of truth, where madness could never be one of the conditions under which thought occurs, because madness is unthinkable, lying outside the boundaries of truth as defined by the cogito. The crucial point for Foucault is that "a line of partition is traced that will soon render impossible the familiar experience in the Renaissance of an Unreasonable reason, of a reasonable Unreason" (Begam 1996:41). In *Murphy,* and in *Madness and Civilization,* both Beckett and Foucault move the battle lines to different ground, away from Cartesian dualism (mind/body) and the desire to coordinate subject and object, to observe and record their points of correspondence, an empirical practice that establishes the system of rationalism, empiricism, and science. Beckett's Murphy desires to move from the cogito to madness, to escape from the weight of subject-object dichotomies, and to will himself into a state of indeterminacy. Again this brings us to the unthinkable, the unthought, and *The Unnamable,* Beckett's 1958 novel that permeated Foucault's thought, a work that sends unreason like a deadly bullet into the center of Cartesian reason and certainty.

For Descartes the cogito begins in absolute doubt and introspection and by this method uncovers a primary certainty, the famous, "I think therefore I am." On the other hand, the Beckettian cogito as manifest in *The Unnamable* confirms only utter confusion about identity: "At no moment do I know what I'm talking about, nor of whom, nor of where, nor how nor why. . . . I doubted my own existence and even still today, I have no faith in it, none" (1965:338, 390–91). Cartesian doubt leads inevitably to certain indubitable truth and the dispelling of all doubt. The Unnamable doubts now and forever and prefers to remain unknowing. As a strict rationalist, Descartes knows he can never be deceived, for thinking, when properly done, operates by rules of reason. In his *Meditations* Descartes declares, "I can already establish as a general principle that everything which we conceive very clearly and very distinctly is wholly true" (1964:92). For the Unnamable the laws of the mind bring only incertitude and failure, impotence, "no need to think in order to despair" (Beckett 1965:367). The opening page of *The Unnamable* twice uses the word *aporia,* which means lack of passage, so that in an aporia the intellect has no passage and can make no headway (Levy 1995:92). In Beckett the path from ignorance to truth and knowledge is permanently blocked by the methods of Descartes, and in turn much of Foucault's work involves exploring other ways of thinking and talking about truth.

Foucault

In *Beyond Good and Evil* Nietzsche asks: "Suppose we want truth: why not rather untruth? and uncertainty? even ignorance?" (1966a:9). Beckett continues this deconstruction of the Cartesian paradigm, and ultimately Foucault spins his own anti-Cartesian web, writing in *The Use of Pleasure* about philosophical activity:

> In what does it consist, if not in the endeavour to know how and to what extent it might be possible to think differently, instead of legitimating what is already known? There is always something ludicrous in philosophical discourse when it tries, from the outside, to dictate to others, to tell them where their truth is and how to find it, or when it works up a case against them in the language of naive positivity.
>
> *(1986:8–9)*

In 1983 Foucault commented that the basic problem he always came back to was the question of truth and how truth is to be told (Rothstein 1994:386–87). Much of Foucault's work points to the need for transgressive counterdiscourses, an endless questioning of the systems of thought in which we are located and hence an opening up of realms of freedom accomplished through speaking the truths of the multiplicities that traverse the self.

Foucault draws us away from Enlightenment ideas of a universal history, atemporal truth, and a human nature that is fixed and timeless. He looks to pluralities, provisional truths, and many changing practices of knowledge. Foucault exhorts us to become free of dogmatic unities and the claimed self-evidence of particular systems of thought. There is no one correct method to explore questions of truth; the imagination is as valid and as precise as scientific measuring instruments. There are no sure truths but only games of truth, nor are there ultimate rational grounds for knowledge or universal prescriptive policies (Rajchman 1985:3–5).

In lectures given in 1973 and 1974 Foucault examines two separate approaches to the truth. One he describes through the use of the word *l'enquête*, meaning inquiry, survey, or inquest; the other by the word *l'épreuve*, revolving around esoteric rituals involving an ordeal, test, or trial. Arriving at the truth through inquiry is a methodological foundation of modernity, a belief that "truth" is objective, that it can be confirmed and reconfirmed through proper methods of scientific inquiry and will produce a truth that is universal. But, as Foucault writes, "We also find profoundly rooted in our civilization another idea of truth repugnant to both science and philosophy" (J. Miller 1993:270). In this countertradition truth emerges from "propitious moments" and "privileged places" where ordeals unfold. One example of a propitious place, as Foucault notes, is Delphi, where Socrates receives the Oracle's prediction that leads to his own lifelong quest to know the truth; another is the ordeal of terminal illness. This interpretation of the truth has enormous transformative potential, for, as Foucault writes,

> One may then suppose in our civilization a whole technology of truth that scientific practice has step-by-step discredited, covered up, and driven out. The truth here does not belong to the order of that which is, but rather of that which happens: it is an event. [Truth] is not given by the mediation of instruments such as those found in modern laboratories; it is rather produced directly, inscribed in the body and soul of a single person. Far from being regulated by rigorous rules of method, "truth" as the outcome of an ordeal is provoked by rituals; it is attained by tricks, one seizes it only by chance: through strategy and not method. The happening of truth thus produced in the individual who lies in wait for it, and is struck by it, creates a relationship, not of an object to a knowing subject, but rather a relationship that is ambiguous, reversible. . . . a relationship of power   *(J. Miller 1993:270–72)*

If we could begin to reflect on truth as emergent and refurbishing, we could perhaps think differently outside the restraints of the Cartesian paradigm. With courage and desire it is possible to create, transcend, and transform all conventional wisdom. Foucault finally realizes that the obligation of truth is ultimately the truth about himself, a confession, a profound interiority. Toward the end of his life, determined to tell the truth about himself more directly, to follow his Nietzschean quest to become what one is, Foucault quoted and talked about what Beckett in *The Unnamable* calls this "wordless thing in an empty place, a hard shut dry cold black place, where nothing stirs, nothing speaks, and that I listen, and that I seek, like a caged beast born of caged beasts born of caged beasts born of caged beasts born in a cage" (1965:386). Truth!

Social Work Under Conditions of Radical Doubt

Whither social work within the world of Nietzsche, Beckett, Foucault, a world without the possibility of final knowledge, a world of multiple truths taking shape from multiple sources? Since early in the twentieth century, social work has located itself within the Enlightenment/scientific paradigm, based on a Cartesian interpretation of the world and knowledge. Nietzsche, Beckett, and Foucault provoke us to think differently, outside the usual social science/positivist framework and to move us away from the empiricist mess, into the postmodern world of disrupted rational grids. A shattering of forms becomes possible if we draw on other sources for our knowledge and practice. What if our main knowledge base was constructed from the humanities? Artist Marcel Duchamp demonstrates the importance of imperviousness to fixed meanings (Tomkins 1996), and novelist Richard Ford thinks of his characters "as being rather unfixed. I think of them as changeable, provisional, unpredictable, decidedly unwhole" (1996:46).

Is it possible to have a professional social work practice under conditions of radical doubt about that practice, a practice historically emplotted within the positivities of Enlightenment reason? One road into this question is suggested by historian Elizabeth Ermarth, who has observed "that the distinction between what is invented and what is real is one that for many reasons we can no longer afford" (1997:47). By abandoning the dualism between invention and reality, and by turning to fiction making as the primary mode of consciousness and the foundation of discourse, we may be able to open up alternative possibilities and many discourses other than rational/Enlightenment ones. With a renewed emphasis on text and language, an "enduring creative power" may emerge from the repressed darkness (Ermarth:62). Samuel Beckett's postmodern writing, for example, can help to diffuse and perhaps even erase received and privileged ideas, especially those associated with the great rationalization of faculties in the Renaissance and Enlightenment and "codified since in a thousand practices across cultures congenial to empiricism and capitalism" (Ermarth:60). The following somewhat long quote from Ermarth (p. 55, emphasis added) captures the idea:

> With "text" and "writing" conceived . . . as modes of discursive engagement, the importance of . . . literary texts and writing becomes obvious: they are among the most highly achieved, most economical exercises of discursive engagement; they take up and improve the forms of discourse we inhabit every day in sloppier, less visible versions; they make the premises of discourse evident. And there is another, less obvious reason to use so-called literary texts. Postmodern narrative language engages pulse and intellect simultaneously and consequently permits no easy escape from *practical problems*. It focuses on *practices*

and refuses in so many ways to accept the distinction between *practice and thought*, between material and transcendental "reality." Such narrative literally recalls readers to their senses by focusing acts of attention on the *actual practices of consciousness and sensibility as they operate in process, and not as they might operate if the world were the rational, logocentric place that so many of our models still describe.* It is arguable that . . . novels articulate the postmodern critique more fully and certainly more accessibly than do most theoretical texts.

Her argument drives to the crux of this chapter: the humanities can assist social work practice in coming to terms with, and making sense out of, the postmodern decline of universalistic discourses and the increasingly accepted polycontextual nature of the world, the pressing and insistent imperatives of diversity and difference.

We live in a world of continuous slippage, where the ground is ceaselessly opening under the present; the humanities can act as a safety net under the fallen structures of the contemporary, the ironic fractures in the system. When we ask what kinds of knowledge will deepen our understanding of ourselves and how we come to know other selves, the arts and humanities can lead us toward understanding, however provisional. Poetry, literature, drama, the visual arts, history and philosophy, and theology inform us as nothing else can of the many dimensions of the human condition, of the kinds of themes—joy, suffering, and the absurdities encountered in everyday social work practice. Howard Goldstein writes that "if we can think of practice as an art, the relevance of the arts and humanities is that much more apparent. Social work practice is often referred to as both an art and a science. But regardless of where science fits into the scheme of the profession, art is what we do, what we use interpretatively, imaginatively, and creatively—that is, if the practitioner is not numbed by a preoccupation with the mechanics of theory, method and technique" (1992:51). Recently, others too have argued that domains of possibility open up to social work once it shifts its orientation from the social sciences to the humanities (Gorman 1993; Falkenheim 1993; Irving 1994).

The humanities set us to creating and recreating truth, although often in ways that are unsettling, as we have seen with Nietzsche, Beckett, and Foucault. The humanities do not provide the same theoretically secure address as empirical knowledge, but outside the realm of utilitarian calculation, aggregate numbers, and quantifiable facts lies the qualitative richness of the world where inner depths count and where there is complexity and contradiction, individual pain and suffering, irony and uncertainty. The humanities provide momentary stays against confusion. History and philosophy enable us to be continually recovering a past and prefiguring a future and can be placed on the mind's scales as something equal to, and corrective of, prevailing conditions. Canadian philosopher George Grant suggests that the humanities can give us intimations of our deprivations (1969:139). Literature enlightens the moral life, and the literary imagination directs the emotions to the creation of livable communities. Poets such as William Blake and W. B. Yeats firmly believed in "the ancient supremacy of the imagination" (Banville 1997:33), and philosopher Mark Kingwell observes that hope's true country is the imagination (1996:351). Social work is a discipline and a practice where the imagination has a role as important as that of the empiricism of the social sciences.

By immersing ourselves in the humanities, and especially literature, we have a much greater appreciation for the interior lives and experiences of other people and are able to begin to imagine the value of their lives—to see the Other as fully human and to understand more fully irony, diversity, and ambiguity. Martha Nussbaum's *Poetic Justice: The Literary Imagination and Public Life* (1995) makes the persuasive case that reading novels encourages us to develop a fully humanistic conception of public reasoning and public well-being and that the literary imagination is an essential ingredient in a democratic society.

Poet Seamus Heaney alerts us to how poetry takes us "from the domain of the matter-of-fact into the domain of the imagined" (1995:xiii). Poetry's truth is "carried live into the heart by passion." Poetry is "a glimpsed alternative, a revelation of potential that is denied or constantly threatened by circumstances. . . . It becomes another truth to which we can have recourse, before which we can know ourselves in a more fully empowered way" (Heaney 1995:4, 8). Heaney affirms "that within our individual selves we can reconcile two orders of knowledge which we might call the practical and the poetic; to affirm also that each form of knowledge redresses the other and that the frontier between them is there for the crossing" (203). Social work needs to undertake this crossing, although it will involve a radical departure from current practice.

When Foucault delivered his inaugural lecture at the Collège de France in early December 1970, he quoted one of his favorite passages from Beckett's *The Unnamable*: "I can't go on, you must go on, I'll go on, you must say words, as long as there are any, until they find me, until they say me" (1965:414). Saying words as long as there are any, and speaking the multitudinous truths of life however troubling until they find us, until they recreate us, may enable social work to withstand the sharp gusts that shake our souls at modernity's end.

REFERENCES

Austin, David M. 1983. The Flexner myth and the history of social work. *Social Service Review* 57, no. 3 (September): 357–77.

Banville, John. 1997. Swan's way: Review of *W. B. Yeats: A Life. New Republic* (June 23): 31–35.

Beckett, Samuel. 1957. *Murphy.* 1938. Reprint, New York: Grove Press.

———. 1958. *Krapp's Last Tape and other dramatic pieces.* New York: Grove Press.

———. 1959. *Watt.* 1953. Reprint, New York: Grove Press.

———. 1965. *Three novels: Molloy, Malone Dies, The Unnamable.* 1958. Reprint, New York: Grove Press.

———. 1984. *Disjecta: Miscellaneous writings and a dramatic fragment.* Edited by Ruby Cohn. New York: Grove Press.

Begam, Richard. 1996. *Samuel Beckett and the end of modernity* Palo Alto, Calif.: Stanford University Press.

Chambon, Adrienne S. and Allan Irving, eds. 1994. *Essays on postmodernism and social work.* Toronto: Canadian Scholars' Press.

Cottingham, John. 1995. René Descartes, 1596–1650. In Robert Audi, ed., *The Cambridge dictionary of philosophy*, pp. 193–96. Cambridge, U.K.: Cambridge University Press.

DeLillo, Don. 1997. *Underworld.* New York: Scribner.

Descartes, René. 1964. *Meditations Concerning First Philosophy: Philosophical Essays.* Translated by Laurence J. Lafleur. New York: Bobbs-Merrill.

Dewey, John. 1920. *Reconstruction in Philosophy.* New York: Henry Holt.

Ermarth, Elizabeth. 1997. Sequel to history. In Keith Jenkins, ed., *The postmodern history reader*, pp. 47–64. London: Routledge.

Falkenheim, Jacqueline F. 1993. The education of a clinical social worker: Finding a place for the humanities. *Clinical Social Work Journal* 21 (1993): 1, 85–96.

Ford, Richard. 1996. The art of fiction. *Paris Review*, no. 140 (Fall): 42–77.

Foucault, Michel. 1965. *Madness and civilization: A history of insanity in the Age of Reason.* Translated by Richard Howard. 1961. Translation, New York: Vintage/Random House.

———. 1973. *The order of things: An archaeology of the human sciences.* 1970. Reprint, New York: Vintage/Random House.

———. 1980. *Power/Knowledge: Selected interviews and other writings, 1972–77.* Edited and translated by Colin Gordon. New York: Pantheon.

———. 1986. *The use of pleasure.* Translated by Robert Hurley. New York: Vintage.

Goldstein, Howard. 1992. If social work hasn't made progress as a science, might it be an art? *Families in Society: The Journal of Contemporary Human Services.* 48–55.

Gontarski, S. E. 1985. *The intent of undoing in Samuel Beckett's dramatic texts.* Bloomington: Indiana University Press.

———. 1995. Introduction. *Samuel Beckett: The complete short prose, 1929–89,* pp. xi–xxxii. New York: Grove Press.

Gordon, Lois. 1996. *The world of Samuel Beckett, 1906–46.* New Haven, Conn.: Yale University Press.

Gorman, Jane. 1993. Postmodernism and the conduct of inquiry in social work. *Affilia* 8 (3): 247–64.

Grant, George. 1969. *Technology and empire: Perspectives on North America.* Toronto: House of Anansi.

Gussow, Mel. 1996. *Conversations with (and about) Beckett.* London: Nick Hern Books.

Harding, Sandra. 1992. The instability of the analytical categories of feminist theory. In Helen Crowley and Susan Himmelweit, eds., *Knowing women: Feminism and knowledge,* pp. 338–54. Cambridge, U.K.: Polity Press.

Harvey, David. 1989. *The condition of postmodernity.* Cambridge, U.K.: Basil Blackwell.

Heaney, Seamus. 1995. *The redress of poetry.* New York: Farrar, Straus and Giroux.

Higgins, Aidan. 1996. Introduction. *Samuel Beckett: Photographs.* New York: George Braziller.

Hill, Leslie. 1990. *Beckett's fiction: In different words.* Cambridge: Cambridge University Press.

Hutchings, Kimberly. 1996. *Kant, critique, and politics.* London: Routledge.

Irving, Allan. 1994. From image to simulacra: The modern/postmodern divide and social work. In Adrienne S. Chambon and Allan Irving, eds., *Essays on postmodernism and social work,* pp. 19–32. Toronto: Canadian Scholars' Press.

Jameson, Frederic. 1991. *Postmodernism or the cultural logic of late capitalism.* Durham, N.C.: Duke University Press.

Jenkins, Keith. 1997. Introduction: On being open about our closures. In Keith Jenkins, ed., *The postmodern history reader,* pp. 1–30. London: Routledge.

Juliet, Charles. 1989–90. Meeting Beckett. *TriQuarterly,* no. 77 (Winter): 9–30.

Kingwell, Mark. 1996. *Dreams of millennium: Report from a culture on the brink.* Toronto: Viking.

Knowlson, James. 1996. *Damned to fame: The life of Samuel Beckett.* New York: Simon and Schuster.

Kuhn, Thomas. 1962. *The Structure of Scientific Revolutions.* Chicago: University of Chicago Press.

Levy, Eric. 1995—96. *The Unnamable:* The metaphysics of Beckettian introspection. *Journal of Beckett Studies* 5, nos. 1 & 2 (Autumn and Spring): 81–105.

Lyotard, Jean-Francois. 1991. *The postmodern condition: A report on knowledge.* Minneapolis: University of Minnesota Press.

Margolin, Leslie. 1997. *Under the cover of kindness: The invention of social work.* Charlottesville: University of Virginia Press.

Marsden, George. 1997. *The outrageous idea of Christian scholarship.* New York: Oxford University Press.

Miller, James. 1993. *The passion of Michel Foucault.* New York: Simon and Schuster.

Miller, Stephen. 1997. The future of disinterest and Foucault's regime of truth. *Partisan Review* 64, no. 1 (Winter): 28–36.

Nehamas, Alexander. 1985. *Nietzsche: Life as literature.* Cambridge, Mass.: Harvard University Press.

Nietzsche, Friedrich. 1966a. *Beyond good and evil: Prelude to a philosophy of the future.* Translated by Walter Kaufman. New York: Vintage.

——. 1966b. *The Birth of Tragedy.* Translated by Walter Kaufman. 1872. Reprint, New York: Vintage.

——. 1968. *The will to power.* Translated by Walter Kaufman and R. J. Hollingdale. New York: Vintage.

——. 1974. *The gay science.* Translated by Walter Kaufman. New York: Vintage.

——. 1979. *Philosophy and truth: Selections from Nietzsche's notebooks of the early 1870s.* Edited and translated by Daniel Breazeale. Atlantic Highlands, N.J.: Humanities Press International.

——. 1983. "On Truth and Lies in a Nonmoral Sense." *Untimely meditations.* Translated by R. J. Hollingdale. 1876. Reprint, Cambridge: Cambridge University Press.

Nussbaum, Martha. 1995. *Poetic justice: The literary imagination and public life.* Boston: Beacon.

Rajchman, John. 1985. *Michel Foucault: The freedom of philosophy.* New York: Columbia University Press.

Rorty, Richard. 1989. *Contingency, irony, and solidarity.* Cambridge: Cambridge University Press.

Rothstein, Eric. 1994. Foucault, discursive history, and the auto-affection of God. *Modern Language Quarterly* 55 (December): 4, 383–414.

Shenker, Israel. 1974. *Words and their masters.* New York: Doubleday.

Tompkins, Calvin. 1996. *Duchamp: A biography.* New York: Henry Holt.

CHAPTER 3

Foucault's Approach: Making the Familiar Visible

Adrienne S. Chambon

This chapter discusses the nature of Foucault's approach by asking the following questions: What is the practice of knowledge that Foucault developed? How does his approach converge or diverge with ways of knowing in social work? What are the challenges that make it difficult, but also productive and liberating, to import Foucault into social work?

Although this is a chapter on "how," it is not a "how to" chapter confined to the technicalities of method. Discussing method in isolation would not be consistent with Foucault, who viewed this form of discussion as historically bound and restrictive. I am proposing a particular reading of a number of conceptual and methodological building blocks in Foucault's work. I seek to show, in an introductory manner, the coherence and the richness of his writings. I believe that the reception of Foucault's work offers a particular challenge to our field. Some objectives and some means he developed will seem strangely familiar to social work readers; others may appear to be profoundly different.

The chapter progresses from broad traits to finer features, in an increasingly narrower order of focalization. I first present the aim of Foucault's project and the role of critical theory in his work. I then discuss the general and specific mechanisms he designed for conducting this type of inquiry, from archaeology and genealogy to the empirical study of micropractices, and link some of his key concepts to his analyses. Finally, I discuss the writing style of Foucault and characteristics of his authoring.

In "What Is an Author?" (1977c) Foucault argues that the original voice of an author is but a vehicle that claims and extends a particular intersection of the thinking of that period. An author occupies a "transdiscursive position" (131). By this token, singling out Foucault limits our understanding. It shows him as the sole source of his work and leaves out the contribution of his predecessors and contemporaries to the intellectual landscape of his time. The roundtable discussion in chapter 4 illustrates the collective nature of such questioning and some of the debates in which Foucault participated. I don't deny these influences (cf. Davidson 1997; Eribon 1994), but the emphasis in this chapter is on Foucault's writings as a particular constellation of ideas and tools of inquiry.

What Was Foucault After?

A Critical Inquiry into Knowledge and Practice

Epistemologically, Michel Foucault set out to critically examine the practices and knowledges that place the person at center stage. His predecessors explored the making of the physical and biological sciences (Canguilhem 1995). Foucault chose to explore the activities that aim to understand, guide, and assist social human beings: (1) the fields of knowledge centered on human action—the social or human sciences, and (2) the practices and institutional arrangements that sustain human conduct—the arena of the helping professions. He wrote on the history of mental illness, medical practices, the transformation of imprisonment practices, and sexuality in the West. These domains overlap with the field of social work and make his writings intriguingly relevant to our discipline.

The purpose of Foucault's investigations was critical and transformative. He questioned the nature and the effects of our activities and the ordinary assumptions and taken-for-granted realities that sustain them. He did not treat the advances made in our fields as simple progress. He "problematized" them. He reflected on how they create and constrain human possibilities. We can draw from his project to identify how routine features of our profession prevent us from envisioning and carrying out fundamental change.

Philosophically, Foucault framed his quest as uncovering the making of contemporary "self" and the mechanisms that constitute this self. Self cannot be understood outside history. It is not a naturally given essence but the dynamic result of events and changing circumstances. Defining *self* is therefore not the beginning of inquiry but rather its endpoint. In a Foucauldian sense social workers do not really start from "where the client is at." Clients do not exist outside the historical activity of social work; they are the result of that activity. The starting point is not inside the client but inside social work.

A link exists between (professional) practices, self, and power. Foucault uncovered the microdynamics of power by examining the particular mechanisms that shape individuals and groups. He stated: "What has been the goal of my work during the last twenty years . . . has not been to analyze the phenomena of power, nor to elaborate the foundations of such an analysis. My objective, instead, has been to create a history of the different modes by which, in our culture, human beings are made subjects" (1982:208).

He concluded by saying, "Thus, it is not power, but the subject, which is the general theme of my research" (209). This is important because commentators have tended to stress power relations in Foucault's work, detached from his focus of interest: the person.

The Unsettling Work of Inquiry

Critical theorists often provide broad explanatory frameworks for understanding, or metamodels. This holds true for the majority of modernist thinkers. Unlike them, Foucault shunned the normative imposition of statements and did not propose a metamodel. It is more helpful to approach his writings as *work that unsettles*. Foucault took the stance that transformative knowledge is disturbing by nature. It disturbs commonly acceptable ways of doing and disturbs the person implementing it. It ruffles the smoothness of our habits, rattles our certainties, disorganizes and reorganizes our understanding, shakes our complacency, unhinges us from secure moorings. It is serious and "dangerous" work, to take up a term that Foucault liked to use.

This unsettling work can become surprisingly useful during historical periods of change, such as now, when established ways of knowing are no longer helpful guides. At those junctures we may find it comforting to step outside our tracks and confront shifting realities. To take up Foucault's challenge with social work today is to take the stance that it may be helpful, and urgently needed, to reflect on the foundations of our profession, rather than merely rearranging the furniture. Foucault's reflexivity is of a basic nature. It is neither an empty exercise in relativistic speculation nor a nihilistic quest. The aim is not to destroy but to redefine and reorient what we do and what we know. It is a commitment to transformation.

Foucault's agenda—how the self is constituted through practices and institutions—represents a formidable challenge. How can we step back from those practices and forms of knowledge that we experience as most natural, that we have been socialized into, and to which we actively contribute as scholars, educators, practitioners, policy makers? What mechanisms do we put in place to breach self-evidence and to shift vantage points?

Making the Familiar Visible Through Archaeological and Genealogical Work

Foucault wrote *Madness and Civilization* (1965) while working in Sweden. He claimed that the range of countries in which he held a position or where he lectured—Poland, Tunisia, Brazil, Japan, and the United States, as well as Sweden—enhanced his grasp of the institutions he was immersed in and brought out the specificity of local arrangements through contrast. In addition to using his geographic estrangement, he purposefully developed a variety of mechanisms for making the familiar unfamiliar and making visible what we take for granted.

He first used the metaphor of archaeology to characterize the approach he used in exploring the origins of contemporary health practices (*The Birth of the Clinic: An Archaeology of Medical Perception,* 1975) and the discourse of social science (*The Archaeology of Knowledge,* 1972). By uncovering buried forms, archaeological work demystifies the dusty material upon which we stand. This slow and careful work starts from the surface and works down through sedimented layers of accumulated knowledge and practice. It is fragmentary work. As each fragment is detached from the whole, it encloses a part-configuration of that whole. Rearranging disparate elements makes visible what we could not see before, which was there but hidden—half covered up, half shining.

Later Foucault emphasized the historical nature of this work, borrowing the notion of genealogy from Nietzsche's *The Genealogy of Morals* (cf. Foucault, 1977b). Whereas a foundational history typically starts from the past and demonstrates the progressive evolution of a field, stressing its accomplishments (a format commonly used to describe professional practice), genealogy starts with a question about the present and works its way in the opposite direction, retroactively through a descent in time. It is a "history of the present," as Foucault called it (*Discipline and Punish* [1979] 1995; see chap. 5 by Parton here). "In my opinion," Foucault said, "recourse to history is meaningful to the extent that history serves to show how that-which-is has not always been; that the things which seem most evident to us are always formed in the confluence of encounters and chances, during the course of a precarious and fragile history" (Foucault 1983:206).

Genealogical work makes no sweeping generalizations. Selecting particular practices and statements, it retraces the "conditions of their existence," or how they came to be what they are and not other. In this manner it identifies new continuities and discontinuities among the ideas and practices of a field. It highlights critical moments, breaks, and departures. As Foucault explained,

> An examination of descent permits the discovery, under the unique aspect of a trait or concept, of the myriad events through which— thanks to which, against which—they were formed. . . . Where the soul pretends unification or the self fabricates a coherent identity, the genealogist sets out to study the beginning—numberless beginnings whose faint traces and hints of color are readily seen by an historical eye.
> *(1977b:146)*

A genealogical approach to social work is an invitation to retrace specific ways of doing and knowing; to illuminate how operating assumptions have clustered together and changed over time; and to identify the events and circumstances that acted as turning points in our profession.

At a time when "case management" is redefining the meaning of a "case," a genealogical inquiry requires that we set aside what we hold to be true about the nature of "the social work case" and that we retrace the history of its development and usage—that we examine the various forms the notion of case took over time, the different types of expertise it generated, and the diversity of responses. Adopting a genealogical perspective is to ask ourselves how we have come to define a case the way we do now and what that presupposes. Other practices can equally be examined, such as the "problem-solving" rationality, or the ways in which we understand and intervene in the family.

Until recently, social work had not applied a genealogical approach to critically examine its practices. Policy analyses take into account the development of systems of welfare over whole periods, emphasizing the progress achieved over time. A closer parallel to genealogical analysis can be found in the practice of case histories. A case history traces a current issue in a client's life to its origin, developmentally; it does so, however, using established psychosocial frameworks of interpretation. There are beginning attempts to use a more genealogical approach that draws from archival documents and agency files (cf. Cree's 1995 work). Laura Epstein's "Origins" project is explicitly positioned as a genealogical study (see chap. 1 here).

The Study of Micropractices: Bridging the Self/Structure Split

Foucault grounded the genealogical perspective in very particular and concrete sets of practices (Gordon 1986). "It may be wise not to take as a whole the rationalization of society or of culture, but to analyze such a process in several fields, each with reference to a fundamental experience: madness, illness, death, crime, sexuality, and so forth," Foucault wrote (1982:210).

Rejecting the two contrastive schools of thought then in fashion—subject-centered phenomenology and structure-centered Marxism—he was careful to stay away from individual consciousness and from general objects such as "the state" or "the economy" (Foucault 1983). Foucault examined instead practices and local circumstances: not institutions but institutional practices; not ideology but statements; not the "subject" but the embodied subject.

Of *Discipline and Punish*, his work on penal institutions, he said:

> In this piece of research on the prisons, as in my other earlier work, the target of analysis wasn't "institutions," "theories," or "ideology," but *practices*—with the aim of grasping the conditions that make these acceptable at a given moment; the hypothesis being that these types of practice are not just governed by institutions, prescribed by ideologies, guided by pragmatic circumstances—whatever role these elements might actually play—but possess up to a point their own specific regularities, logic, strategy, self-evidence, and "reason." It is a question of analyzing a "regime of practices" . . . not a history of the prison as institution but of the *practice of imprisonment.*   *(1987:102–103)*

By examining practices close-up through a magnifying lens (cf. Gordon 1986), Foucault brought together into a single fold the two poles of the social work profession that are traditionally kept apart, the micro- and macrolevels of the person and the environment. He made visible the linkages between individual and society: how institutional practices generate social identities, which in turn trigger new knowledge and practices. This approach is a profound departure from social work ways. It opens new ways of understanding.

The Status of Practice and Discourse

Forms of practice and forms of knowledge, although distinct, often converge in their consequences. Practices codify actions and prescribe how to deal with individuals, groups, families, and communities. Knowledge produces formulations of "truth." We come to "see" things in particular ways through the concepts and theories we develop about them: how we name, characterize, explain, and predict. Understanding is imposing a view upon reality: "We must conceive discourse as a violence that we do to things, or at all events, as a practice we impose upon them; it is in this practice that the events of discourse find the principle of their regularity" (Foucault 1972:229). Things do not exist outside our naming them. It is the act of naming that creates things. Foucault's use of the term *discourse* never reduces to the sense of "the discourse of youth" or "discourse of sexuality." Saying this would imply that youth or sexuality are solid entities that exist before we speak of them. Foucault argued instead that we are able to conceive of youth and sexuality only as a result of historical ways of knowing (see Halperin 1994 and chap. 8 by Wang here).

Once we adopt the language of stress, for example, we adopt a particular logic, with assumptions about the nature, source, and consequences of situations. We set aside an alternative cluster of ideas, such as exploitation, with which we associate different sets of facts, different sources of evidence, and different concepts. Edelman (1988) discusses how we variably construct social problems, social actors, and social solutions. Similarly, once we adopt the language of causality, we group events and circumstances in a singular fashion; we include the principle of prediction, and we exclude whatever does not fall under that logic. More than ways of naming, discourses are systems of thought and systematic ways of carving out reality. They are structures of knowledge that influence systems of practices. "Discursive practices are characterized by the delimitation of a field of objects, the definition of a legitimate perspective for the agent of knowledge, and the fixing of norms for the elaboration of concepts and theories. Thus, each discursive practice implies a play of prescriptions that designate its exclusions and choices" (Foucault 1977c:199).

The two realms of knowledge and practice, although not fully in sync, influence one another. Regimes of truth and regimes of practice are systemically structured and therefore can be studied with similar means. The structures are not apparent. They need to be uncovered. Foucault analyzed the minute features of discourse, as he did practice. By closely examining language, we can see that local sets of statements follow certain rules, share a common logic or rationality, and vary historically as distinct "discursive formations" (Foucault 1972).

Because social work is a professional discipline, we expect knowledge and practice to come together, at least within our field. Yet we regularly decry their distinctiveness and complain about the unbridgeable chasm of two worlds: how academics are disconnected from the field; how practice wisdom cannot be formalized into a theory. Laura Epstein reframed the terms of this debate in her 1996 discussion of empiricism and social work. She argued, within a Foucauldian perspective, that research and practice wisdom have a much greater commonality than we are willing to concede. Beneath the apparent differences lies a common logic: "The gulf that divides researchers and practitioners is very complicated and partly an illusion. Research heads and practitioner heads seem to live in different worlds in which one does not recognize the other. Yet they are, in my opinion, more alike than they admit" (Epstein 1996:114). Arguing that "the difference is more apparent than real" (116), she alleged that their shared assumptions act as common constraints: "They conceive the world in the same restricted way. Thus, they both limit their ability to identify and work on issues about the nature and role of social work" (115). She then proposed that we revisit the principles that underlie our practice and research.

The Surprising Status of Subjectivity/ies

The notion of subject in Foucault's work is one of the most contentious issues for social work (unlike other disciplines, such as cultural studies, for instance). Social work has historically placed the person (not "the subject") at center stage as the core purpose of social work's activities by leaning on a humanistic conception of universal human needs and individualistic notions of personality, motivation, autonomy, and self-determination. These values are best encapsulated in the social work case as the focal object of practice. Despite periodic revisions of the concept of self to accommodate knowledge in the wider society (e.g., Nurius 1993), social work persistently seeks to salvage the individual at the center of its world.

Recent trends have begun to depart from that norm. Constructivism, critical feminist theory, race and multicultural perspectives, and—to varying degrees—the concept of empowerment (Hartman 1993; Laird 1993; Saleeby 1994; Sands and Nuccio 1992) have begun to dislodge monolithic ways of defining self and to locate clients and workers within cultural and institutional arrangements and within systems of power.

Foucault took a more radical stance. He historicized the self. Separating selfhood from the individual, he traced the constitution of a uniquely bounded (and rational) individual to the Enlightenment period (see chap. 2). His point is that this individual self makes certain choices possible but restricts alternative forms of expression.

Although Foucault rejected the naturalness of *individual* self, his studies are full of detailed accounts of experienced self and particularly of *embodied* self—the multiple imprints that institutions make on our bodies. "In thinking of the mechanisms of power, I am thinking of its capillary form of existence, the point where power reaches into the very grain of individuals, touches their bodies and inserts itself into their actions and attitudes, their discourses, learning processes and everyday lives" (Foucault 1980:39). Feminist thinkers have taken up the body as the juncture between the personal and the political realms and have acknowledged the work of Foucault in doing so (Bordo 1989; Probyn 1991; Sawicki 1991). How we sit and how we stand, how we study and how we play, how we talk to one another, how we wish and how we despair, and how institutional regulations mold our selves in the deepest way. Foucault's writings express deeply felt experiences and are thus paradoxically very much person centered—while, in his perspective, individuality remains only one historical manifestation of the self.

Detailed Documentary Work

Genealogy is one means of achieving defamiliarization; finely detailed documentary work is the other. The vantage point shifts from everyday vision to the infinitely small and the seemingly unimportant. Foucault did not apply a theory to reveal the details of practice. Instead he derived an understanding of social forms from the documentation of such details. By examining concrete practices in their most minute details, we can question institutional mechanisms and gain a new understanding.

As an illustration, in *Discipline and Punish* Foucault focused on the innovative organizations that served as models for the establishment of the modern prison and other key institutions. He pored over archives and quoted at length from legislation, regulations, articles, and manuals for children. He drew upon architectural sketches and diagrams, artistic lithographs, satirical drawings, coins, and other artifacts. In that book Foucault examined how the organization of physical space and the regimen of rules of conduct prescriptively shape ways of being and social interactions. He gave detailed descriptions of the architectural layout of jails, army barracks, schools, and hospitals. He reproduced the hourly schedules of a prisoner, factory worker, and child in school. He broke down the gestures that constitute acts of "examination," extending his "microphysic" documentation (see Gordon 1986) to minute codes of behavior, including body posture.

The philosopher Gilles Deleuze and historians such as Arlette Farge and Paul Veyne have all emphasized the meticulous attention with which Foucault focused on the very obvious and the very fine, if not insidious, mechanisms of control and norm setting, and we can draw parallels with contemporary norms of professional training. His work can be likened to that of an entomologist, or at least an ethnographer (see chaps. 9 and 10). Indeed, Foucault's writing is compatible with the work of institutional ethnographers working within a critical theory paradigm, such as Erving Goffman (1961) or Dorothy Smith (1987).

The details of institutional practices and statements exposed by Foucault often offer something surprising. In treating details of practice as "tactical" constituent elements of strategies of influence (Foucault 1995:139), Foucault often selected the least expected features, those that tend to be overlooked as insignificant, the details that "don't matter." Through dissection, ordinary features of routine activity become exquisite and glaring—at times even unbearable. This was a systematic strategy on his part. By magnifying otherwise dull details, Foucault made public a more hidden, intimate view of reality. He created a form of gossip, showing us the underside of things, what tends to be left unsaid and unaddressed. His depictions have a scandalous flavor. At times staging a theater of cruelty, he displayed features that, once uncovered, can no longer be eluded.

Not surprisingly, Foucault's critics have questioned his selection of features and the ones he left out. He answered that he did not aim to account for every aspect of a phenomenon but purposefully chose to trace selective patterns and collected only those sets of features associated with them: "There can be no question here of writing the history of the different disciplinary institutions, with *all* their individual differences. I simply intend to map on a series of examples some of the essential techniques that most easily spread from one to another" (1995:139, emphasis added; see also Foucault 1983).

This aspect of Foucault's work, the close examination of practices and unearthing of daily details, is highly compatible with social work. Since the publication of Mary Richmond's *Social Diagnosis* in 1917, social workers have developed a mastery of details through the activity of data collection. Gathering rigorous evidence for professional purposes requires a systematic gleaning of a multitude of small facts (behaviors, thoughts, wishes) from ever-expanding areas of life (health, school, economic, domestic): "Social evidence may be defined as consisting of any and all facts as to personal or family history which, taken together, indicate the nature of a given client's social difficulties and the means to their solution" (Richmond 1917:43). And more crucially: "What do we mean by the word fact? It is not limited to the tangible. . . . Thoughts and events are facts" (53).

Detailed documentation is necessary to build a case. It must be multi-faceted and as thorough as possible. Social workers do more than inquire. They sift through evidence in clients' lives. They assess, weigh, and discard sets of information. As they collect data, they simultaneously draw inferences and interpret their findings. Social workers have been highly skillful in searching for the detail that will tell it all, details that will make the point for us, that will convince authorities to act. As Richmond put it,

> Social evidence, like that sought by the scientist or historian, includes all items which, however trifling or apparently irrelevant when regarded as isolated facts, may, *when taken together*, throw light upon the question at issue; namely, as regards social work, the question what course of procedure will place this client in his right relation to society?
>
> *(1917:39, emphasis added)*

Expanding on this idea, she added:

> Facts, having a subjective bearing . . . are especially characterized by their cumulative significance. Variations between people . . . display themselves ordinarily not in a few conspicuous acts, but in a trend of behavior evidenced by innumerable trifling remarks or by a succession of decisions and impulses each unimportant in itself. Evidence of this cumulative sort, therefore, is essential wherever, as in social work, decisions rest upon intimate understanding of character.　　*(40)*

Foucault's finite observations are thus quite consistent with social work skills. However, by bringing out unexpected details, studying Foucault expands the scope of our attention and opens up new lines of inquiry. What is open to scrutiny in social work? What details do we document, and what small facts do we overlook? Do we scrutinize our own practice to the same extent that we scrutinize clients? Foucault invites us to survey our spaces of actions and our territories of wording beyond the ways in which we commonly reflect upon our practice.

To document micropractices in social work is, for instance, to break down the practice of intake to its finer actions (see chap. 9): to document what a social worker does at her desk as she fills out a form; what categories of information the form elicits, and which information is missing; how the worker conducts an intake session; what happens during "case consultation"; the small decisions and interactions that accompany the placement of a child in care or that accompany discharge planning (see de Montigny 1995). Discursively, what types of reasoning and argumentation constitute a case in an expert way? What considerations are off-limits for particular client groups in given organizational settings? How do different sets of legal and policy statements combine to define the range of options for clients? How are regular cases made and exceptional circumstances evoked? How do new theories encourage a focus on particular aspects of our clients' lives?

Beyond Description: Organizing and Making Sense of Details

Dreyfus and Rabinow (1982) saw the selection of details and the relation between part and whole, this interpretative aspect of Foucault's approach, as hermeneutically related. Although he positioned himself radically outside this tradition, Foucault paid extreme attention to the meaning of features, immersing himself in texts or practices. It is worth noting that, in the earlier stage of his career, Foucault took part in translating the writings of a German hermeneut, Leo Spitzer (1970). Spitzer focused on the most minute details of language and on nuanced actions performed through language in literary forms. Foucault may have adopted his subsequent close reading of texts and practices from such sources. However, unlike Spitzer, Foucault did not believe that such analysis reveals the unity of a text, of a practice, or of a self. A practice, a set of statements, a self has no single center; it has multiple directions. It is fraught with tensions and contains several possibilities. For Foucault, as perhaps for the more postmodern authors, the work of deciphering reveals complex configurations.

How did Foucault identify relevant patterns from rich details? Stressing the principle of scarcity, he argued that specific practices are restricted to a narrow range of human possibilities. Starting from the practices themselves, and refusing to apply a predetermined grid of analysis, he first described and then derived "series" of comparable features that present "regularities." Foucault multiplied the examples, buttressing a solitary example with others. He piled them up to show how their persistence structures action in a consistent manner. The juxtaposition of architectural features, time schedules, and rules of proper behavior reveals a common logic of operation. The structure of a timetable imposes a pace on the activity and a degree of effort on the part of the participants; it also differentiates between one activity and the next. In social work we can think of the rationing of time and the pace of appointments, or the planning of client activities, as constitutive processes.

The importance of grounded details in Foucault's work explains why he has been characterized by some as the quintessential empiricist. According to the historian Paul Veyne, Foucault avoids diluting specificities into general notions; he stays close to detailed descriptions of actions and suspends interpretation. Staying close to what people actually do, to actual practices, is hard work.

> The method followed here . . . consists in describing in quite objective terms what a paternalistic emperor does, what a head herdsman does, without presupposing anything else at all. . . . Practice is not some mysterious agency, some substratum of history, some hidden engine; it is what people do. . . . If practices are, in one sense, "hidden" and if we may provisionally call them the "concealed base of the iceberg," it is quite simply because "practice" shares the fate of nearly all our behavior and that of universal history: we are often aware of it, but we have no concept for it. . . . Judging people according to their actions means not judging them according to their ideologies; it also means not judging them according to lofty eternal notions such as the governed, the State, freedom, or the essence of politics, notions that trivialize the originality of successive practices and render it anachronistic.
>
> *(Veyne 1997:153–54)*

The point here is that details are not mere illustrations. Attended to at close range, the fine level of detail or microscopic aspect of description encapsulates the very mechanisms we are trying to understand.

From documenting repetition and minor variations, Foucault extracted original working concepts, such as "docile bodies," that collapse into a single notion a complex combination of shaping and acquiescence in embodied behaviors, stemming from "disciplinary" actions. Plate 10 in *Discipline and Punish* shows a 1749 drawing of a tree with a crooked trunk that has been attached to a post for straightening. The caption reads: "Orthopaedics or the art of preventing and correcting deformities of the body in children." The drawing and its caption explicitly state that redress is a form of influencing that produces effects of betterment through effort and strain—if not pain. This statement links the body and the soul. It ties mastery to control, improvement to "discipline."

As this orthopedic example suggests, Foucault identified strategies of influencing in their obvious and veiled manifestations. A different example would be to consider as positive the creation of protected environments (as in educational or welfare systems) when they replace repressive forms of confinement. They can also be thought of as alternative forms of enclosure and as a mechanism for exercising control (1995:141–42). Foucault's approach is therefore particularly useful whenever we want to examine the less obvious forms of power—not when we impose force where it is not wanted but when we exercise our influence in apparently wanted ways–a point that I will take up later in this chapter in regard to the shaping of the self.

Deleuze (1986) called Foucault a "cartographer" who did not hesitate to slice "laterally" across domains of practice, to draw new maps, delimit new boundaries, and define new objects of study. By examining the distribution (what Foucault called the "dispersion") and variation of features across contexts, Foucault showed unexpected parallels among institutional domains. Again, in *Discipline and Punish* he identified features of technology shared by what would seem to be quite distinct regulating systems: the army, penitentiary, hospital, and school. His findings were jarring, for they invalidated the commonsense distinction between authoritarian institutions and "enabling" or "caring" ones. For social work this raises the important question of how the functions of control and of caring can actually coexist within a single context, how they are separate or joined in professional practices.

This distributional or structured mode of analysis in Foucault's writings was often complemented with complex figures of displacement, reversals, and decenterings, making this aspect of his work reminiscent of therapeutic readings of clients' narratives. This parallel between Foucauldian analyses and interpretive clinical work may partly explain the appeal of Foucault to clinicians. Foucauldian analyses show the unexpected applicability of clinical reading skills to an understanding of institutional practice.

This is where the more structuralist aspect of Foucault's work can be read. Notwithstanding the debate as to whether Foucault was or not a structuralist, whether he claimed to be so at an earlier stage of his work, and disclaimed it later on, it can be argued in a general way that an organizational understanding of features is structuralist when it stresses structures and relations among features. His work is even semiotic in its analysis of features as "signs" and of the structuring of systems of difference and complex relations among signs. Foucault's work is also poststructuralist in the sense that it deals with open, and not predetermined, structures that are inductively arrived at. He continuously incorporated in his analyses the historical circumstances of their structuring and traced their transformations.

Delimiting Patterns Through Circumstances and Effects

Foucault's studies do more than delimit patterns of actions. They encompass sets of circumstances and effects. We can say that his approach is process oriented. Foucault did not conduct causal analysis, nor did he make predictive statements. He took those terms to express a particular type of rationality, a singular form of simplification, a system of belief. Foucault was not deterministic. He believed in multicausality and chance in human affairs and the possibility of interpreting complex circumstances. Trends cannot be predicted, but they can be detected and mapped out after the fact.

He documented the circumstances that make actions and statements possible, their "network of contingencies" (Foucault 1983:206) or conditions of existence. Discussing the tracing of discursive forms, he stated: "Taking the discourse itself, its appearance and its regularity, we should look for its external conditions of existence, for that which gives rise to the chance series of these events and fixes their limits" (1972:229). In material and institutional terms this means asking the question: What organizational changes, policy directions, economic and social developments contribute to the development of particular practices?

Whereas detailed descriptions illuminate the regularities of practice, their nature is additionally revealed through their consequences. Foucault studied the *effects* of practice and discourse. This is where Foucault introduced a series of core concepts that have become associated with his work and have by now become part of common usage: *normalization, governmentality,* and *discipline.*

Clusters of practice (more than individual actions) differentially shape the range of actions possible. Foucault extended the use of the notion of government beyond the fields of politics and ideology to encompass broad and diffuse techniques for shaping behavior and ways of being:

> This word must be allowed the very broad meaning which it had in the sixteenth century. "Government" did not refer only to political structures or to the management of states; rather it designated the way in

which the conduct of individuals or of groups might be directed: the government of children, of souls, of communities, of families, of the sick. It did not only cover the legitimately constituted forms of political or economic subjection, but also modes of action, more or less considered and calculated which were destined to act upon the possibilities of action of other people. To govern, in this sense, is to structure the possible field of action of others.   *(1982:221)*

By defining government and control as diffuse and polysemic (taking up a multiplicity of forms), Foucault opened up a broad field of "studies in governmentality" that examine the range of shaping (or regulating) practices. This is an important trend developing today. It underscores the relevance of such questions for contemporary times (see Rose and Miller 1992; "Liberalism" 1993).

Disciplines are clusters of means and diverse technologies that guide behavior at a microlevel. As Foucault said, "'Discipline' may be identified neither with an institution nor with an apparatus; it is a type of power, a modality for its exercise, comprising a whole set of instruments, techniques, procedures, levels of application, targets; it is a 'physics' or an 'anatomy' of power, a technology" (1995:215).

The process of normalization through particular disciplines does not reduce to negative influences. It not only restricts or erases unwanted behavior, it also shapes wanted behavior: "Let us say that discipline is the unitary technique by which the body is reduced as a 'political' force at the least cost and maximized as a useful force" (Foucault 1995:221).

In *The Birth of the Clinic* (1975) Foucault argued that the development of medicine did not limit itself to knowledge of illness and disease but extended its influence to ordinary behaviors, creating knowledge about the body and health and defining normality:

> Medicine must no longer be confined to a body of techniques for curing ills and of the knowledge that they require; it will also embrace a knowledge of *healthy man*, that is, a study of *non-sick man* and a definition of the *model man*. In the ordering of human existence it assumes a normative posture, which authorizes it not only to distribute advice as to healthy life, but also to dictate the standards for physical and moral relations of the individual and of the society in which he lives.   *(34)*

Here Foucault is questioning the mechanisms and the effects of "negative" and "positive" shaping (see chap. 7). On that basis we can view the rapid expansion of health promotion models (Lupton 1995), and even contemporary ethics, as current attempts to extend a normalizing influence over individuals and populations.

Practices, Subjectivities, and Relational Power

Foucault elicited a series of distributional effects that result from normalizing practices. The latter function as "dividing practices." They constitute polarities between self and other, good and bad, normal and pathological. They create classes of features and categories of people: "If the science of man [social sciences] appeared as an extension of the science of life, . . . the very subjects it devoted itself to (man, his behaviour, his individual and social realizations) therefore opened up a field that was divided up according to the principles of the normal and the pathological" (Foucault 1975:36).

The making of specific or local systems of difference partition self and other in various ways: "The objectivizing of the subject in which I shall call 'dividing practices,' the subject is either divided inside himself or divided from others. . . . Examples are the mad and the sane, the sick and the healthy, the criminals and the 'good boys'" (Foucault 1982:208). These divisions expand into elaborate classification systems with internal gradations. They locate individuals within series and assign them a relational rank. They partition age groups and break the difficulty of tasks into subtasks. They define degrees of development and hierarchies of deviance. They establish the multiple processes of affirmation and reward, surveillance and exclusion (cf. *Discipline and Punish*).

Taking a discourse example, the notion of risk (developed in chap. 5 here) guides the judgment of clinicians in assessing individuals and serves to define programmatic and policy priorities. This expert modality splits the population along multiple dimensions. All this happens without consideration for its implications. As the notion enters into general calculations of rationality and efficiency, it is taken for granted; its effects become unnoticed.

Practices further divide those who are served from those who serve, the helpers, establishing a particular structure of relation: "The madman tends to form with the doctor, in an unbroken unity, a 'couple' whose complicity dates back to very old links" (Foucault 1984:162). With the proliferation of people-centered practice, the development of one group is linked to the development of the other. In *The Birth of the Clinic* Foucault argued that the institutional development of a corps of health experts grew side by side with disease classifications and with the categorization of "the ill." Each set of practices creates the conditions for a specific constellation of relations. He argued in *Madness and Civilization* that the emergence of modern psychiatric practices created a relation of dependence between patient and therapist, which combines features of intimacy with features of control: "All nineteenth-century psychiatry really converges on Freud, the first man to accept in all its seriousness the reality of the physician-patient couple, the first to consent not to look away nor to investigate elsewhere . . . the first to follow its consequences with absolute rigor" (1984:165).

Institutional activities simultaneously create clients and workers, as two sides of the same coin. This complementary process is made explicit in the working contract between client and worker. The contract encourages clients to enlist in a client subjectivity (become a voluntary client) and to agree to a particular kind of work upon themselves. It defines the worker's actions and ways of relating to the client. The practices of intake and crisis intervention constitute client and worker in a different manner. Changing practices modify the participants. These changes do not happen without struggles, as an old "naturalness" is abandoned for a new one.

Dividing practices are not only imposed from the outside but implicate the self through concrete mechanisms of involvement. In *Madness and Civilization* Foucault argued that, contrary to what took place in earlier periods, modern institutions are characterized by less overt coercion. Disciplinary practices recruit the willing participation of individuals in the constitution of their identity. In other words, the self contributes to its own making.

One mechanism of recruitment consists of the development of self-awareness: "The form of awareness that the madman must have of his own madness" (Foucault 1984:145). Self-awareness contributes to the creation of the moral subject:

> The obscure guilt that once linked transgression and unreason is thus shifted; the madman, as a human being originally endowed with reason, is no longer guilty of being mad; but the madman . . . must feel morally responsible for everything within him that may disturb morality and society, and must hold no one but himself responsible for the punishment he receives.
>
> *(1984:145)*

These "modern" norms are characterized by self-control and responsibility, commitment to self-knowledge and to self-change. They are fostered through a number of activities such as the practice of "confession."

Clinical social work relies heavily on the practice of self-talk by the client in the presence of, and with assistance by, the worker. Clients may be given homework that is designed to encourage them to modify their activities and to reflect upon their self. Professional supervision mirrors the self-knowledge expected from clients. Professionals are trained to adopt a self-observing stance and to reflect upon their actions, emotions, and sense of self. Classroom education replicates this principle by including an important component of self-reflection. All these activities share a number of assumptions: We do not simply act, but we reflect upon our doings. We shape our selves to be congruent to the task. Thus social work promotes a fit for both client and worker between the self and the task.

Multifaceted Practices, Agency, and Change

Foucault explored the multifaceted nature of practices and statements. In *Madness and Civilization* he argued that mental health practices aim to humanize a space of relations while they implement subtle forms of control (see Epstein 1994 and chap. 1 here). He further commented that a single practice often combines apparently contradictory functions. This in part explains how the effects of discipline can be veiled.

In the second chapter of *Discipline and Punish* Foucault discussed a historical practice that existed under the monarchy. More and more in the eighteenth century and leading up to the French Revolution, justice was rendered publicly, with public display of torture and execution of the condemned. Public display satisfied a primary function of punishment and retribution aimed at the perpetrator. But this function could hardly explain the excessive means resorted to, such as extending acts of torture and dismemberment beyond the criminal's death. Those actions that seem gratuitous and unreasonable made sense only by invoking a different function, this time aimed at the public. Public execution also served the purpose of instilling horror and fear in the audience. More than setting an example, and beyond the specifics of the crime, it served to impress the power of the authorities and enlist social obedience.

In an interesting twist Foucault remarked that such public displays periodically led to the opposite effect than the one intended. They could move the crowd assembled to shows of sympathy and solidarity with the accused because of their similar social backgrounds. More and more in the eighteenth century such manifestations often resulted in acts of public disobedience that challenged the legitimacy of the authorities beyond the specific case. Eventually, the increasing number of riots led to terminating this practice in an effort to contain the crowds. Justice was subsequently rendered hidden from view.

This illustration shows how, for Foucault, practices express complex functions. A social form contains its counterform and can create opportunities for deviation and innovation (see chap. 8). In this instance, specific features of domination triggered unrest. In other words, Foucault demonstrates that in deciphering social phenomena it is useful to look for reactive traits, particularly the more obvious figures of reversal.

A recurrent critique of Foucault's work is that it leaves no room for agency. What is left for initiating personal and social change if practices and knowledge constitute the self? This is a central argument made by feminist scholars (e.g., Fraser 1989). Extending the previous example, if normative practices constitute forms of subjectivity, change is to be found in counterforms or alternative forms of knowledge and of practices. An avenue of research and practice consists of looking for the deployment of actions and subjectivities at variance with the norm. Foucault claimed that forms of opposition or innovation are intrinsically linked to dominant forms, as derived expressions. They need not be dramatic departures. They can be minor changes. This is where notions of strategies, tactics, and resistance can be useful. Though he declined to offer a normative prescriptive program of action for change (see Fraser's critique on this point), Foucault offered a host of clues to how to develop such alternative strategies.

More fundamentally, Foucault spoke to the *transformative* potential of his work. Transformative work shows that the present is not natural and need not be taken as inevitable or absolute. Change can come from the realization of the precarious nature of established ways and by inviting the development of alternatives. This holds true for the client and for the worker and is of particular relevance to the academic social worker, researcher, and educator. We come close here to the definition of the role of the intellectual, as well as its limits: "The work of the intellectual . . . is fruitful in a certain way to describe that-which-is by making it appear as something that might not be, or that might not be as it is" (Foucault 1983:206). Foucault concluded:

> These [forms of rationality] reside on a base of human practice and human history; and that since these things have been made, they can be unmade, as long as we know how it was that they were made. . . . Any description must always be made in accordance with these kinds of virtual fracture which open up the space of freedom understood as a space of concrete freedom, i.e., of possible transformation.   (206)

Because power is productive, it is up to us to produce new forms, after seeing through that which is all too familiar, and to realize that those new forms will generate new possibilities as well as new constraints.

Destabilizing and Productive Language in Foucault's Writings

Writing in the human sciences is caught within discursive rules and changing norms. Both the concepts in use and the structure of arguments contribute to standard forms. Geertz (1988) has shown for anthropology how each school of thought develops its modes of credibility through particular rules of argumentation and even through its writing style. Each canon in turn becomes an obstacle to change.

Asking how Foucault writes is not about the originality of his style. It means treating his style as a discursive practice. What principles does he follow in writing, and what does his style accomplish? Can writing unsettle the reader and be an invitation for change? Can writing be a subversive and transformative practice? Is there any correspondence or continuity between Foucault's writing style and the nature of his query?

I argue that a number of the conceptual and methodological features discussed earlier can be found in Foucault's writing style. The way Foucault used language is far from standard. His language disturbs and confuses some, stimulates and inspires others (Megill 1990; O'Neill 1994). His style has been described as ambiguous and literary.

Foucault actively questioned established codes of discourse in the human sciences. He valued the unusual writing of Nietzsche and sought to expand this repertoire. Foucault also wrote extensive literary and art critiques during the first part of his career. According to Judith Revel (1994), Foucault saw literature as subversive language, as rebelliousness against the norm. She even argued that Foucault's subsequent decreased interest in literature coincided with his involvement in the prisoners' movement against the jail system and later in movements against totalitarian regimes.

Taking the same point of departure as Revel, I see literature for Foucault as a subversive language. Further, I see Foucault's style as strategic. In reading his works closely I came to realize that the transgressive intent in his literary essays could be found directly in his style. Foucault seems to have incorporated some of the potentialities of poetic language in his writing. His style removes the comfort we take from rational analyses of reality. Using stylistic rhetorical means that stray from conventional ones, he aims to disturb and to mobilize us.

In *Death and the Labyrinth: The World of Raymond Roussel* (1992) (entitled simply *Raymond Roussel* in the French original), Foucault discussed the
poetic mechanisms put in place by Roussel, an experimental author. What
Foucault said of Roussel is strikingly reminiscent of the writing style Foucault later developed.

Foucault claimed that Roussel destabilizes the reader through rhetorical
means that breach current language norms. Both writing and reading
become unsettling experiences: "His work as a whole . . . systematically
imposes a formless anxiety, diverging and yet centrifugal, directed not
toward the most withheld secrets but toward the imitation and the trans-
mutation of the most visible forms" (Foucault 1992:11).

Roussel explored language effects that stretch our common understandings. He offered new options for understanding reality by taking words and
images as texture to be reinvented and worked through. Words were material that he disassembled and reassembled so that familiar phrases became
unfamiliar. He drew words from various registers, the formal and the experiential, from realistic and from fantastic worlds. He juxtaposed words to
create new structures of thought and experience. He named things in unexpected ways. He played with rhythm and resonance. There is no reason that
those properties of language should be excluded from the arena of the social
and health sciences.

Mixing Stylistic Genres

Foucault's style is unusual in the social sciences. It combines different writing genres in a single text, alternating between the rational exposition of
arguments, the language of immediate experience, poetic expression, and the
language of revolt.

The historian Arlette Farge, with whom Foucault wrote some of his
archival studies (Farge and Foucault 1982) made the same point, arguing that
this discursive mechanism interrogates the reader forcefully. Of the language
of *Discipline and Punish*, she said:

> a vocabulary which plays on two very distant registers, and whose
> simultaneous use reinforces the violence of the demonstration. The
> one, sumptuous, poetic, at times incantatory, almost fascinated, uses
> strong words in spurts, like atrocious, fright, abominable, terror,
> unleashing and refers to paroxysmal images and figures, in which
> naked suffering is deployed before our eyes. . . . The other register,

used at times simultaneously, at times sequentially, is more interpretative: it sets in place a technical vocabulary (new to the times), where we
find terms, by now so familiar, like "apparatus," "principles of rationality," "systems," "forms of enunciation." . . . The interplay between
these two levels of statements triggers for the reader moments of rup-
ture, dislocations, shocks, and it structures the book with force,
because it creates formidable tensions between the discourse of per-
ceptions and that of elucidation, between the discourse of the body,
and the discourse by the body. *(Farge 1992:184; my translation)*

Those genres are truly combined in his work. They can be found in a
single paragraph and even within a sentence. By juxtaposing aesthetic or
emotional language with rational language, by combining sensibilities and
logics, Foucault transgressed the unwritten rule that effectively divides
poetry from science.

By jolting our accepted ways of saying, Foucault stretches our capabil-
ity of seeing. His writing simultaneously exposes and analyzes power and
powerlessness and underscores hidden forms of violence. Using other-than-
rational language, he relays the emotional effect of practices upon selves and
conveys their constraining effects experientially. He further transgresses conventions when in his writing he equally associates beauty with the morally
"good" and with unwanted features. He shows us, as disturbing as this is,
how forms of constraint can also be appealing—just as caring work can also
be controlling. He makes the reader, if not complicit in the crime, at least a
close participant.

This mixture has a destabilizing effect on the reader—for some irritat-
ing, for others inspiring. His writing style has been critiqued for that extreme
character. He argued that the prisoners to whom he had shown his texts on
the jail system, and who experienced the institutional practices firsthand,
recognized themselves in his depictions. They claimed contextual validity.

Needless to say, this mixture of genres is at odds with the writing norms
in social work (Bloom, Wood, and Chambon 1991). Social work carefully
distinguishes between emotional expression and analytical reasoning. In
their writings social workers mark a stylistic boundary between illustrative
vignettes and the analytic segments of texts. Vignettes and analysis are spa-
tially set apart, their respective styles generally contrasted. This distinction
reinforces the divide between the experience of clients and the expert understanding of workers. The dividing line applies particularly to violent language. Social work texts reserve violent language for clients. Clients demand,

dominate, or aggress. Reference to workers is made in the language of reason and relies on neutral, objective terminology such as *balance, functioning,* or *coping.*

By contrast, Foucault used more passionate language. He enlists our emotions as readers so that we respond to the unbearable nature of a situation. This unconventional writing style has some readers feeling deeply uncomfortable. They cannot reconcile this style with scientific merit. Yet disclaiming the style is also a way of dismissing the nature of the arguments.

Some scholars have suggested that social workers should draw from literature to extend our understanding of the complexity of human nature in the social world and to expand the language of the profession (see chap. 2 by Irving; Turner 1991); a few examples exist of social workers' exploring alternative ways of writing. This has become an increasingly popular option among feminist scholars, as well as for those interested in narrative and postmodern approaches (see, for instance, Gorman 1993 and Irving 1994).

The point is not to adopt Foucault's style for ourselves or to introduce emotional language indiscriminately. It is to consider that rational language is neither neutral or transparent. It affects its audience and operates as a constraint (as well as a possibility). It distances the reader from actual experiences and understandably *fails to mobilize us for change.* Students who become socialized to professional and academic writing styles often lose the stronger challenging voice they expressed when they entered the field. At times, in order to maintain that voice they have to actively resist the acquisition of a more distanced professional language and the corresponding skills.

Deploying Arguments

Foucault built his arguments too—his rhetoric—in a highly unusual manner. In keeping with mixed genres, he did not separate the descriptive elements of his studies from his more interpretive and critical comments. He alternates between detailed descriptions and reasoning, images, and ideas. He mixes two actions, showing and telling.

Showing is not simply an act of illustration. For Foucault, showing is a way of telling. Images condense patterns of relations. In his discussion of the panopticon as an architectural mode of surveillance (*Discipline and Punish*), Foucault took great pains to describe what the mechanism looks like and how it operates and to impress upon the reader the many facets of repression through the details of the imagery and the development of arguments.

Social work texts commonly use vignettes to illustrate the dynamics of a case. They are an entry point into dailiness and bring into view the particulars of the human situation. They also serve to establish credibility with the reader, whether the texts are addressed to practitioners or to learners. They serve to confirm the interpretation. Whenever statistics are lacking, vignettes are to be expected.

Foucault used the vignette in a somewhat different manner; more than an illustrative tool, it becomes an interpretive tool. It offers clues for interpretation and provides the basis for an analogical expansion. Foucault's discussions circle around the object (presented in the form of a vignette) and, amplifying certain features, consider the many ramifications of a particular form. He takes us on a voyage through the vignette. As in his discussion of the panopticon in *Discipline and Punish,* he reproduces for and with the reader the steps of discovery in elucidating a structure of experience.

The attention Foucault paid to details is rhetorical and serves the purpose of his demonstration. Foucault draws the reader in, with the details set into relief. The accumulation of details builds a compelling picture (Deleuze 1986) and imposes the interpretation as evidence. Foucault first shows and then tells. He often briskly concludes a point by coining a new term to name a phenomenon, having gained (or not) our assent to his argument. The unusual sequence of showing, then telling accounts for the discomfort of the more conventional readers. They experience being ensnared by the author until they can no longer resist his line of argumentation. Is this a mirroring of practice, or is this manipulation?

Foucault further enlists readers by using the rhetorical means of repetition, variation, and distribution of the arguments themselves, in accordance with the mechanisms he proposes to uncover reality.

The Resonance of Words

Language is also rhythm and sound. Foucault used the evocative function of words and built on their musical resonance. Choosing the words carefully, and adding repetition to alliteration, he uses the reader's body as an echo chamber. Evidence comes to be perceived in an embodied way. Of Roussel's writing, he said, "It is a system which proliferates with rhymes, in which not only syllables are repeated but also words, the entire language, things, memory, the past, legends, life" (1992:56). He concluded, illustrating in his language what he claims about Roussel: "By the marvelous power of repetition hidden in the words, the bodies of men are transformed into cathedrals of sound" (57).

Foucault often juxtaposed unexpected words in phrases and imposed new, often complex, meaning. As an example, in coining the phrase "docile bodies," he juxtaposed terms that do not usually go together. *Docile* is more generally associated with *people* than with *bodies*. His term *docility* refers to a complex function, the acquisition of abilities through new mastery, while losing power and becoming subjected (Foucault 1995:138). What happens when we replace a term more commonly used in social work, like *compliance*, with the notion of docility?

Foucault used *body* to refer to two apparently distinct realms, to physical and subjective bodies, and to society, as the "social body." Juxtaposing the two sets of meanings can be seen as ambiguity or fuzziness on his part. He strategically draws from the multifunctionality or polysemy inherent in language. In this ambivalent use of the term body, Foucault blurred the distance between the personal and the social domains. He invited us to see our participation in the latter as a sensory act. Institutions mobilize us in intimate ways, including and particularly through our bodies. Conversely, he could discuss the hurtful effects of institutional practices on the collective (the social body) in an intimate personal way.

The elasticity of his language points to continuities where we usually see discontinuities. Of Roussel too, Foucault said: "The scattering of words allows an improbable joining of beings" (1992:36). He commented further on exploring this idea as a conscious stylistic mechanism:

> The identity of language—the simple, fundamental fact of language, that there are fewer terms of designation than there are things to designate—it itself a two-sided experience: it reveals words as the unexpected meeting place of the most distant figures of reality. It is distance abolished; at the point of contact, differences are brought together in a unique form: dual, ambiguous, Minotaur-like.   *(14)*

Foucault further supported this argument by quoting the eighteenth-century grammarian Dumarsais: "Thus by necessity and by choice, words are often turned away from their original meaning to take on a new one which is more or less removed but that still maintains a connection. This new meaning is called 'tropological'" (15).

Language presents, represents, and conveys. Foucault invites us to go beyond standard terminologies and to construct powerful concepts as tools in order to be able to see the world differently. Once we borrow a concept like examination or discipline to think of our daily practices, we start perceiving and understanding our everyday gestures in a new way. One could ask: Does this not distort the nature of the activity? Is this not giving a bad name to a gentle or reasonable act?

Social work tends to use the particular register of reasonable language by privileging harmony, rationality, and the scientific approach through notions of balance or functionality. The use of rational language inhibits challenge to social work's activities and obscures their effects. When social workers examine the procedural forms that they regularly use, they often fail to notice that the statements in those forms use the language of command: "Sign here," "Fill in the right box," "Don't forget." The form's graphics reinforce this function. Statements are boxed into allocated spaces bounded by lines. Filling in the form is already an imperative act. Noticing this pattern reveals the hidden use of power and its everyday intrusion in our defining gestures.

We can sometimes pick up some of these effects through the reactions of clients and the responses of students when they are newly socialized to those ways of thinking. Students can actively resist using a language that feels removed from experience and places them at a distance from their clients, as a distinct breed of people—whether through diagnostic language or the current economic language of restructuring, delocalization, or flexibility. A Foucauldian way of dealing with the reality hidden in those terms would be to examine more closely the responses of newcomers to the professional language of the field. I would also argue that advanced practitioners tend to develop a hybrid language of experience for talking to clients, with a view to bridging that gap.

It remains that Foucault's language is often difficult to grasp, addressed as it was to a particular audience at a particular time. This raises the question of inventing a new accessible language for dealing with change.

Foucault's playfulness with style is to be taken as a serious act, which means attending to language differently. He makes us aware that language shapes the reality that we see.

In summary, I would like to suggest that Foucault's approach to social issues was systematic, even though it did not lend itself to a summary or a blueprint. The intent of his work and of his key concepts needs to be understood; otherwise, the risk is to lose and distort his project.

I believe we can draw principles from his work in the form of building blocks and directions for social inquiry. Those ideas can be freeing and exhilarating:

1. Taking seriously the notion of scientific inquiry as "unsettling work," and of theory as an "unsettling practice." Moving away from preestablished models will open up new avenues of questioning.

2. Historicizing our understanding of reality by retracing how particular practices and forms of knowledge have been created and adopted over time and treating these as results and not as truths. This is a serious invitation to conduct archival work and explore earlier voices and circumstances through agency materials such as case files.

3. Examining practices and texts in a detailed manner to reveal hidden patterns and effects in order to enhance our grasp of the different ways in which power is manifested; concurrently, to consider the multifunctionality of practices and discourses.

4. Linking subjectivity to actions and knowledge to help us better understand how doing constitutes the doer, how social work activities create clients and workers. This also translates as perceiving forms of knowledge and practice as permissible options with their systems of rules—and conceiving that those can be modified and transgressed.

5. Exploring new possibilities in the naming of things, in complex descriptions, in the effects of our writing and our relation to our audiences, as practitioners and scholars.

Foucault combined beauty with discipline, possibility with constraint, control with caring. We tend to rebel against accepting these mixed forms, those mixed functions. We refuse, as scholars and practitioners, our own duplicity. One part of our rejection of Foucault is most likely our resistance to the arguments he is making. We respond with mixed emotions to the effects of his arguments.

REFERENCES

Bloom, Martin, Katherine Wood, and Adrienne S. Chambon. 1991. The six languages of social work. *Social Work* 36 (6): 530–34.

Bordo, S. R. 1989. The body and the reproduction of femininity: A feminist appropriation of Foucault. In Alison M. Jaggar and Susan R. Bordo, eds., *Gender/body/knowledge*. New Brunswick, N.J.: Rutgers University Press.

Canguilhem, George. 1995. On *Histoire de la folie* as an event. *Critical Inquiry* 21 (Winter): 282–86.

Cree, V. E. 1995. *From public streets to private lives: The changing task of social work.* Aldershot, U.K.: Avebury.

Davidson, Arnold, ed. 1997. *Foucault and his interlocutors.* Chicago: University of Chicago Press.

Deleuze, Gilles. 1986. *Foucault.* Paris: Les Editions de Minuit.

de Montigny, G. A. 1995. *Social working: An ethnography of frontline practice.* Toronto: University of Toronto Press.

Dreyfus, H. L. and Paul Rabinow. 1982. *Michel Foucault: Beyond structuralism and hermeneutics.* Chicago: University of Chicago Press.

Edelman, Murray. 1988. *Constructing the political spectacle.* Chicago: University of Chicago Press.

Epstein, Laura. 1994. The therapeutic idea in contemporary society. In Adrienne S. Chambon and Allan Irving, eds., *Essays on postmodernism and social work*, pp. 3–18. Toronto: Canadian Scholars' Press.

——. 1996. The trouble with the researcher-practitioner idea. *Social Work Research* 20, no. 2 (June): 113–17.

Eribon, Didier. 1994. *Michel Foucault et ses contemporains.* Paris: Fayard.

Farge, Arlette. 1992. Un récit violent. In Luce Giard, ed., *Michel Foucault: Lire l'oeuvre*, pp. 181–87. Grenoble: Jérome Millon.

Farge, Arlette and Michel Foucault, eds. 1982. *Le désordre des familles: Lettres de cachet des archives de la Bastille.* Paris: Gallimard/Juillard.

Foucault, Michel. 1965. *Madness and civilization: A history of insanity in the age of reason.* Translated by Richard Howard. New York: Vintage/Random House.

——. 1972. *The archaeology of knowledge* and *The discourse on language.* Translated by A. M. Sheridan Smith. New York: Pantheon.

——. 1975. *The birth of the clinic: An archaeology of medical perception.* Translated by A. M. Sheridan Smith. New York: Vintage.

——. 1977a. History of systems of thought: Course description of Foucault's first year at Collège de France. In D. F. Bouchard, ed., and D. F. Bouchard and Sherry Simon, trans., *Language, countermemory, practice: Selected essays and interviews*, pp. 199–204. Ithaca, N.Y.: Cornell University Press.

——. 1977b. Nietzsche, genealogy, history. In D. F. Bouchard, ed., and D. F. Bouchard and Sherry Simon, trans., *Language, countermemory, practice: Selected essays and interviews*, pp. 139–64. Ithaca, N.Y.: Cornell University Press.

——. 1977c. What is an author? In D. F. Bouchard, ed., D. F. Bouchard and Sherry Simon, trans., *Language, countermemory, practice: Selected essays and interviews*, pp. 115–38. Ithaca, N.Y.: Cornell University Press.

——. 1980. Prison talk. Interview by J. J. Brochier. Translated by Colin Gordon. In Colin Gordon, ed., *Power/Knowledge: Selected interviews and other writings, 1972–77*, pp. 37–54. New York: Pantheon.

——. 1982. The subject and power. Afterword to H. L. Dreyfus and Paul Rabinow, eds.,

Michel Foucault: Beyond structuralism and hermeneutics, pp. 208–26. Chicago: University of Chicago Press.

Foucault, Michel. 1983. Structuralism and poststructuralism: An interview with Gérard Raulet. *Telos: A Quarterly Journal of Critical Thought* 55 (Spring): 195–211.

——. 1984. The birth of the asylum. In Paul Rabinow, ed., *The Foucault reader*, pp. 141–67. 1965. Reprint, New York: Pantheon.

——. 1987. Questions of method: An interview with Michel Foucault. In Kenneth Baynes, James Bohman, and Thomas McCarthy, eds., *After philosophy: End or transformation?* pp. 100–24. Translated by Alan Bass. Cambridge, Mass.: MIT Press.

——. 1992. *Death and the labyrinth: The world of Raymond Roussel.* Translated by Charles Ruas. New York: Doubleday.

——. [1979] 1995. *Discipline and punish: The birth of the prison.* Translated by Alan Sheridan. New York: Vintage.

Fraser, Nancy. 1989. *Unruly practices: Power, discourse, and gender in contemporary social theory.* Minneapolis: University of Minnesota Press.

Geertz, Clifford. 1988. *Works and lives: The anthropologist as author.* Palo Alto, Calif.: Stanford University Press.

Goffman, Erving 1961. *Asylums.* New York: Doubleday.

Gordon, Colin. 1986. Question, ethos, event: Foucault on Kant and Enlightenment. *Economy and Society* 15, no. 1 (February): 71–87.

Gorman, Jane. 1993. Postmodernism and the conduct of inquiry in social work. *Affilia* 8 (3): 247–64.

Halperin, David H. 1994. Historicizing the subject of desire: Sexual preferences and erotic identities in the pseudo-Lucianic erotes. In Jan Goldstein, ed., *Foucault and the writing of history*, pp. 19–34. Cambridge, Mass.: Blackwell.

Hartman, Ann. 1993. The professional is political. Editorial. *Social Work* 38 (4): 365–66, 504.

Irving, Allan. 1994. From image to simulacra: The modern/postmodern divide and social work. In Adrienne S. Chambon and Allan Irving, eds., *Essays on postmodernism and social work*, pp. 19–32. Toronto: Canadian Scholars' Press.

Laird, Joan, ed. 1993. *Revisioning social work education: A social constructionist approach.* New York: Haworth Press.

Liberalism, neoliberalism, and governmentality. 1993. *Economy and Society* 22, no. 3 (August).

Lupton, Deborah. 1995. *The imperative of health: Public health and the regulated body.* Thousand Oaks, Calif.: Sage.

Megill, Alan. 1990. Foucault, ambiguity, and the rhetoric of historiography. *History of the Human Sciences* 3 (3): 343–63.

Nurius, Paula. 1993. Human memory: A basis for better understanding the elusive self-concept. *Social Service Review* 67 (2): 261–78.

O'Neill, John. 1994. *The posthumous eye: Eye-work in Foucault.* Paper presented at the International Congress: Michel Foucault and literature. Victoria University, Toronto, October 15.

Probyn, Elspeth. 1991. This body which is not one: Speaking an embodied self. *Hypatia* 6: 111–24.

Revel, Judith. 1994. *Invention de soi, parole réfractaire et passage à la limite: Michel Foucault et la littérature de la transgression.* Paper presented at the International Congress: Michel Foucault and literature. Victoria University, Toronto, October 14.

Richmond, Mary. 1917. *Social diagnosis.* New York: Russel Sage Foundation.

Rose, Nikolas and Peter Miller. 1992. Political power beyond the state: Problematics of government. *British Journal of Sociology* 43 (2): 173–205.

Saleeby, Dennis. 1994. Culture, theory, and narrative: The intersection of meanings in practice. *Social Work* 39 (4): 351–59.

Sands, R. G. and Kathleen Nuccio. 1992. Postmodern feminist theory and social work. *Social Work* 37 (6): 489–94.

Sawicki, Jana. 1991. *Disciplining Foucault: Feminism, power, and the body.* New York: Routledge.

Smith, D. E. 1987. *The everyday world as problematic: A feminist sociology.* Toronto: University of Toronto Press.

Spitzer, Leo. 1970. *Études de style.* Translated by Eliane Kaufholz, Alain Coulon, and Michel Foucault. 1947. Reprint, Paris: Gallimard.

Turner, Margaret. 1991. Literature and social work: An exploration of how literature informs social work in a way social sciences cannot. *British Journal of Social Work* 21: 229–43.

Veyne, Paul. 1997. Foucault revolutionizes history. In Arnold Davidson, ed., *Foucault and his interlocutors,* pp. 146–82. Translated by Catherine Porter. 1978. Translation, Chicago: University of Chicago Press.

Social Work, Social Control, and Normalization: Roundtable Discussion with Michel Foucault

This roundtable discussion was originally published in French in 1972 as part of a special issue of the journal Esprit. This was a unique event. The editors had organized a series of discussions and invited papers to debate the status of the social work profession, all grouped under the title "Why Social Work?" The roundtable was later reprinted in *Dits et Écrits* (Foucault 1994).

Roundtable participants whose work has appeared in English were the sociologist Jacques Donzelot, known particularly for *The Policing of Families* (1979), and the architect Paul Virilio, who writes extensively on questions of technology and society. The other participants were the sociologists Philippe Meyer and Jean-René Tréanton (the latter was then the director of the *Revue Française de Sociologie*), the historian Jacques Julliard, and the writer René Pucheu, as well as Director Jean-Marie Domenach and Chief Editor Paul Thibaud of *Esprit*.

At the time Domenach, Donzelot, and Foucault were active members of the Groupe d'Information sur les Prisons (GIP), an advocacy coalition that worked with prisoners to reform the prison system between 1971 and 1973 (see, for instance, Macey's 1993 account in his biography of Foucault). *Esprit* contributed to the dissemination of those ideas.

This English version is an original translation by Adrienne S. Chambon. A different version appeared in Lotringer's *Foucault Live* (1989) under the title "Confining Societies." The translation in this volume deviates from that version on a few points and includes a number of segments that had been left out. Some arguments, which seemed to delve specifically into the French context, have not been included.

Internment and Capitalism

DOMENACH: Until recently, asocial or antisocial behaviors were thought of and dealt with in legal terms (prisoners, the confined, the alienated, the outcasts.) Today, they are increasingly conceived of in clinical terms (personality disorders, psychopaths, the mentally ill). How do you account for this development?

DONZELOT: How you state the question troubles me. I would prefer to reverse the order of the arguments. Aren't you putting the cart before the horse when you speak first of asocial or antisocial behavior, whereas behaviors are determined foremost by institutional frames? People are placed in those institutions because of power relations, which the legal and clinical spheres comply with, in conjunction with one another.

MEYER: Yes, but doesn't it make a difference whether the priority is placed upon the legal sphere, as was happening in the past, or upon the clinical sphere, which is the situation today?

FOUCAULT: I would like to introject a small historical specification, which may or may not cast the problem in a different light. Like Donzelot, I believe that the legal categories of exclusion are usually accompanied by medical or clinical corollaries. What masks this relation is that, for a number of reasons, legal terminology is more or less stable, whereas, by contrast, clinical categories are relatively unstable and change rapidly.

It is true that the notion of personality disorder is a recent one. But this does not imply that the backing of the legal system by the clinical sphere, or the transformation of a legal category into a clinical one, are recent phenomena. Indeed, before personality disorders appeared on the scene, there were the degenerates and before them the monomaniacs; these notions are just as legal as medical. Still, a wide police selection (or triage) took place in the West starting, I believe, in the fifteenth century, with the hunting down of vagrants, beggars, and the idle; this practice of selection, of exclusion, of police internment remained outside the scope of the judiciary, of the legal system.

For a number of years, the Parliament of Paris was responsible for policing drifters and beggars in the city, but this prerogative was quickly abolished, and the responsibility de facto lay with institutions and mechanisms that were totally outside the regular legal apparatus. Then, at the beginning of the nineteenth century, all police practices of social selection were reincorporated in the legal system with extensive coordination (within the Napoleonic state) between police, justice, and penitentiary institutions. At the very moment when these practices were being integrated into the judiciary or police domains, at that point in time emerged new psychological, psychiatric, and sociological categories that served to justify them. Functioning as an overlay, they provided a new reading of these practices (although not a different understanding).

MEYER: Let me add a couple of comments: It seems that the difference between the personality disorders of today and the degenerate of previous times is that the degenerate did not mobilize a whole slew of technicians specializing in relationship management, rehabilitation, and adaptation. Besides, you say that the penal apparatus came first and was backed later on by the psychiatric apparatus; do they not stand today in a reverse relationship?

FOUCAULT: I very much agree with you. Definitely, the relation between the penal and the psychiatric spheres, or the legal and the psychological, has changed considerably in the last hundred and fifty years. Nevertheless, I believe that both originated in social practices of selection and exclusion; they derive from police practices that were incorporated at a late date in the legal domain. You are right when you say that there are technicians now who are responsible for rehabilitating personality disorders, whereas degenerates were not considered treatable. But at the time when the large prisons and the large psychiatric hospitals were simultaneously created, in the 1820s and 1830s, jurors were very confused when they were asked to take a position about crimes such as parricide or the murder of a child. They had to choose between the prison and the hospital, two solutions that, in the final analysis, were somewhat equivalent. The problem was: This individual needs to be locked up. Which form of internment is the safer of the two, the prison or the hospital? The medical-police connection is an old one.

MEYER: In working on the representation of madness in the public at large among the "noncrazy," I was struck by the fact that a large number of people thought of themselves as potentially mentally ill. This is clearly an effect of the diffuse influence of psychoanalysis. It becomes apparent that this new representation of madness, linked with the determination to "clinicize" the sphere of the social, creates a new means for transmitting the law.

DONZELOT: At the beginning of the nineteenth century, a sort of essentialist conception prevailed, exemplified in the categories of relegated, outcasts, segregated, et cetera, and knowledge served purely to confirm such a segregation. Whereas now, it is as though this knowledge offers a somewhat transparent and more fluid view of illness and of its categories and starts to convey a new type of surveillance. In other words, knowledge becomes an instrument; it is no longer an alibi. That is what you were saying when you spoke of new representations: everyone sees themselves as potentially sick. It became possible, then, to establish a system of prevention that induces such representations.

VIRILIO: I caught on to something that Foucault was saying earlier that interests me very much: that "sociatry" came before psychiatry. This leads to the following questions: Where are asylums located today? Are they closed or open? This is particularly important in light of the recent decree passed by the House of Commons in Great Britain to close down all asylums in the next twenty years. It takes us back to a similar situation to the one you described in *Madness and Civilization*—back to the Middle Ages, before internment was established but not exactly under the same conditions. The mad and the deviant are now "liberated" on the English soil but on a territory that, this time, is completely controlled and greatly different from what it was in medieval times. What do you think of a broad notion of sociatry as preceding psychiatry?

FOUCAULT: The decision of the House of Commons is indeed remarkable. It is even astonishing. And I wonder whether they have a clear vision of what this will lead to; unless they know too well what it cannot accomplish. Capitalist societies, and until now this holds true for societies that call themselves noncapitalist, are in any case enclosing societies.

If we classify societies according to how they get rid of—not their dead—but rather their living, we obtain a classification into massacring-type societies, or societies with ritualistic murder; societies practicing exile; societies favoring reparation; and societies practicing internment. This seems to me to be the four main types.

I think it is difficult for us to explain why capitalist society is characterized by internment. Why, indeed, is it necessary for a society in which one sells her or his force of labor to be of the internment-type? Idleness, vagrancy, migrations of those who seek better wages elsewhere—all lead to the systematic gridlike control of these masses and the possibility of putting them back to work. All this is inscribed in the very practice of internment, to the extent that when a capitalist society such as the British declares the abolition of internment at least for the mad, I wonder: Does this mean that the whole other side of internment, the prison system, is going to disappear, or, on the contrary, is it going to take up the empty space left behind by the asylum? Will Britain be led to do the opposite of what the Soviet Union did? The Soviet Union generalized the psychiatric hospital, treating it as a prison system. Will England expand the role of its prisons, even if they are considerably improved?

MEYER: In an article in the journal *Topique*, Donzelot spoke of a general devaluation of internment among advanced industrial societies. Does he think, like Virilio, that the devaluing of internment is accompanied by the development of a network of people whose task is social control, "social controllers," as it were?

DONZELOT: I don't think we are dealing with the end of internment. I simply think that it is being devalued and that we are witnessing an external dissemination of internment procedures, while the spaces of internment are maintained as a security backup. Fewer prisons, but on the basis of a system of control and surveillance that keeps people in their rightful places and that will ultimately fulfill the same function.

FOUCAULT: That is why your question interested me so much, but I hesitate. If we reduce the problem to these two notions: the legal and the psychological, it leads us to take one of two positions: (1) Either the psychological discourse uncovers the truth of what the legal practice did blindly—this is a positivist view, which one often finds among historians of medicine and among psychologists when they tell you: What were sorcerers? They were neurotics. (2) Or if one conducts an analysis in purely relativistic terms, we recognize that the legal and the psychological are two readings of a single phenomenon. The mode of reading that was primarily legal in the nineteenth century is now psychological in the twentieth century, without the psychological being more firmly grounded than the legal used to be. And for me, I would add a third term, which by approximation I call policing: a selective, exclusive, and enclosing practice upon which one can observe the development of legal and psychological practices and discourses.

DONZELOT: Previously, things were done with the means available; these were exclusionary practices. Today, a very effective system of confinement exists in the school system. Schools, as we know them, enable people to stay in their assigned places according to the requirements of the system, that is, based on their social origin. Baudelot and Establet's book on the Capitalist School tells the story quite well. It speaks of two networks of schooling: the secondary-and-above network, and the primary and professional network. There may be a third one, the legal-clinical network, a sort of new educational layer that absorbs to a certain degree the old products of exclusion.

　　We could talk of a form of dialectic—although I don't like that word very much—between exclusion and confinement. When things are going well, under conditions of available resources, confinement takes place through the school system. When this is not sufficient, exclusionary means take over. This is the problem as far as I see it. It is no more complicated than that.

JULLIARD: In other words, internment in the way we mean it is a substitute to previously closed societies. To the extent that these societies are opening up, they no longer maintain these internal mechanisms of regulation, which were characteristic of precapitalistic societies. At that point, we witness the development of the asylum and the prison as forms of internment.

FOUCAULT: It has been an important technique in the growth of capitalism, more prevalent by far than during the period of early capitalism.

Social Work and Police Control

DOMENACH: Social work is constantly expanding its field of activity. Initially developed as volunteer assistance to interventions aimed at eradicating tuberculosis and venereal diseases, social work was later transformed into a professional modality of social assistance aimed at the underclass or paraproletariat. Today, it has become widely established in the industrial and service sectors. Its latest developments, particularly in urban contexts, consist of community interventions with "regular" populations.

Do you see the extension and evolution of social work as a function of the nature and development of our economic system? Is there truly a continuity between the type of social work derived from police, psychiatric, or rehabilitative interventions with deviants and broad social action aimed at the general population? What do we mean today by social work?

JULLIARD: I will start with a commonsensical observation that may be worth stating. There is no doubt that our societies are moving to increase the functional isolation of groups. Until recent times, a large number of societies operated on the basis of distinct groupings. In contrast it seems that today, leaving aside the situation of marginalized populations, the isolation of the elderly and of young people who are not yet able to work has resulted in the creation of social groups such as "children," the world of "adults," and the "elderly," which correspond respectively to distinct productive functions. To the extent that we are dealing with social groupings defined by relations of production more than by any other factor, there is a need for social interventions that target each of these groupings, since they reach their equilibrium solely on the basis of their function, externally defined.

VIRILIO: As an illustration, in some neighborhoods of Paris and in the suburbs, there already exist local agents whose involvement in "social" action consists in inspecting basements and hanging out on the doorsteps of apartments on a regular basis.

MEYER: In the suburban areas around Paris, housing units are divided into "blocks" along the Anglo-American model. To each housing block are assigned one youth worker, one social worker, and—I didn't make this up—one police officer who are known in the neighborhood. They are just as likely to intervene by carrying groceries for sick elderly women as by stopping delinquents from harming the public. What will these youth workers and social workers do? As Julliard pointed out, and this is reflected in the general discourse, everyone already perceives that the social fabric is coming apart. It is believed—that is the argument put forward by those concerned and by the decision makers to protect themselves—that those youth workers and those social workers are placed in those neighborhoods to foster sociability.

What do they really do? Let me give you a concrete example. A group of youth workers in a housing block came up with the following project: They are going to visit all the homes of the underclass in the neighborhood—their neighborhood is heavily "delinquent prone"—and they will explain to the mothers how to raise their infants so that these do not end up in the street when they become teenagers. This is an instance of "clinical reductionism." Various theories promote the limitation of the concept of delinquency to a purely clinical notion. These youth workers and these social workers will not only fail to produce sociability, as is officially claimed; on top of that, they will reinforce the process of dismemberment and atomization of the social fabric. And that to me seems catastrophic—independent of the function of social control that they are asked to play through this new regulation.

DONZELOT: A form of responsibility is taken up. Something is taken over, a takeover of power that leads to the dispossession of all available means to achieve concerted forms of collective life. It is a deliberate counterstrategy, which in the guise of community mobilization institutes social control and surveillance on a broad scale!

PUCHEU: . . . I would like us to identify *who* is behind this development. I am a bit afraid of this "who." I don't have the sense that the state is organized well enough to be able to master the totality of the social processes with such Machiavellian genius as to make us believe that someone, somewhere, is directing the social agents surreptitiously. Who wishes the transformation of social mobilizers into controllers? The collective unconscious or what?

DONZELOT: I wasn't postulating a transcendental subject who manipulates society directly. I simply stressed that the system of assistance that once was relatively autonomous is systematically tied today to the judiciary. There is a continuity between prevention assistance, assistance within the court system, et cetera. And so, by and large, we have two sets of facts: on the one hand, a much greater connection for a number of agents to the judicial apparatus, and on the other, the dissemination of a systematic model of interpretation of human problems, psychologism, which operates mainly through ideology.

TRÉANTON: I believe that the great diversity that exists among social workers prevents consciousness raising on their part, and this contributes to
the crisis. They have great difficulty [trying] to become unionized. They
have great difficulty in developing collective agreements. They attempt
to understand their problems and the problems that they are required
to deal with through highly diversified structures. They are employees
of sorts, wage earners of small and midsize firms within a society in
which problems are now located at the level of large organizations. Still,
I do not agree with overgeneralizing.

FOUCAULT: ... I think that a number of individuals in this situation are
saying no and denouncing the system. This does not protect them
against exclusion or the fact that their exclusion is now accepted by
everyone, not only obviously by the bureaucracy but also by their colleagues. This proves the extent to which social work has become programmatic and institutionalized.

THIBAUD: Wherever there is social work, the social worker is always tied to
a source of authority. I think that this is an absolute rule. That is clearly
the situation in prisons and also in industry. Social workers don't actually possess authority. They have some freedom of action but no real
authority.

PUCHEU: There are degrees of autonomy.

JULLIARD: I believe that the word *police* led to an erroneous debate. The
relationship to the police, as a particularly functional means of coercion,
is very clear in the case of the prison. If we take teachers—we can consider them as "social workers" for the purpose of our discussion—we can
see how they are becoming aware, in larger numbers, that next to their
explicit function of communication, they have the implicit function of
maintaining order. I wouldn't use the term policing function, because it
is too restrictive, too polemical, and it muddies the debate instead of
clarifying it. But there is clearly a function of maintaining the status
quo.

It seems to me that the problem stems today from how this implicit
function has become explicit to a number of people. They now realize
that a number of the activities they wish to conduct in the purview of
their explicit function, and that are needed and perfectly legitimate, lead

them to question their implicit function. They are then confronted with the external authorities that define them, and that, I wouldn't quite say direct them at a distance, but that, in the final analysis, sustain their legitimacy.

MEYER: I would like to add a word concerning the expanding field of social work. We need to reflect upon this extension. We can presently find side by side archaic forms of social work—those that are purely and simply charitable interventions (to provide bread and that sort of thing)—with the more modern forms of "mobilization" of "regular" populations. These two poles seem to me to be the two extremes in the profession and account for the increasing numbers of social workers and for their broadened scope of activity.

PUCHEU: So, is the community worker necessarily a police person in our society?

MEYER: No, but that person's mandate is that of a controller.

VIRILIO: So the social worker is part of a general challenge addressed to us all: We no longer know how to mobilize ourselves or how to recreate ourselves. That is terrible. This trade-off that is addressed to us all through the population of the social workers, we cannot accept it. That is the problem with social work. We make believe that it is not up to society to create itself, as if it was being treated, acted upon, solely from the outside. It looks as if we are going through three stages: the self-regulation of ancient societies, the regulation of our societies, and now we are going toward a kind of "deregulation" through urbanization, as you were saying earlier, a new phenomenon associated with world cities (globalization).

FOUCAULT: I would like to add a word along Julliard's statement. Obviously, we have never said that a particular social worker, or the social worker as individual, is subsidized by the police. That isn't what our discussion is about. What is important is that social work is inscribed within a larger social function that has been taking on new dimensions for centuries, the function of surveillance-and-correction: to surveil individuals and to redress them, in the two meanings of the word, alternatively as punishment and as pedagogy.

This function of surveillance-correction was already implemented in the nineteenth century through diverse institutions, among them the church, and later by elementary school teachers. It is commonly thought that social work originated in the volunteer assistance to eradicate tuberculosis and venereal diseases. I wonder if its origin isn't to be found instead in the "educator" function, more specifically with elementary school teachers. They have had this role, next to the priests. . . .

The great treason that intellectuals performed in their relation to the bourgeois state is sanctioned in the fact that social workers are now expected to play the role that elementary school teachers, high school teachers, and intellectuals have ceased to fulfill for some time. The paradox in all this is that these social workers have been educated by these very intellectuals. This is why social workers cannot but transgress the function that they are required to fulfill.

Working Classes and Dangerous Classes

DOMENACH: Concerning the political influence of social work, how are we to locate or define within social theories those who are considered as maladjusted? Are they problems or subjects? Are they subjects of capitalism or agents of change?

TRÉANTON: There is growing unease among most social workers who are becoming aware of their unwilling contribution—mainly implicit—to maintaining the status quo. There is an internal tension there. I find it extremely interesting to study the ways in which this internal tension is manifested. We are not dealing with isolated instances but with a widespread realization. We could ask students in schools of social work. It would be interesting to conduct a survey among them and find out how many ask themselves these questions.

One of the main aspects of this crisis is linked to the way they are taught, on the whole, to deal with problems on an individual case-by-case basis. Most of the time, they realize that they are forbidden from reflecting or intervening at a collective or more general level. They are not allowed to reach the political arena or perform collective action. They are told that their task is exclusively to care for individuals. There is the rub. Therefore, many of them come to realize that to intervene at the individual level is totally illusory unless political problems are addressed. And they fail to see any way out of this dilemma.

JUILLARD: . . . There remains the issue as to whether marginalized people, delinquents, prisoners, or the mentally ill, can become major agents in a political action. That is the question. Personally, I would be cautious. I fail to see how these marginalized groups could become the core of a true political action. . . .

This action can be integrated insofar as "normal" people are able to perceive that the problems faced by marginal groups have become their own. The issue isn't to change the working class or to change the nature of social action. I don't well see how that can be done. If the aim of political action remains to exercise or to achieve power, this can only be accomplished by groups that already occupy significant positions in society, the producers who hold a specific social and economic function.

We are discovering that there are no longer two categories, marginals and producers. A growing number of producers are being marginalized and are experiencing various forms of exclusion. There lies, maybe, the possibility of reintegrating real marginals into social and political action, which would be common to all workers.

DONZELOT: I tend to agree with this view of a general process of fragmentation and categorization of people. I think we should identify the main dividing lines. One of them is crucial: What separates the respectable, unionized worker who has a job from the disreputable, incarcerated nonunionized worker? Indeed, this fundamental line of partition sustains the economic and political system. I don't think the issue is to change the working class. That is a pitfall to be avoided. However, it is upon this breaking point, this dividing line, that we need to place our efforts.

FOUCAULT: . . . Where I don't follow you is when you say: There is the working class on one hand, and the marginals on the other, and you include in this category the incarcerated, the mentally ill, delinquents, et cetera. Should we be defining the nonworking masses by this list of mentally ill, et cetera? Wouldn't it be more accurate to say that there is a divide between the working class and the underclass? So that, instead of saying, "There is the working class and the marginals," we would say, "Within the overall lower class, there is a divide between those who work and those groups who are not part of the system of production." The institution of police, the legal system, and the penal system are one of the means used to deepen this partition, which is needed by capitalism.

In the end, what capitalism fears, rightly or wrongly since 1789 and so on, is social revolt and riots; people in the streets with their knives and guns, ready to engage in violent action. The bourgeoisie has been haunted by this vision, and it wants to send the message to the working class that that is no longer an option. "Surely, in your own interest, you cannot ally yourself with people who are ready to spearhead insurrections."

And all this mobile population, always ready to come down to the streets, to riot, has been earmarked as a negative example by the penal system. All the legal and moral devaluing made of violence, theft, et cetera, all this moral education that the elementary school teacher provided to the workers in positive terms, the judicial system has made its own in negative terms. Thus the divide is continuously reproduced and refashioned between the working class and the nonworking world, since it was thought that their contact could potentially be the catalyst of riots.

DONZELOT: The function of any apparatus or institution is to delimit a territory and to define its boundaries, i.e., to divide. The function of social workers is to partition. A family visited by a social worker becomes a designated family. It now belongs to an excluded or potentially excludable population, to which an individual would no longer want to belong since it is now outside the law.

TRÉANTON: Do the social worker's actions have a stigmatizing effect? Do they result in a public act of labeling?

FOUCAULT: There are two ways to erase the dividing line between the nonworking lower class and the working class. One is to intervene upon the lower class and to teach it certain values, principles, and norms so that it accepts without critical examination those values that belong to the bourgeoisie and those that the bourgeoisie has inculcated to the working class. This will disarm the lower class. It will lose its specificity and will cease to be a dangerous ferment of riots and revolt.

Another way to overcome the divide is to address the working class and the lower class together. The system of values that you are taught, what is it exactly if not a system of power, an instrument of power in the hands of the bourgeoisie? When you are told it is bad to steal, you are offered a certain definition of private property that is given the value the bourgeoisie assigns to it. When you are taught not to like violence, to make peace, not to seek vengeance, to prefer justice to a struggle, you are taught to prefer bourgeois justice to social struggle. You are taught that a judge is better than vengeance. That is the work that has been accomplished so well by those intellectuals and elementary school teachers and is now being pursued in their own way by the social workers.

THIBAUD: This type of alliance between the working class and the underclass traditionally takes place during periods of violent revolution. However, this alliance is ephemeral. Past the shaky period when one power replaces another, things tend to fall back upon the traditional system of exclusion. The heroes of the riots end up in jail. The issue then is how to establish an alliance between the working class and the underclass based on something other than the value of revolt, upon a common social project. Without it, their alliance will show itself to be fragile and fake once the angry days are gone.

FOUCAULT: When I said earlier that the problem was precisely to show the working class that the system of justice that it is offered and imposed is really an instrument of power, it was for that reason, so that the alliance with the lower class would not simply be a tactical alliance of a day or an evening, but that there could take place—between a proletariat that does not share at all the ideology of the lower class and the lower class that does not share the social practices of the working class—something other than a circumstantial encounter.

DONZELOT: I believe that an encounter can take place between an insurrectional lower class and a working class burdened by bourgeois values, outside the professional arena around housing problems, unemployment, neighborhood life, social isolation, health problems, or confrontations with police control. It is at the level of these activities that the connection can be made.

THIBAUD: What is interesting is that then we have to say that people's social location in the system of production is not a determining factor. We are raising a new problem, the distinction between the social and the economic spheres.

It seems to me that the disjuncture between the social and the economic becomes clear once we start to talk about social work as a global action performed upon society as a whole, rather than as a series of dispersed activities, each one linked to a major social function (production, education). The crisis of the social democratic welfare state—a democratic political power controlling production for the benefit of society through programs or planification—this crisis is spreading to all the components of this system. As a result, there is a certain autonomy of the social sphere that formulates more direct claims (as illustrated by the theme of quality of life).

REFERENCES

Donzelot, Jacques. 1979. *The policing of families.* Translated by Robert Hurley. New York: Random House.
Foucault, Michel. 1989. *Foucault live (Interviews, 1966–84).* Edited by Sylvère Lotringer. New York: Semiotext(e).
——. 1994. *Dits et Écrits, 1954–88.* Edited by Daniel Defert and François Ewald. Paris: Gallimard.
Macey, David. 1993. *The lives of Michel Foucault.* London: Vintage.
Table ronde. 1972. *Esprit* no. 4–5 (Avril–Mai) (Pourquoi le travail social?): 678–703.

Part Two
Social Work Practices and Knowledge Reconsidered

Reconfiguring Child Welfare Practices: Risk, Advanced Liberalism, and the Government of Freedom

Nigel Parton

The purpose of this chapter is to analyze and reflect upon the current state of child welfare policy and practice and how this has changed in recent times. Although the primary focus is Britain, I also suggest that similar developments are evident throughout the Western world, particularly the United States. In doing so I am attempting to outline a "history of the present," drawing on a number of ideas developed by Michel Foucault in his later work related to governmentality and how we can understand and think about the relations of force that shape our present, particularly in terms of liberal rule.

A number of writers have suggested that we are experiencing a period of major crisis in child welfare (Lindsey 1994; N. Parton 1996a, 1997) and that this particularly arises from the need to respond to the increasing numbers of child abuse allegations. Thus we have the requirement to investigate and police families but in the context where the primary mandate is to provide a supportive, preventative service to children and families in need. Currently, child welfare services are subject to considerable overload so that resources have to be prioritized and responses rationalized in such a way that the tensions and problems can be addressed in day-to-day policy and practice (Parton, Thorpe, and Wattam 1997).

A central part of my argument is that new strategies are emerging that do not focus on either meeting the needs of children or responding to child abuse but rather on assessing and managing risk. The new strategies dissolve the notion of a subject or a concrete individual and put in its place a concern with a combination of risk factors. As a result, the essential focus of policy and practice no longer takes the form of a direct face-to-face relationship between the social worker and the client but resides in establishing flows of the population, primarily related to the family and the household, based on the collation and monitoring of a range of abstract factors deemed liable to produce risk for children. However, although the notion of risk gives the impression of calculability and objectivity, it is inherently contingent and open to differing and sometimes conflicting interpretations (Armstrong 1995; N. Parton 1996b). In the process the role and accountability of professional social workers are recast and subject to a variety of forms of audit in which the role of the manager or administrator becomes key. As Castel has argued, "The specialists find themselves now cast in a subordinate role, while managerial policy formation is allowed to develop into a completely autonomous force, totally beyond the surveillance of the operative on the ground who is now reduced to a mere executant" (1991:281). I argue further that these developments have a wider significance, because they both reflect and feed into an emerging configuration of governmentality associated with "advanced liberal" societies and thus provide a small but significant instance of the state we are in, the essential contours of our current sphere(s) of operation, and offer important insights into the complex politics of child welfare.

What I am arguing is that the problem of risk provides a key point of entry for investigating and understanding contemporary "advanced liberal" strategies for governing conduct in the area of child welfare policy and practice, and this is qualitatively different from what went before.

Destabilizing the Present

Although Foucault may be regarded as making a significant contribution to opening up debates now associated with poststructuralism, postmodernity, and postmodernism (Boyne and Rattansi 1990; Smart 1993), more recently a number of commentators have tried to distance his work and approach(es) from such developments in social theory, particularly as they tend toward totalization and attempting to identify the essence of various epochs (Barry, Osborne, and Rose 1996). Foucault's major contribution is seen in terms of the conceptual devices and tools that he made available for understanding the contingencies of the systems of power in which we live and that thereby inhabit us today. Concepts are deployed to demonstrate the negotiations, tensions, and accidents that have contributed to the fashioning of ourselves and our times. Following Barry, Osborne, and Rose (1996), two elements can be seen to characterize Foucauldian histories of the present: the general ethos of the approach and the concern with liberalism.

Foucault always attempted to introduce an "untimely" ethos to the present, thereby adding a sense of its fragility and contingency and demonstrating it does not necessarily have to be like this. In the process we can think about the present differently and act in new and creative ways (Bell 1994). The present is not seen as necessary, inevitable, or homogeneous but as something to be decomposed, problematized, and acted upon. Destabilizing and fragmenting the present opens up a space for the work of freedom and change (Rose 1993). The purpose is to bring into the open the problems that have particular relevance for our contemporary experiences and in so doing uncouple our experiences from their conditions. The ethos is thus one of a permanent questioning of the present and a commitment to uncertainty—not to establish the limits of thought but to locate where they might be transgressed and thus arrive at novel ways of thinking and acting.

The second characteristic of the Foucauldian approach that I draw upon is the concern with the vicissitudes of liberalism in shaping the political contours of the present. Here the notion of governmentality takes on some significance. In the late 1970s Foucault began to explore what he called "the art of government." Recognizing that disciplinary power and government have coexisted for some time, he suggested that the liberal forms of freedom may not be in conflict with the exercise of discipline but be dependent upon it (Foucault 1991; Gordon 1991). He was concerned with linking the analysis of the constitution of freedom with the exercise of rule. He was considering the extent to which freedom has become, in "free" liberal democratic societies, a resource for, and not merely a hindrance to, government—a notion that is closely aligned with the emergence of post-Enlightenment thinking.

The "science of police" flourished in the late eighteenth and early nineteenth centuries as a vigorous branch of political economy and saw as its problematic the understanding of all kinds of crime and disorder and the development of appropriate policies for their prevention and control (Pasquino 1978; Reiner 1988). The term *police* was much broader, referring to more than the activities of a group of people in uniforms employed to control and prevent crime. Police connoted the whole craft of regulating the social order by economic, social, and cultural policy. The science of police was concerned with the whole business of domestic government and regulation and dreamed of a time when the sovereign state could regulate social order in fine detail via a closely calibrated and centralized series of interrelated economic, social, and cultural policies.

Liberal government abandoned such an approach for a vision of society in which government would be based on the exercise of freedom and in which the relationship between liberty and discipline and freedom and rule, while interdependent, was subject to continual renegotiation and fine balancing. In this respect, then, we can see the tensions and questions that today characterize the "crisis" of child welfare and that strike at the core of liberal forms of government as they have emerged since the early nineteenth century. Namely, how can we devise a legal basis for the power to intervene in the private sphere of the family in order to protect children but in a way that does not undermine the family and convert all families into clients of a sovereign state? The demand to ensure that the family is autonomous and free and the primary sphere for rearing children poses just that question, while recognizing the need for intervention in the families that are failing in this primary task (N. Parton 1991). However, this question engenders answers that vary by time and place and, as I have already suggested, the responses are undergoing significant mutation.

The Problematics of Government

As Gordon has demonstrated, Foucault used the concept of government in two senses (Foucault 1991; Gordon 1986, 1991). His first objective was to draw attention to that part of our experience, not necessarily modern, that is constituted by all those ways of reflecting and acting that aim to shape or regulate people's conduct according to certain principles or goals. The conduct of conduct. What makes these forms of reflection governmental, rather than theoretical or philosophical, is their wish to be practical. Thought becomes governmental to the extent that it tries to insert itself as a practice.

Foucault also uses the term in a more limited way, to analyze the problematics of rule as they have taken shape in the West during the last three hundred years as a way of moving beyond the problems posed by the science of police and associated with liberalism as a mentality of rule. Here the notion of governmentality addresses itself specifically to the domain of the political, not as a domain of state or a set of institutions and actors but in terms of the varieties of political reason.

Foucault argued that the idea of governmentality has increasingly dominated politics since the early nineteenth century. Governmentality refers to the "ensemble formed by the institutions, procedures, analyses and reflections, the calculations and tactics, that allow the exercise of this specific albeit complex form of power" (Foucault 1979:20). The regulation of the population has proved to be the unending concern of governmentality. Such an approach does not reduce the exercise of political power to the actions of the reified sovereign state but draws attention to the range of mechanisms through which different groups and forms of knowledge regulate, and thereby constitute, the lives of individuals, families, and the community. This conception of political power is both wider and more complex than analyses that reduce politics to the activities, priorities, and decisions of the state. Similarly, such a conception does not attempt to reify the state as necessarily functional, autonomous, or monolithic, or as wholly concerned with social control and discipline (Cohen and Scull 1983).

Foucault's concept of governmentality both broadens and redirects the analysis of political power. It recognizes that the exercise of power takes place through an ever shifting set of alliances of political and nonpolitical authorities. Professionals and other "experts" are crucial to its operation, but they also have their own interests and priorities, which means that day-to-day policies and practices are not unified, integrated, or easily predictable. Similarly, social regulation, while discursively constrained, is not simply imposed from above in the form of direct constraint or imposition but by encouraging and supporting individuals to exercise their freedoms and choices, thereby allowing government "at a distance." As Rose and Miller put it,

> Power is not so much a matter of imposing constraints on citizens as of 'making up' citizens capable of bearing a kind of regulated freedom. Personal autonomy is not the antithesis of political power, but a key term in its exercise, the more so because most individuals are not merely the subjects of power but play a part in its operation. *(1992:174)*

According to Rose and Miller, government is best understood as a domain of cognition, calculation, experimentation, and evaluation. This domain is inextricably linked to the activities of experts and their fields of knowledge in which human conduct is analyzed, rendered calculable, and administered. These activities are carried out through various, often competing, "local tactics of education, persuasion, inducement, management, incitement, motivation and encouragement" (1992:175).

The concept of governmentality implies that the very existence of a field of concerns we call *policy* should itself be treated as in need of explanation. It highlights the diversity of power and knowledge entailed in rendering fields of practice knowable and amenable to intervention (Foucault 1986). Policy should be analyzed in two ways. First, policy should be located in discussions about the proper ends and means of government. These discussions articulate the shifting political rationalities and justifications for what should be done, by whom, at what cost, for/to whom, with what overall conception of the "good society," and the desirable directions and methods of social change. But, second, policy should also be analyzed in terms of the technologies of government—how the particular technical devices of writing, listing, numbering, computing, and so on render an issue a knowable, calculable, and administrable object. If issues or areas of concern are to be transformed into new areas of government, the information must be available—statistics, reports, and so on—for evaluation, calculation, and intervention. Similarly, intervention requires certain techniques or "technologies" that provide the particular mechanisms through which the object of concern can be modified. Such technologies may appear quite mundane and refer to the

> techniques of notation, computation and calculation; procedures of examination and assessment; the invention of devices such as surveys and presentational forms such as tables; the standardisation of systems for training and the inculcation of habits; the inauguration of professional specialisms and vocabularies; building designs and architectural forms—the list is heterogeneous and is, in principle, unlimited.
>
> *(Miller and Rose 1990:8)*

This analysis of governmentality takes as central the discursive field within which concerns, needs, and problems are defined, delineated, and given priority and the way they are responded to. It is concerned with the analysis of discourses and their changing character. By referring to *discourses*, this approach gives weight to the linguistically constituted character of reality. This does not mean that discourses are "mere words." Discourses are structures of knowledge, claims, and practices through which we understand, explain, and decide things. In constituting agents, they also define obligations and determine the distribution of responsibilities and authorities for different categories of people, such as parents, children, social workers, doctors, lawyers, and so on. They are impersonal forms, existing independently of any of these people as individuals (Foucault 1977b, 1978). They are frameworks or grids of social organization that make some social actions possible while precluding others. A discourse is best understood as a system of possibility for knowledge and for agency (Philp 1985; Woolgar 1986). A system of possibility allows us to produce statements that can be either true or false.

Both the nature of and the priorities for social work in the child welfare field have undergone important changes in recent years. How has this come about, and what are the essential elements of contemporary policy and practice? An analysis of discourse will not only outline the significance of changes in language in social work but will also provide insights into the nature of contemporary policy and practice itself. What forms of policy and practice have emerged in social work and what types of knowledge inform this? An analysis of the changes in social work discourse in child welfare will outline how the sphere of operations for social work has been circumscribed and prioritized and how in the process new possibilities for social workers and those on the receiving end have opened up. In attempting such an analysis, we need to identify the shifting conditions of possibility for social work and the nature of the space it occupies, and how this might be changing. This space is both theoretical and practical, providing the rules for the formation of statements and the changing rules and priorities of day-to-day practice. Similarly, through this space the nature of social work is related to the changing rationalities and technologies of government.

Social Work and the Birth of "The Social"

One of Foucault's central concerns was to provide a critique of the way modern societies regulate and discipline their populations by sanctioning the knowledge claims and practices of the new human sciences—particularly medicine, psychiatry, psychology, criminology, and social work—that provided the opportunity for the emergence of the "psy" complex (see also Ingleby 1985; Rose 1985). He argued that these new disciplines legitimated new knowledge claims and forms of social regulation that subverted the classical order of political rule based on sovereignty and right. They instituted a regime of power exercised through disciplinary mechanisms and the stipulation of norms for human behavior. The normal family, the healthy child, the perfect wife, and the proper man both inform ideas about ourselves and are reproduced and legitimated through the practices of the psy complex. According to Foucault, these new knowledges have so colonized the old powers since the late eighteenth century that they have transformed the more traditional forms of law and judicial rights. No longer were the crucial decisions made in the courtroom according to the criteria of judicial rights but in the hospital, the clinic, or the welfare office, according to the criteria of "normalization." Even decisions made in the courtroom were increasingly colonized by the psy complex according to these same criteria (Foucault 1977a).

Normalizing disciplinary mechanisms, which attempt to subject the individual to training, require a knowledge of the whole person in that person's social context and depend on medicosocial expertise and judgments for their operation. They depend on direct supervision and surveillance, and they emphasize the need to effect change in character, attitudes, and behavior in an individualized way. They are concerned with underlying causes and needs and attempt to contribute to the improvement of those being served as well as to social defense. Because the psy professions have the exclusive insight into the problems, knowledge, and techniques required, they are allowed wide discretion to diagnose and treat and thereby normalize.

Foucault identifies three processes involved in discipline: hierarchical surveillance, normalizing judgment, and the examination. Hierarchical surveillance provides a nonreciprocal monitoring gaze in which the bearers of power are able to create individual knowledge about human bodies on a continuous basis (Foucault 1977a:170–76). Normalizing judgment involves a continuous discretionary evaluation of conduct in the context of standards that float between positive and negative poles, which allows the application of detailed impositions and privileges (1977a:177–83). According to Foucault, the examination "combines the techniques of an observing hierarchy and those of normalising judgment. It is a normalising gaze, a surveillance that makes it possible to qualify, to classify and to punish. It establishes over individuals a visibility through which one differentiates them and judges them" (184).

Such a disciplinary mode of power embodies many of the activities of the "dividing practices" whose central concern is constructing, modifying, and operationalizing classification systems. Medicine and social work are seen as prime examples.

The primary elements of the disciplinary society emerged from the early nineteenth century, and surveillance, classification, examination, ordering, and coding techniques of power began to pervade the social body. The new forms of knowledge, such as medicine, psychiatry, and social work (or philanthropy, as it was constituted then), were directly related to the exercise of power and helped create new objects of concern, investigation, and intervention and thus accumulated new bodies of information (Miller 1987).

A number of writers (Cohen 1985; Garland 1985; Rose 1985) have argued that the central elements of the changing forms of social regulation originally identified by Foucault grew in significance during the late nineteenth century and throughout the twentieth century. While the old institutions—

such as the prison—have remained, new community-based initiatives have developed, thus expanding the system of noncustodial social regulation and taking in new and more diverse areas of social life while increasing the intensity of the old ones. The visibility, ownership, and identity of the systems of social regulation have become vague as the boundaries between them, and between them and the community, become blurred. The family, the school, and the community itself are absorbed into and permeated by the newly developing and increasingly pervasive mechanism of social regulation. Such changes are legitimated by the inevitable failures of the old mechanisms to fulfill their objectives, and the system becomes self-perpetuating. With more and more areas of expertise brought in, with their different knowledges, priorities, and interests, the system becomes ever more complex, making integration and mutual understanding more difficult. As a consequence, the systems of classification, to allocate cases and demarcate areas of responsibility, become ever more sophisticated and central.

The emergence of philanthropy and subsequently social work in the area of child welfare during this period has provided a particular set of policies and practices that have both refined and complicated discipline, together with the modern rationalities and technologies of government. More particularly, this emergence has provided a particular dimension of and contribution to what Jacques Donzelot (1980) has referred to as the "social." The emergence of the social, and social work in particular, is associated with the transformations that took place from the mid-nineteenth century onward around a growing grid of intersecting and interrelated concerns and anxieties about the family and the community more generally. The social discourse developed as a hybrid in the space identified between the private and the public spheres—an intermediary zone. It produced and was reproduced by new relations between the law, administration, medicine, the school, and the family. Central to its emergence was the incorporation of a range of philanthropists into the judicial process with respect to children and young people, and the emergence of psychiatry as a specialty that informed not only judicial decisions but the practice of the successors to the philanthropists—social workers.

The emergence of the social and the practices of social workers, who were its primary technologists, was a positive solution to a major problem posed for liberalism (Hirst 1981), namely: how can the state establish the health, development, and hence the rights of individual family members who are weak and dependent, particularly children, while promoting the family as the "natural" sphere for caring for those individuals and thus not intervening in all families, which would destroy the autonomy of the private sphere? Philanthropy, and subsequently social work, developed at a midway point between individual initiative and the all-encompassing state. It provided a compromise between the early liberal vision of unhindered private philanthropy and that of the all-pervasive and all-encompassing police or socialist state, which would take responsibility for everyone's needs and hence undermine the responsibility and role of the family.

Issues in relation to the child exemplify these difficulties: for children to develop their full health and sensibilities, they could not be left to the vagaries of the market and the autonomous patriarchal family (Dingwall and Eekelaar 1988). The emergence of the social was seen as the most appropriate way for the state to maintain its legitimacy while protecting individual children. For liberalism "the unresolved problem is how child rearing can be made into a matter of public concern and its qualities monitored without destroying the ideal of the family as a counterweight to state power, a domain of voluntary, self-regulating actions" (Dingwall, Eekelaar, and Murray 1983:214–15).

Originally, with the emergence of modern industrial society this activity was carried out by voluntary philanthropic organizations. Donzelot (1980) argues that two techniques were of significance in the philanthropist's relationship with families, particularly on behalf of children—what he calls "moralization" and "normalization." Moralization involves the use of financial and material assistance as leverage to encourage poor families to overcome their moral failure. It was used primarily for the deserving poor who could demonstrate that their problems arose for reasons beyond their control. Normalization applied to attempts to spread specific norms of living through education, legislation, or health and involved a response to complaints, invariably from women about men, and hence provided a means of entry into the home. In return for this guidance, and moral and minimal material support, philanthropic workers were given an insight into what was happening inside the home and leverage to bring about changes in behavior and lifestyle. Clearly, however, there were problems if individuals did not cooperate or did not approach the worker in the first place, so that children and other weak and dependent family members were left to unbridled parental devices.

In the late nineteenth and early twentieth centuries in Britain, such philanthropic activities were increasingly absorbed into the formal institutions of the state. This process continued through to the early 1970s with the introduction of local social service departments as the "fifth social service"

(Townsend 1970).[1] Although moralization and normalization were to be the primary forms of contact, this was increasingly framed in legislation that would also provide for the possibility for coercive intervention. "Tutelage," as Donzelot calls it, based on the notion of preventive intervention, would combine a number of elements, though coercive intervention would be used for the exceptional circumstances in which the techniques of moralization and normalization had failed.

During much of the twentieth century the growth and formalization of modern child welfare social work and its absorption by the state were based on attempts to develop new strategies of preventive penology on behalf of young people who were identified as actual or potential threats. Social work was concerned about the growth of crime and delinquency and the apparent failures of the more traditional judicial and community forms of social regulation that provided the central rationale for the growth of social work (Hall 1976; Cooper 1983; Harris and Webb 1987). Only since the early 1970s have concerns about child abuse and child protection dominated policy and practice (N. Parton 1985, 1991).

However, the space occupied by child welfare social work has always been complex. As I suggested earlier, it both interrelated with and was dependent on a number of other more established discourses, particularly law, health/hygiene, psychiatry, and education. Although the space social work occupied between the public and the private was a crucial one, a variety of discourses impinge on and interpenetrate it. It is for this reason that social work is potentially such a contested area and one subject to diverse and sometimes competing rationales and definitions. Thus, although it was important that social work had a diffuse mandate so that it could be interpreted and operated in a variety of ways, that diffuse mandate leaves it in an ambiguous position. Perhaps most crucially, this ambiguity arises from the sphere of operation itself: between civil society, with its allegiances to individuals and families, and the state, in the guise of the court and its "statutory" responsibilities. Child welfare social work is in an essentially ambiguous, uncertain, and contested arena.

This ambiguity captures the central, if sometimes submerged, element of social work as it emerged from the late nineteenth century. Social work essentially occupied the space between the respectable and the deviant or dangerous classes, as well as the space between those with access to political and speaking rights and those who are excluded (Philp 1979). It fulfills an essentially mediating role between those who are actually or potentially excluded and the mainstream of society. In the process it mediates not only between the excluded and state agencies but crucially between other diverse state agencies and discourses, together with a wide range of private, voluntary, and other philanthropic agencies, and the diverse overlapping discourses that inform and construct them.

The goal of much child welfare social work is to go beyond the dividing practices—the normal and deviant—implied by discipline to the processes that were of central concern to Foucault in his later work, whereby human beings turn themselves into subjects (Foucault 1979). Social work alluded "to the underlying character, the hidden depths, the essential good, the authentic and the unalienated" (Philp 1979:99).

In doing so, the social worker produces a picture of the individual client as a subject that is not immediately visible to the doctor, courts, or social security officer but that exists as he or she "really" or potentially "is." The concern with discipline shifts toward that of regulation. If discipline is modeled on the gaze and based on the examination, the normalizing judgment, and hierarchical observation, regulation operates through interiorization, the confession, and talking through which individuals both take on and express themselves as subjects. While discipline produces knowledge by constituting individuals as objects of scientific discourse, regulation provides knowledge of subjects in their subjectivity. Whereas the former relies on experts who draw on more traditional, objectivized, positivistic science, the latter relies on experts who draw upon interpretative knowledge and use themselves and their insights and understanding of relationships as their primary technologies of practice. This was the primary form that social work took with children and families through much of the twentieth century.

Child Welfare and the Spread of "Welfarism"

Although the sphere of government was wide ranging and complex at the turn of the century, and social work strategies formed only a small element within it, they were nonetheless a crucial part of the process that drew individuals and families into the sphere of government. This was done essentially not through repression "but through the promotion of subjectivity, through investments in individual lives, and the forging of alignments between the personal projects of citizens and the images of social order" (Miller and Rose 1988:172). Social work provided an important but ambiguous strategy to enable "government at a distance," or indirect methods of social regulation, to take place. This was important for achieving the liberal ideal of maintaining autonomous free individuals who were governed at the same time.

For social work to operate quietly and in an uncontested way, it required a supportive social mandate and an internal professional confidence and coherence. The latter, particularly in the period following World War II, was provided primarily by a body of knowledge borrowed from neo-Freudianism and ego psychology, while the field's professional aspirations veered toward medicine and psychiatry (Payne 1992). Similarly, the growth of social work in Britain after the late nineteenth century paralleled and, especially after the war, was interrelated with the development of social interventions associated with the establishment of the welfare state—what Rose and Miller refer to as "welfarism." According to Rose and Miller, the growth of welfarism is best understood not simply in terms of the growth of the interventionist state but as a particular form of government through which a variety of political forces "seek to secure social and economic objectives by linking up a plethora of networks with aspirations to know, programme and transform the social field" (1992:192).

The key innovations of welfarism lay in the attempts to link the fiscal, calculative, and bureaucratic capacities of the apparatus of the state to the government of social life. As a political rationality, welfarism was structured by the wish to encourage national growth and well-being through the promotion of social responsibility and the mutuality of social risk and was premised on notions of social solidarity (Donzelot 1988). Both the rationality and central technologies of welfarism were given particular articulation through the twin and closely interrelated approaches developed around the work of John Maynard Keynes and William Beveridge. The emergence of welfarism rested on twin pillars—one Keynesian and the other Beveridgian in the postwar period.

The Keynesian element stood for an increase in government in terms of attempts to manage economic demand in a market economy through judicious intervention, for example, by increased public expenditure during a recession, especially with the aim of maximizing production and maintaining full employment. Keynesianism stood for state intervention from the demand side of the economy to ensure a high level of economic activity and full employment. We might say this provided the economic component of welfarism. On the other hand, the Beveridgian notion of insurance (in its widest sense) against the hazards of a market economy formed the social component. Unlike the Keynesian economic argument, the social argument for welfarism was now new. Since the days of Bismarck in Germany and

Lloyd George in Britain, most capitalist countries had developed forms of social protection underwritten and coordinated by the state. What was new in the postwar period was that the principle of state intervention was made explicit, and the institutional framework that would make state responsibility for maintaining minimum standards became a reality. This involved pooling society's resources and spreading the risks. Social insurance summed up this departure. Universality of population coverage, comprehensiveness of risks covered, adequacy of benefits, and the citizenship notion of state social services (provided as a right to all and not as a form of charity to the few) were the hallmarks of the Beveridge approach.

Social insurance fundamentally transformed the mechanisms that integrated the citizen into the social order. Not only were individuals to be protected from the evils of 'want, disease, idleness, ignorance, and squalor' but they would be constituted as citizens bound into a system of solidarity and mutual interdependence. Social insurance was seen as a scientific and statistical method of encouraging passive solidarity among its recipients. Everyone would contribute and everyone would benefit, though some more than others. The overall rationale of welfarism was to make the liberal market society more productive, stable, and harmonious; the role of government, while more complex and expansive, would be positive and beneficent.

A number of assumptions characterize the development of welfarism in the twenty-five years after World War II, and these were taken for granted by a wide range of academics, politicians, administrators, and professionals. They saw the institutional framework of social services as the best way to maximize welfare in society and assumed that the state worked for everyone and was the best way of furthering this process. Social services were instituted for benevolent purposes, to meet "social needs," compensate socially caused "diswelfares," and promote "social justice." Their underlying functions were ameliorative, integrative, and redistributive. Social progress would continue to be achieved through the agency of the state and professional interventions. Increased public expenditure, the cumulative extension of statutory welfare provision, and the proliferation of government regulations, backed by expert administration, represented the main guarantors of equity and efficiency. Social scientific knowledge was given a preeminence in ordering the rationality of the emerging professions, which were seen as having a major contribution to developing individual and social welfare.

Not surprisingly, during this period child welfare social work was imbued with a degree of optimism that measured and believed that significant improvements could be made in the lives of children and families with judicious professional interventions. In the context of the institutional framework of the other universal state welfare services, social work was based on a positive and optimistic view of those it was working with and what could be achieved, although the field was constituted as a residual service. The development of child welfare work continued to be located in the space between the respectable and the dangerous classes, but the latter had been reconstituted. In the context of full employment, rapid growth, and universal social services, not only did these people no longer constitute a "class" but they were no longer dangerous. A major assumption of welfarism was that, except for a very small number, everyone was treatable or could be rehabilitated, because the depraved were essentially deprived or misguided. Social problems were located in a few families and could be treated. The consensus was that social work with children and families was a positive development in the context of the development of welfarism (Packman 1981; N. Parton 1985).

This consensus had a number of dimensions. It was assumed that the interests of the social worker, and hence of the state, were similar to, if not the same as, those of the people they were trying to help. The relationship was essentially benign but paternalistic. Interventions in the family were not conceived as a potential source of antagonism between social workers and individual family members. The assumption was not only that many problems had their genesis within the family but that their resolution resided there as well. When a family required modification, this would be primarily on the basis of the normalizing techniques of counseling, help, and advice. Because the social worker was working on behalf of a beneficent state, individuals' arrival in state care was assumed to be necessarily in their interest. Child welfare work was seen as a positive experience for all concerned (Packman 1981).

Child Welfare and "Advanced Liberalism"

However, just as child welfare social work began to play an important role in the welfarist project, welfarism itself was experiencing considerable strains in both its political rationality and technological utility. As a consequence, the rationale and activities of social work with children and families were particularly vulnerable to criticism and reconstitution, because these seemed to personify all that was problematic with welfarism.

The problems with welfarism were seen as being encompassed by both the economic and social spheres from the mid-1960s onward. In the economic sphere they included a slowdown in economic growth (particularly in Britain, compared to its Western competitors); increased difficulties in controlling inflation; a gradual increase in unemployment, which became rapid in the 1970s; and a growth in the public sector relative to the private, so-called productive sectors of society. In the social sphere they included the rediscovery of poverty and significant areas of continued and growing social deprivation; the growth of violence in terms of crime, trade union militancy, and social indiscipline generally; a decline in individual responsibility and attachments to the traditional nuclear family; and a failure of the various social sciences and the various experts who operated them to contribute to social well-being (N. Parton 1985, 1994).

Approaches informed by the New Right provided the possibility of supplanting welfarism with a new rationality of government (Levitas 1986; Gamble 1988) and were increasingly dominant from the mid-1970s onward. The central element of both the critique and recommendations for change was that both the political rationalities and technologies of government pursued by welfarism were central to the problems and thus required fundamental change. Increasingly, scholars, as well as politicians and journalists, argued that welfarism needed to be rethought in terms of its moralities, explanations, vocabularies, and technologies, a situation indicative of the need for a new form of government and new discursive practices.

As a consequence, we can identify the emergence in the late 1970s of a range of new strategies of government that we can term "advanced liberal" (Rose 1993a) and that include the following key elements: extending market rationalities—contracts, consumers, competition—to domains where social, bureaucratic, or professional logic previously reigned; governing at a distance; formally separating the activities of welfare professions from the apparatuses of federal and local government and the courts and developing new systems of audit, devolved budgets, and codes of practice to govern the welfare professions; and giving individuals new freedoms by making them responsible for their present and future welfare and the relations that they have with experts and institutions. No longer is the emphasis on governing through society, the social, but through the calculating choices of individuals (Rose 1996a) as exemplified by the marketplace. In this context we need to understand the development of new strategies for governing child welfare, a key to which is England's Children Act of 1989 (which took effect in October 1991).

However, we should not see the criticisms of child welfare policy and practice in Britain as simply arising from the antiwelfare New Right (Clarke 1993). Some criticisms that emanated from within social work itself concerned the apparent poor and even deteriorating quality of child welfare practice in the newly created local social service departments (Parker 1980). However, a variety of different concerns were developing more widely, and these became increasingly important in influencing the parameters of the debate as it developed, prompting a fundamental rethinking of child welfare policy and practice (N. Parton 1991).

First, beginning in the 1960s the growth of the women's movement and the recognition of violence in the family led to the recognition that not only may the family not be a haven of tranquility but that women and children were suffering a range of abuses at the hands of men. Much early campaigning was directed at improving the position of women, and only after the mid-1970s, with the growing concerns about sexual abuse, was much of the energy directed to the position of children (C. Parton 1990). Such critiques helped to disaggregate the interests of individual family members and supported the development of the children's rights movement (Freeman 1983; Franklin 1986, 1995). Also emerging from the late 1960s was a critique more obviously inflected with civil liberties that concentrated on the apparent extent and nature of intervention in people's lives that was allowed, unchallenged, in the name of welfare (see Taylor, Lacey, and Bracken 1980; Morris et al. 1980; Geach and Szwed 1983). Increasingly, lawyers drew attention to the way the administration of justice was unfairly and unjustly applied in various areas of child care and the need for a greater emphasis on individual rights.

During the mid-1980s the parents' lobby gained its most coherent voice with the establishment of Parents Against INjustice (PAIN). This organization proved influential in ensuring a place on the political and professional agendas for the rights of parents and of children to be left at home, free of state intervention and removal. The result was that state intervention, as practiced by health and welfare professionals, was identified as actively and potentially abusive.

However, child abuse inquiries provided the major catalyst for venting major criticisms of policy and practice in child welfare and the competencies of social workers. While child abuse inquiries became more commonplace after the 1973 death of a child named Maria Colwell (Secretary of State 1974; N. Parton 1985),[2] they gained a new level of intensity during the mid-1980s because of the inquiries into the deaths of Jasmine Beckford (London Borough of Brent 1985), Tyra Henry (London Borough of Lambeth 1987), and

Kimberley Carlile (London Borough of Greenwich 1987). These public inquiries provided the vehicles for political and professional debate about what to do about child abuse in the full glare of the media (Franklin and Parton 1991; Aldridge 1994). They resulted in detailed accounts of what had gone wrong in the particular cases as well as more general critical commentary on and recommendations for improvement of policy and practice (Department of Health and Social Security [hereafter DHSS] 1982; Department of Health 1991).

Until the mid-1980s more than thirty inquiries were undertaken, and all were concerned with the deaths of children at the hands of their parents or caretakers. All the children had died as a result of physical abuse and neglect and had often suffered emotional neglect and failure to thrive. The child welfare professionals, particularly social workers, were seen as having failed to protect the children, with horrendous consequences. Rather than see the deaths as resulting simply from individual professional incompetencies, they were usually seen as particular reflections of policy, practice knowledge and skills, and the way systems operated and interrelated (Hallett and Birchall 1992).

The recommendations stressed that social workers should be encouraged to use their legal mandate to intervene in families to protect children and that they needed to become knowledgeable of the signs and symptoms of child abuse so they could spot it in day-to-day practice.

However, the Cleveland inquiry (Secretary of State 1988) provided a quite different set of concerns and circumstances and seemed to provide different interpretations of what was wrong and how we should respond. This time, it seemed that professionals—pediatricians as well as social workers—had failed to recognize the fights of parents and had intervened prematurely in families where authorities had concerns about sexual abuse.[3] Although the reasons for the problems were again seen as residing primarily in interagency and interprofessional misunderstandings, poor coordination and communication, and the legal context and content of child abuse work, the emphasis was rather different. Now the recognition was not only that the law needed to be changed but that professionals should be much more careful and accountable in identifying the legal evidence for what constitutes sexual abuse and child abuse in general. It was not simply a question of getting the right balance between family autonomy and state intervention but also getting the right balance between the power, discretion, and responsibilities of the various judicial, social, and medical experts and agencies (Ashenden 1996). In this respect the juridical experts were seen as central—the law and legal thinking needed to be brought to bear in decisions that have such dramatic consequences for children and parents, and thus the family, which was seen as being fundamentally undermined by the events in Cleveland.

Thus, although quite different in their social location and their focus of concern, we can see a growing set of constituencies starting to develop in the late 1970s that criticized the postwar welfarist consensus in relation to child welfare and the medicoscientific dominance in relation to child abuse. These were most forcefully articulated in and through child abuse inquiries. What emerged were arguments for a greater reliance on individual rights, firmly located in a reformed statutory framework that placed a greater emphasis on legalism. Within this emphasis, the rule of law, as ultimately judged by the court, takes priority over those considerations that may be deemed, by the professional experts. as optimally therapeutic or "in the best interests of the child."

Freedom, although central, is constructed in negative terms as freedom from unnecessary interference. Clearly, however, a fine balance has to be struck between protecting the innocent and weak and protection from unwarrantable interference—particularly from the state. In such circumstances the law becomes crucial in defining and putting into effect both natural rights and natural responsibilities. It must provide the framework for the underwriting of contracts between individuals and between individuals and the state, and its goal must be to provide a more explicit rationale for state intervention and to hold agents of the state more accountable for their actions.

In many respects the Children Act of 1989 on the surface did not seem consistent with other pieces of social legislation that were being introduced at the time, because many of its key principles seemed much more consistent with the premises of welfarism. The act took much of its inspiration from a government report, *Children in Care*, also known as the "Short Report" (Social Services Committee 1984), and the *Review of Child Care Law* (DHSS 1985). Consequently, the act's central principles encouraged negotiation with families and involving parents and children in a plan. The accompanying guidance and regulations encouraged professionals to work in partnership with parents and young people. Similarly, the act strongly encourages the role of the state in supporting families with children in need, by providing preventative services and thus keeping the use of statutory proceedings and emergency interventions to a minimum.

However, the act was centrally concerned with trying to construct a new set of balances related to the respective roles of various state agents and the family in the upbringing of children. Although it would be inappropriate to see the legislation as a direct consequence of concerns arising from public inquiries regarding child abuse, its central focus and concern were child protection issues (N. Parton 1991). Notions of individual rights and legalism framed the legislation in several ways.

The other key elements to emerge were the criteria to be used for making decisions and therefore for establishing priorities. The assessment of high risk has become central (N. Parton 1991, chaps. 3 and 5). The Children Act frames high risk in terms of significant harm. The criteria for state intervention include that the child is suffering, or is likely to suffer, significant harm (sec. 31[2][a]). This had not been a criterion before.

Assessments of actual or potential high risk become the central concern and activity. However, in a context in which the knowledge and research for assessing and identifying high risk are contested and in which the consequences of getting that decision wrong are considerable, it is not surprising that legislators would not leave that decision to the health and welfare experts alone. The decisions and the accountability for making them must be lodged with the court and be based on forensic evidence. So, although assessments of high risk are central, they are framed in terms of making judgments about what constitutes actual or likely significant harm. The implication is that the legal gaze and the identification and weighing of forensic evidence cast a shadow throughout child abuse work and child welfare more generally, but subjected to a variety of checks and balances set in place because of the need to work in partnership with children and families and with a range of agencies and professionals. Social workers are still central, not as caseworkers or counselors but as case managers or key workers, coordinating and taking central responsibility for assessing risk and monitoring and evaluating progress. The law sets out the process for carrying out the work, thereby potentially making policy and practice more explicit and accountable.

Concerns about risk, particularly about child abuse, now lie at the heart of child welfare policy and practice (Parton, Thorpe, and Wattam 1997), and developments in Britain parallel similar changes in the United States, where the trends and issues are perhaps even more evident (Lindsey 1994). We can now summarize the essential factors that have contributed to this situation.

First, the problem of how to respond to child abuse has dominated child welfare for thirty years, and the term has been officially broadened well beyond its original conception of the battered baby syndrome (Dingwall 1989). Now it includes neglect and physical and emotional abuse (Home

Office 1991). The definitions are essentially broad and all inclusive; although we do not have a mandatory reporting system, as in the United States, health and welfare professionals may be found morally and organizationally culpable if they do not report their concerns to an appropriate investigating agency, essentially local social services departments or the police (N. Parton 1996b).

Second, and directly related to the first point, is that public, professional, and political awareness has grown considerably. This was reflected in the 1980s by the tremendous increases in the number of cases on child protection registers (N. Parton 1995). What is of greater significance, however, is the dramatic increase in allegations requiring investigation—now estimated at more than 160,000 per year (Dartington Social Research Unit 1995).

Third, the broadening definition and growth in awareness and allegations have taken place in a context in which social workers now have a clear responsibility not only to ensure that children do not suffer in the family but also not to undermine parental responsibility and family autonomy. The notion of child protection subsumes within it the protection of the child from significant harm as well as the protection of the parents and family privacy from unwarrantable state interventions.

Fourth, these developments have taken place in a changing economic context that has had a direct effect on social service departments and social work practice with children and families. The amount of need and number of potential clients have grown as increasing sections of the population have become marginalized from the mainstream economy and the incidence of poverty, deprivation, and social exclusion has increased (Barclay 1995; Hills 1995; Oppenheim and Harker 1996). However, other state health and welfare services have had insufficient resources to meet these demands, and social service departments have been subject to continual constraints, cutbacks, and reorganization of their resources.

This increased demand in the context of reduced resources means that state child welfare agencies are finding it almost impossible to develop the more wide-ranging preventative family support strategies included in the Children Act of 1989. Priorities and choices have to be made, not just between the more traditional child welfare responsibilities and responding to child abuse but in relation to child abuse itself. In this respect the investigation of "high risk" takes on its particular urgency and gets at the heart of what it means to be a child welfare worker today. The focus becomes one of differentiating the high risk from the rest, so that children can be protected, parental rights and responsibilities can be respected, and scarce resources can be directed to where they will, in theory, be most effective. Resources and skills are focused on investigating, assessing, and sifting out high risk, particularly when high risk cannot be clearly demarcated. Where there is insufficient knowledge to demonstrate that the family or situation is safe, systems of monitoring, observation, and surveillance take on major significance.

The child protection system has been set up essentially to identify actual or significant harm, and this is dominating the provision and priorities of child welfare services more generally. Increasingly, the priorities are framed according to legalistic criteria that make the identification of forensic evidence central even when the case is not strictly provable. Where cases cannot be so constructed, or where the weight of evidence is not sufficient, the case is quickly filtered out of the system (Gibbons, Conroy, and Bell 1995). The current system provides mechanisms and rationales—however administratively and professionally time consuming—for controlling demand and thereby prioritizing work, and it is the notion of risk that lies at its heart.

Risk and Contemporary Child Welfare

The notion of risk is indicative of a move toward a logic in which the possibility of incurring misfortune or loss in the future is neither to be left to fate nor to be managed by the providential state. An analysis of risk helps us to understand a number of related features of contemporary child welfare policy and practice.

The first concerns the way in which the subjects, or consumers, of child welfare services are to be thought about and constrained to act. Individuals are increasingly held responsible for their fate and that of their children through a kind of calculation about the future consequences of present actions, trying to make the future calculable. Risks are to be identified, assessed, monitored, reduced, insured against by the prudent citizen, effective professional, or well-organized agency (O'Malley 1992; Alaszewski and Walsh 1995; Kemshall and Pritchard 1996). Individuals are constrained to think about their conduct in terms of risks to be calculated, averted, or monitored so that social workers have become not so much concerned with subjects and their relationships of social existence; social workers now tend to be advisers or managers of personal risk. According to Rose (1996b), individuals are invested with the responsibility to manage their risk and take responsibility for failures to manage it. Risk management thus becomes a technique of the prudent self. In terms of government, new relations are set in place between the technologies for the government of others and the modes in which human beings are to understand and govern themselves.

As a consequence, child welfare policies and practices are crucially concerned with dividing and sifting the prudent from the imprudent, the self able to manage itself and high-risk situations, and those who must be managed. By definition, all children are potentially imprudent, so the key focus becomes the situations they are in and the parents or caretakers who have the responsibility for managing and monitoring risk on the child's behalf (Parton, Thorpe, and Wattam 1997). This art of the management of risk to children is key to understanding the sphere of operation for child welfare at the junction of the self-managed world of the affiliated and the twilight world of the marginalized and excluded, particularly certain sections of the poor in terms of single-parent households, substance abusers, the homeless, and certain ethnic groups that comprise the biggest proportion of the clients of child welfare services. The ordered world of social problems has been displaced by the fragmented world of the excluded. This fragmented terrain becomes the sphere of operation for child welfare workers captured by concerns about risk. In the process the will to cure or rehabilitate becomes little more than the exculpation of a particular type of relation to the self-prudent in terms of self-management, making and honoring contracts, setting and achieving recognizable targets, and learning the skills of managing the "family."

However, the new mentalities of risk do not only reconstitute the nature and focus of child welfare work and the nature of relationships between social workers and their clients, particularly women. The centrality of risk is also significant in terms of the way workers think about and organize themselves and are organized—their obligations and the way they are made accountable. Risk management, the identification, assessments, elimination, or reduction of possibility or consequence of loss or misfortune become an essential element of the raison d'être of the professionals themselves. The government of risk takes place through a transformation of the priorities systems and thus the subjectivities of social workers themselves.

For within these new strategies of the government of child welfare, audit becomes a key mechanism for responding to the plurality of expertise and the inherent impossibility of deciding among the various truth claims. As Michael Power (1994a, 1994b) has argued, audit in a range of different forms has come to replace the trust once accorded to professionals both by their clients—now users and customers—and the authorities who employ, legitimate, and constitute them. Audit responds to failure and insecurity by attempting to manage risk.

Risk is rendered manageable by new relations of regulation between the political centers of decision making and the front-line social worker by introducing a variety of new procedures, forms, devices, and systems for making and noting decisions and thereby making them visible. In the process the entities to be audited are transformed in order to make them auditable. Where the key concern is risk, the focus becomes not making the right decision but making a defensible decision—one that demonstrates that the processes and procedures have been followed and that allows the child welfare agency to prioritize and contain the range of misery and need coming its way. In the United States formal risk assessment models have proliferated in the area of child protection and now are used by more than forty states (Berkowitz 1991). They have arisen in response to the growing number of cases and the stagnant resources available for child welfare agencies (English and Pecora 1994). Although neither as advanced nor as formalized, similar systems and technologies are being developed in Britain (Cleaver, Wattam, and Cawson 1995). As Castel (1991) has suggested, we are approaching a situation in which a general system for predicting the risk for children in crisis is becoming a formula into which is plugged a range of abstract and statistical factors—age of mother, previous history, household composition, employment status; if the formula yields certain results, a service is allocated or the child protection agencies intervene. In effect, information gathered from a variety of sources is brought together to consider the nature and significance of risk for the child.

The significance of such developments therefore is not only in terms of their implications for children and their caretakers but for the professionals themselves and how their policies and practices are judged. Procedures and mechanisms for risk assessment and risk management change the role of professionals, who become governed at a distance. They face the prospect of legal or organizational sanctions if they fail to follow the designated steps to ensure that all the risks are investigated and accounted for. In the process they have the responsibility to play their part in the strategy of reducing risk and minimizing harm—to the child, the family, and the organization—under threat of sanction and blame if things go wrong (Parton 1996b).

Thus I have argued here that the increasingly central concerns with risk in child welfare agencies in Britain and across the Western world point to important changes in both the way social workers think about and constitute their practices and the way social work is itself thought about and thereby constituted more widely. I have argued that not only can risk be seen to characterize contemporary child welfare policies and practices but that, following Foucault, it provides a small but significant instance of the important changes in the government of freedom in and of advanced liberal rule.

NOTES

1. The four social services—health, education, social security, and public housing, were established in Britain in the late 1940s, following World War II.

2. Maria Colwell, seven, died on January 7, 1973; she was one of nine children. She spent more than five years in the care of social services and was fostered by her aunt but was returned to her mother and stepfather at the age of six years, eight months. The family was placed under the supervision of the local social services department in Brighton, in the south of England. A variety of social workers visited the family, and her teacher and neighbors expressed concern about Maria on numerous occasions. However, she was beaten to death on the night of January 6–7, 1973, and was found to weigh about three-quarters of what would have been expected for her age and height. Her stepfather was convicted of manslaughter and sentenced to eight years' imprisonment. The local and national media mounted a campaign that was highly critical of social workers and social services, and the secretary of state set up a public inquiry in May 1973, which reported in September 1974.

3. The Cleveland affair and subsequent public inquiry, which broke in the spring and early summer of 1987, focused on the activities of two pediatricians and social workers based in a hospital in Middlesborough, a declining chemical and industrial town in the northeast of England. In the course of a few weeks they removed more than a hundred children from their families to an emergency place of safety (the hospital) on the basis of what the media, which quickly took hold of the story, saw as questionable diagnoses of child sexual abuse. A number of new techniques for diagnosing and identifying sexual abuse, developed by pediatricians and child psychiatrists, were subjected to close scrutiny, particularly the anal dilation test, the use of anatomically correct dolls, and "disclosure" work. This was the first scandal and public inquiry into possible overreaction, as well as the first on sexual abuse and in which medical science and social work were scrutinized (see N. Parton 1991 for a more detailed analysis).

REFERENCES

Alaszewski, Andrew and Mike Walsh. 1995. Literature review: Typologies of welfare organizations. *British Journal of Social Work* 25 (6): 805–15.

Aldgate, Jane and Jane Tunstill. 1995. *Making sense of section 17: Implementing services for children in need within the 1989 Children Act.* London: Her Majesty's Stationary Office.

Aldridge, Meryl. 1994. *Making social work news.* London: Routledge.

Armstrong, David. 1995. The rise of surveillance medicine. *Sociology of Health and Illness* 17 (3): 392–404.

Ashenden, Sarah. 1996. Reflective governance and child sexual abuse: Liberal welfare rationality and the Cleveland inquiry. *Economy and Society* 25, no. 1 (February): 64–88.

Barclay, Peter. 1995. *Joseph Rowntree Foundation inquiry into income and wealth.* Vol. 1. York, U.K.: Joseph Rowntree Foundation.

Barry, Andrew, Tom Osborne, and Nikolas Rose, eds. 1996. *Foucault and political reason: Liberalism, neoliberalism, and rationalities of government.* London: University College Press.

Bell, Vikki. 1994. Dreaming and time in Foucault's philosophy. *Theory, Culture, and Society* 11: 151–63.

Berkowitz, Stephen. 1991. *Key findings from the state survey component of the study of high risk child abuse and neglect groups.* Washington, D.C.: National Center on Child Abuse and Neglect.

Boyne, Roy and Andrew Rattansi, eds. 1990. *Postmodernism and society.* London: Macmillan.

Castel, Robert. 1991. From dangerousness to risk. In Graham Burchell, Colin Gordon, and Peter Miller, eds., *The Foucault effect: Studies in governmentality.* London: Harvester Wheatsheaf.

Clarke, John, ed. 1993. *A crisis in care? Challenges to social work.* London: Sage.

Cleaver, Heidy, Corinne Wattam, and Pat Cawson. 1995. *Assessing risk in child protection.* Final Report submitted to the Department of Health. London: National Society for the Prevention of Cruelty to Children.

Cohen, Stanley. 1985. *Visions of social control: Crime, punishment, and classification.* Cambridge, U.K.: Polity Press.

Cohen, Stanley and Andrew Scull, eds. 1983. *Social control and the state: Historical and comparative essays.* Oxford: Basil Blackwell.

Cooper, Joan, 1983. *The creation of the British personal social services, 1962–74.* London: Heinemann.

Dingwall, Robert. 1989. Some problems about predicting child abuse and neglect. In Olive Stevenson, ed., *Child abuse: Public policy and professional practice.* Hemel Hempstead, U.K.: Harvester/Wheatsheaf.

Dingwall, Robert and John Eekelaar. 1988. Families and the state: A historical perspective on the public regulation of private conduct. *Law and Policy* 10 (4): 341–61.

Dingwall, Robert, John Eekelaar, and Topsy Murray. 1983. *The protection of children: State intervention and family life.* Oxford: Basil Blackwell.

Donzelot, Jacques. 1980. *The policing of families: Welfare versus the state.* London: Hutchinson.

——. 1988. The promotion of the social. *Economy and Society* 17, no. 3 (September): 395–427.

English, D. J. and P. J. Pecora. 1994. Risk assessment as a practice method in child protective services. *Child Welfare* 73 (5): 451–73.

Foucault, Michel. 1977a. *Discipline and punish.* London: Allen Lane.

——. 1977b. *The archaeology of knowledge.* London: Tavistock.

——. 1978. Politics and the study of discourse. *Ideology and Consciousness*, no. 3 (Spring): 7–26.

——. 1979. *An introduction*, vol. 1 of *The history of sexuality*. London: Allen Lane/Penguin.

——. 1986. Space, knowledge, and power. In Paul Rabinow, ed., *The Foucault reader*. Harmondsworth, U.K.: Penguin.

——. 1991. Governmentality. In Graham Burchell, Colin Gordon, and Peter Miller, eds. *The Foucault effect: Studies in governmentality*. London: Harvester Wheatsheaf.

Franklin, Bob, ed. 1986. *The rights of children*. Oxford: Basil Blackwell.

——. 1995. *The handbook of children's rights: Essays in comparative policy and practice*. London: Routledge.

Franklin, Bob and Nigel Parton, eds. 1991. *Social work, the media, and public relations*. London: Routledge.

Freeman, M. D. A. 1983. *The rights and wrongs of children*. London: Francis Pinter.

Gamble, Andrew. 1988. *The free economy and the strong stake*. London: Macmillan.

Garland, David. 1985. *Punishment and welfare: A history of penal strategies*. Aldershot, U.K.: Gower.

Geach, Hugh and Elizabeth Szwed, eds. 1983. *Providing civil justice for children*. London: Arnold.

Gibbons, Jane, Sue Conroy, and Christine Bell. 1995. *Operating the child protection system*. London: Her Majesty's Stationary Office.

Gordon, Colin. 1986. Questions, ethos, event: Foucault on Kant and Enlightenment. *Economy and Society* 15, no. 1 (February): 71–87.

——. 1991. Governmental rationality: An introduction. In Graham Burchell, Colin Gordon, and Peter Miller, eds., *The Foucault effect: Studies in governmentality*. London: Harvester Wheatsheaf.

Hall, Phoebe. 1976. *Reforming the welfare: The politics of change in the personal social services*. London: Heinemann.

Hallett, Christine and Elizabeth Birchall. 1992. *Coordination and child protection: A review of the literature*. London: Her Majesty's Stationary Office.

Harris, Robert J. and David Webb. 1987. *Welfare, power, and juvenile justice: The social control of delinquent youth*. London: Tavistock.

Hills, John. 1995. *Joseph Rowntree Foundation inquiry into income and wealth*. Vol. 2. York, U.K.: Joseph Rowntree Foundation.

Hirst, Paul. 1981. The genesis of the social. In *Politics and power*, no. 3. London: Routledge and Kegan Paul.

Ingleby, David. 1985. Professions as socializers: The "psy complex." In Andrew Scull and Steven Spitzer, eds., *Research in law, deviance, and social control 7*. New York: JAI Press.

Kemshall, Hazel and Jacki Pritchard, eds. 1996. *Good practice in risk assessment and risk management*. London: Jessica Kingsley.

Levitas, Ruth, ed. 1986. *The ideology of the new right*. Cambridge, U.K: Polity Press.

Lindsey, Duncan. 1994. *The welfare of children*. New York: Oxford University Press.

Miller, Peter. 1987. *Domination and power*. London: Routledge and Kegan Paul.

Miller, Peter and Nikolas Rose. 1988. The Tavistock program: The government of subjectivity and social life. *Sociology* 22 (2): 171–92.

——. 1990. Governing economic life. *Economy and Society* 19, no. 1 (February): 1–31.

Morris, Alison, Henri Giller, Elizabeth Szwed, and Hugh Geach. 1980. *Justice for children.* London: Macmillan.

O'Malley, Pat. 1992. Risk, power, and crime prevention. *Economy and Society* 21, no. 3 (September): 283–99.

Oppenheim, Carey and Linda Harker. 1996. *Poverty: The facts.* 3d ed. London: Child Poverty Action Group.

Packman, Jean. 1981. *The child's generation.* 2d ed. Oxford: Basil Blackwell and Martin Robertson.

Parker, Roy, ed. 1980. *Caring for separated children: Plans, procedures, and priorities: A report by a working party established by the National Children's Bureau.* London: Macmillan.

Parton, Christine. 1990. Women, gender oppression, and child abuse. In Violence Against Children Study Group, *Taking child abuse seriously.* London: Unwin Hyman.

Parton, Nigel. 1985. *The politics of child abuse.* London: Macmillan.

——. 1991. *Governing the family: Child care, child protection, and the state.* London: Macmillan.

——. 1994. "Problematics of government," (post)modernity, and social work. *British Journal of Social Work* 24 (1): 9–32.

——. 1995. Neglect as child protection: The political context and the practical outcomes. *Children and Society* 9 (1): 67–89.

——. 1996a. The new politics of child protection. In Jan Pilcher and Steve Wagg, eds., *Thatcher's children: Politics, childhood, and society in the 1980s and 1990s.* London: Falmer Press.

——. 1996b. Social work, risk, and "the blaming system." In Nigel Parton, ed., *Social theory, social change, and social work.* London: Routledge.

——., ed. 1997. *Child protection and family support: Tensions, contradictions, and possibilities.* London: Routledge.

Parton, Nigel, David Thorpe, and Corinne Wattam. 1997. *Child protection: Risk and the moral order.* London: Macmillan.

Pasquino, Pasquale. 1978. Theatrum politicum: The genealogy of capital: Police and the state of prosperity. In *Ideology and consciousness* no. 4. London: Routledge and Kegan Paul.

Payne, Malcolm. 1992. Psychodynamic theory within the politics of social work theory. *Journal of Social Work Practice* 6 (2): 141–49.

Philp, Mark. 1979. Notes on the form of knowledge in social work. *Sociological Review* 27 (1): 83–111.

——. 1985. Michel Foucault. In Quinton Skinner, ed., *The return of grand theory in human sciences.* Cambridge: Cambridge University Press.

Power, Michael. 1994a. *The audit explosion.* London: Demos.

——. 1994b. The audit society. In A. G. Hopwood and Peter Miller, eds., *Accounting as social and institutional practice.* Cambridge: Cambridge University Press.

Reiner, Robert. 1988. British criminology and the state. *British Journal of Criminology* 29 (1): 138–58.

Rose, Nikolas. 1985. *The psychological complex: Psychology, politics, and society in England, 1869–1939.* London: Routledge and Kegan Paul.

———. 1993a. Government, authority, and expertise in advanced liberalism. *Economy and Society* 22, no. 3 (August): 283–99.

———. 1993b. Toward a critical sociology of freedom. Inaugural lecture. Goldsmiths College, London.

———. 1996a. The death of the social? Refiguring the territory of government. *Economy and Society* 25 (3): 327–50.

———. 1996b. Psychiatry as a political science: Advanced liberalism and the administration of risk. *History of the Human Sciences* 9, no. 2 (September): 1–23.

Rose, Nikolas and Peter Miller. 1992. Political power beyond the state: Problematics of government. *British Journal of Sociology* 43 (2): 173–205.

Smart, Barry. 1993. *Postmodernity.* London: Routledge.

Taylor, Laurie, Ron Lacey, and David Bracken. 1980. *In whose best interests?* London: Cobden Trust/Mind.

Townsend, Peter. 1970. *The fifth social service: A critical analysis of the Seebohm proposals.* London: Fabian Society.

United Kingdom. Dartington Social Research Unit. 1995. *Child protection: Messages from research.* London: Her Majesty's Stationary Office.

United Kingdom. Department of Health. 1991. *Child abuse: A study of inquiry reports, 1980–89.* London: Her Majesty's Stationary Office.

United Kingdom. Department of Health and Social Security. 1982. *Child abuse: A study of inquiry reports, 1973–81.* London: Her Majesty's Stationary Office.

United Kingdom. Department of Health and Social Security. 1985. *Review of child care law: Report to ministers of an interdepartmental working party.* London: Her Majesty's Stationary Office.

United Kingdom. Home Office in conjunction with the Department of Health. 1991. *Memorandum of good practice on video recording interviews with child witnesses for criminal proceedings.* London: Her Majesty's Stationary Office.

United Kingdom. London Borough of Brent. 1985. *A child in trust: Report of the panel of inquiry investigating the circumstances surrounding the death of Jasmine Beckford.* London: London Borough of Brent.

United Kingdom. London Borough of Greenwich. 1987. *A child in mind: Protection of children in a responsible society: Report of the commission of inquiry into the circumstances surrounding the death of Kimberley Carlile.* London: London Borough of Greenwich.

United Kingdom. London Borough of Lambeth. 1987. *Whose child? The report of the panel appointed to inquire into the death of Tyra Henry.* London: London Borough of Lambeth.

United Kingdom. Secretary of State for Social Services. 1974. *Report of the inquiry into the care and supervision provided in relation to Maria Colwell.* London: Her Majesty's Stationary Office.

United Kingdom. Secretary of State for Social Services. 1988. *Report of the inquiry into child abuse in Cleveland.* London: Her Majesty's Stationary Office.

United Kingdom. Social Services Committee. 1984. *Children in care (HC 360).* London: Her Majesty's Stationary Office.

Woolgar, Steve. 1986. On the alleged distinction between discourse and proxies. *Social Studies of Science* 16: 309–17.

CHAPTER 6

Contested Territory: Sexualities and Social Work

Carol-Anne O'Brien

Youth sexualities have been the focus of considerable attention in social work practice and academic publications, frequently within such contested categories as "adolescent sexuality" and "teenage pregnancy." In this chapter I explore what the work of Michel Foucault can offer to an analysis of social work discourses on youth sexuality. In turning to Foucault's work I am guided by Jeffrey Weeks's suggestion (1991) that we use Foucault's theories as he used the work of Nietzche and others, as a "box of tools" rather than an orthodoxy. I am interested in the ways Foucauldian analyses can intersect with queer theory and contribute to debates within social work and social welfare about the sexuality of young people. I discuss Foucault's key concepts concerning sexuality and draw on them to analyze social work practices and literature related to youth sexuality and the subjugated discourses that may be found in these sites.[1]

Sexual Science and Social Work

Let us first consider the ways in which social work discourses about youth sexualities can be considered "sexual science" in Foucauldian terms. In the first volume of *The History of Sexuality* ([1978] 1990) Foucault argues that the domain of sexuality has been increasingly constructed in terms of scientific knowledge, which he termed "scientia sexualis." Sexual science has been concerned with classifying, analyzing, and examining sex in minute detail, with conducting causal studies, and other work that constitutes sex as a problem of truth. Foucault suggests that scientific discourses about sexuality are particularly incited in fields concerned with human subjects, such as social work and social welfare.

In *The History of Sexuality* Foucault explores the processes through which sexuality was developed and deployed as a central domain in power and knowledge relations and in the formation of the subject through different historical periods. Foucault debunks what he calls "the repressive hypothesis," arguing that the history of sex is not one of increasing openness and freedom from religious and Victorian control but rather the multiplication of discourses inciting sex in polymorphous forms while declaring sex to be society's most profound secret and the key to each individual's deepest self and identity. Foucault notes that European societies have been speaking about sexual silence and criticizing sexual hypocrisy for a long time.

In this chapter I also follow Foucault's use of the term *discourse*. Foucault conceptualizes discourse as meaning "the relations between statements" (1972:31) and "practices that systematically form the objects of which they speak" (49). A particular discourse not only reflects and sets limits on what can be known and said, it also constitutes knowledge, communication, and practices. Thus I argue that academic social work discourse about youth sexualities not only mirrors what is taught, said, and practiced in relation to social work with young people. It also contributes to the development of social work discussions about sexuality and helps to constitute the paradigms of social work knowledge on the topic.

In *The History of Sexuality* Foucault suggests that in recent centuries sex increasingly became the object of "bio-power," that is the administration of life. Bio-power has evolved in two forms, or "poles of development." The first is "anatomo-politics," or "disciplinary power," which operates on the human body as a machine, attempting to optimize its capabilities, efficiency, usefulness, and political docility. The second pole of bio-power is "regulation of the population." This form of power is concerned with biological processes such as births, mortality, and probabilities of life; its instruments have included economic interventions and public health campaigns. Each pole of bio-power has its correlative fields of knowledge, and sexual science is a field of knowledge that has become increasingly significant in constituting discourses of sexuality.

Foucault's concept of sexual science is useful in understanding how sexuality is constructed in social work research and theorizing about youth. Social work academic literature in general is concerned with constituting professional knowledge, whereas scholars who focus on youth and sexuality contribute to the construction of particular knowledges about youth and social work and about sex and social work.

I found that in social work publications about youth and sexuality since the mid-1980s the authors typically constitute sexuality as an object of scientific knowledge and themselves as experts in that knowledge. Thus the introductory sections of these articles frequently deploy statistics concerning the sexual activities of young people. For example, Gibbs (1986) begins an investigation of the sexual activities and attitudes of a group of young women aged twelve to sixteen by suggesting that "adolescent sexual attitudes and behaviors" have changed since World War II: "Several studies of teenage sexuality indicate an increasing trend in premarital intercourse since 1967. . . . Accompanying this increase has been a steady decline in the average age at first intercourse, particularly among black females, who initiate sexual activities about a year earlier than whites" (81).[2]

Wodarski (1987) and Chilman (1983, 1988, 1989) cite statistics that purport to estimate the "occurrence" of "coitus" among young women. Other scholars deploy statistics to argue that higher percentages of black girls than white girls give birth while single (see Chilman 1985, 1988; Armstrong 1991; A. Butler 1992; Plotnick 1993), and have "sex" at an earlier age (see Gibbs 1986; Chilman 1988; Armstrong 1991).

As Foucault suggests, considerable attention is devoted to elucidating the "causes" of these events in young people's lives. In her 1986 article, which attempts to find "correlates" between urban girls' sexual attitudes and their sexual activities, Gibbs suggests that in addition to the influences of ethnicity, class, religious, and other social factors, "sexual activity among adolescents has also been correlated to deviant behavior, substance abuse, educational achievement, family relationships and peer group influences" (93). Hall sought to examine the extent to which sexual activity among young people (actually, young women) was associated with "a lack of sex knowledge, maternal distancing, attempts to fulfill dependency needs, attempts to cope with developmental tasks, peer pressure, [and] problems in familial interaction, such as conflict, communication, intimacy, role diffusion" (1986:25). In a similar vein Chilman argues that "social, psychological, and biological factors all play a part in nonmarital adolescent coitus" (1988:39). Causal factors put forward by other authors include youthful moves toward independence (Cervera 1993b) or rebelliousness (Trad 1993), whereas Taylor turns feminist analysis against young women when she cites research that she suggests shows that "early initiators have lower grades in school and are more likely to have dropped out. . . . They have lower expectations for themselves and expect to accomplish little. They are more susceptible to being manipulated by boyfriends . . . and hold stereotypical views of sex roles, seeing women in very traditional ways" (1990:78).

I would argue that the sexual scientific knowledge deployed by social work scholars is not monolithic but rather continually contested. This is particularly clear in analyses of one of the most contentious political issues of the 1990s in the United States, namely, childbearing by young women and girls. Shifman and colleagues (1986), Wodarski (1987), Bergman (1988), and Combs-Orme (1993) cite research to argue that this practice causes "health risks," "medical problems," "psychological stress," and "social problems." "Causes" for childbearing by girls and young women are found by Rubenstein, Panzarine, and Lanning (1990) and Taylor (1990) in failure or refusal to use birth control; by Trad (1993) in rebelliousness; by Donaldson, Whalen, and Anastas (1989) in childhood sexual abuse; by Freeman (1992), Carlson, Abagnale, and Flatow (1993), and Resnick, Chambliss, and Blum (1993) in male irresponsibility (it is the "irresponsibility" of black males that they discuss); and by Stafford (1987) and Plotnick (1993) in the availability of welfare programs. The Resnick study of male teenagers who "caused a pregnancy" reported that they were more likely to show "acting-out behavior (e.g., substance use, risk of unintentional injury, delinquency, and absenteeism)" (1993:371).

Contesting these discourses, some scholars deploy statistics to critique the view that rates of childbearing by teenagers are increasing (see Chilman 1983, 1985, 1989; Wood and Nuttall 1987; A. Butler 1992). Klerman, Jekel, and Chilman (1983) argue that an association between early pregnancy and health, social, and economic problems does not mean that a causal relationship exists, whereas Weatherley and Cartoof (1988) say that teenaged parents have no greater problems than older ones of comparable socioeconomic status, and Massat (1995) finds that they are not overrepresented among those who abuse or neglect their children.

In sum, Foucault's concept of sexual science is apt in understanding this social work literature on youth sexuality. I would argue that social work scholars constitute sexuality as an object of scientific knowledge and themselves as experts in that knowledge. Claims are made about the "occurrence" and the "causes" of sexual activities among young people, although this discourse is contested rather than monolithic.

Pedagogization of Youth Sexuality

Foucault (1990) identifies four "strategic unities" that emerged through the deployment of sexuality in eighteenth-century Europe, each articulating in different ways the two poles of bio-power. These strategic unities were the "hysterization" of women's bodies, the "socialization of procreation," the "pedagogization" of children's sexuality, and the "psychiatrization of perversions."

I found that the strategic unity in the deployment of sexuality that Foucault named the "sexualization of children," or the "pedagogization" of children's sexuality, was particularly relevant to my analysis of the social work literature on youth sexuality. Foucault argues that children's sexuality came to be seen as "preliminary," as preparing for adult sexuality and requiring the guidance of (if not control by) parents and professional experts in education and medicine. Foucault describes how this was historically articulated at the level of the regulation of populations through moral campaigns that denounced precocious sexuality, particularly masturbation, as a menace to collective welfare and to the health of the "race." At the level of the discipline of the body, children were constituted as sexual through, for example, boarding school architecture and the supervision of schoolboys' activities in bed. The rationale for these campaigns was paradoxical, suggesting both that children's sexuality was "natural" and at the same time that it was "contrary to nature." Parents, teachers, doctors, and other professionals were called on to "take charge . . . of this precious and perilous, dangerous and endangered sexual potential" (Foucault 1990:104).

My reading of this area within social work discourse revealed that a frequent motif was the sexual potential of youth as being both "dangerous and endangered." Wodarski suggests that the procreative activities of youth are "one of the critical social problems facing our society" (1987:175). Shifman and colleagues (1986) see these as a "national concern," whereas Meyer says they are "probably the most pressing social issue on the national agenda" (1994:334). Chilman (1983) puts forward the danger of "contagious" lesbianism (discussed in greater detail shortly). Hall argues that the "rise in teenage sexual activity and parenthood have increased public concern for the vulnerability of all adolescents" (1986:23). Gibbs is interested in determining which young women are "vulnerable to early sexual activity" (186:90), suggesting that sexual activity is dangerous. By the late 1980s the "dangers" of teen sex are constructed as even more serious. An editorial by Shapiro and Allen-Meares (1989) suggests that in "this era of AIDS" the "consequences of sexual expression go far beyond the familiar outcomes of unplanned pregnancy, premature parenthood, and treatable sexually transmitted diseases" to "sexually transmitted diseases that may be untreatable and even life-threatening" (xiii). Thus "sexual expression" as a whole, rather than unprotected contact with particular bodily fluids, is rendered potentially deadly.

I found that early childbearing was usually constructed in morally negative terms. For example, Moyse-Steinberg suggests that "being a teen parent is not a good idea" (1990:58). Jaccard and Dittus (1993) link "teen pregnancy" with other "deviant" behaviors such as drug and alcohol use. Shifman and colleagues appear to promote an educational exercise used with young women (who were African American), which included the following question: "Karen is a teenager having a baby. What are the bad things that might happen to her or the baby?" (1986:45). "Good things" are not discussed. Hall refers to (predominantly African American) young women who gave birth more than once as "recidivists" (1986:25), a term usually reserved for those who commit repeated criminal acts. As the following quotation shows, the procreative activities of teenage women are constituted as dangerous, both to themselves and to society:

> Health risks increase for both the mother and the child both before and after delivery. Babies born to teenage mothers are more likely to have a low birth weight, be premature, and suffer from congenital defects. Teenage mothers are more likely to develop cervical cancer and uterine diseases. Associated sociopsychological problems also occur. Teenage mothers are more likely to have troubled marriages, and some studies have reported that they are more likely to abuse or neglect their children than are older parents. These findings may relate to the fact that teenage parents are very likely to suffer from severe financial difficulties and associated emotional strain. The economic costs to society must be considered as well. Fully half of all payments made under the Aid to Families with Dependent Children Program (AFDC) go to women who bore children during their adolescent years.   (Stafford 1987:471)

Combs-Orme's comment that "both professionals and the public agree that pregnancy is undesirable for adolescents" (1993:344) is an explicit statement of a central assumption that frames social work discourse on youth sexuality. Yet other scholars offer competing analyses. Chilman (1985) does not agree with the argument that teenaged childbearing is always a problem, positing that the consequences depend on a woman's individual qualities, family support, and social and economic factors, rather than the age of the mother alone. Luker (1994) suggests that young African American women who choose to have their children early may be making quite rational decisions. Meyer (1994) argues that only girls who lack financial resources suffer public opposition and the whims of policy changes.

Most social work scholars propose strategies for working with young people in which the efforts of social workers and other service providers are directed at reducing their clients' (particularly girls') sexual activities (see Kirby, Peterson, and Brown 1982; Diamond and Diamond 1986; Gibbs 1986; Quinn 1986; Striar and Ensor 1986; Freeman 1989). For example, Scales argues that it is "usually preferable for adolescents to refrain from sexual intercourse" (1983:223), and Moyse-Steinberg suggests that young women should be encouraged to delay this activity "until after high school or until marriage" (1990:59).

One strategy in social work's approach to youth sexualities and procreation is "prevention": "Prevention is defined as the act of discouraging a problematic behavior or illness before it actually happens or before it becomes a problem. . . . Prevention is especially appropriate to dealing with the problems of the adolescent. It provides an early developmental focus for intervention which may forestall development of future problems" (Wodarski 1987:206, 205).

Gibbs discusses strategies for preventing young women from becoming sexually active, including a "focus on the interrelationship between sexual activity and other deviant behaviors in adolescent females" (1986:94). Preventative programs are often aimed at pregnancy prevention (e.g., Quinn 1986; Shifman et al. 1986; Moyse-Steinberg 1990; Taylor 1990; Freeman 1992; Carlson et al. 1993; Jaccard and Dittus 1993; Plotnick 1993; Resnick et al. 1993). Weatherley and Cartoof (1988) present a rare example of a discussion of pregnancy prevention that is located within a broader strategy of social and economic change.

Schultz also suggests that social workers "need to put our pro-family values up front and recognize that the family (including the single parent) is the most important source of sexual learning" (1986:18). But I found that while social work scholars depict parents as having the right to be the primary influence over their children's sexuality, scholars also depict parents as being inadequate to the task without the intervention of professionals. Parents are "probably inadequately prepared to be helpful sex educators for their children" (Shapiro and Allen-Meares 1986:xi). Thus "we should teach sexual value[s] to parents, not just to adolescents" (Schultz 1986:20).

Because social work scholars see parents as a weak link in the pedagogization of their children's sexuality, some strategies address the regulation of parents. The "joint parent-child sex education program" described by Kirby and colleagues (1982) is partly motivated by an effort to avoid parental opposition to sex education programs for youth. It also aims to provide parents with expert-authorized knowledge that they can impart to their children, encourages parents to take an active role in educating their children about sex at home, and "can greatly improve parent-child communication on sexual topics and substantially reduce anxiety and awkwardness" (107). Scholars argue that such programs are particularly important because research cited shows that "interventions aimed at fostering more effective parent-child (especially mother-daughter) communication around sexual issues have a good record in the important areas of delaying the onset of sexual activity among teenagers and of encouraging contraceptive use among sexually active teens" (Quinn 1986:101).

Jaccard and Dittus argue that promotion of parent-child communication about sex will permit a "family-based approach to adolescent-pregnancy prevention," which will be a "politically viable and potentially effective method for making an impact on teenage pregnancy" (1993:342).

I would argue that the discourse of parent-child communication ignores unequal relations between parents and children and is concerned with helping parents to influence their children's behavior, that is, with enhancing parental power. It does not aim to help parents listen to their children or to understand and facilitate young people's desires to be sexually active. One exception is an editorial that urges social workers to listen to young people and help parents "balance the needs for autonomy/dependence declared by their adolescent members" (Shapiro and Allen-Meares 1986:xii). Social work and social welfare scholars rarely align with youth against parental power. Gochros (1982) is unusual in drawing on the discourse of sexual oppression to critique adults' denial of young people's sexual rights and the inculcation in children of obedience toward adults.

If youth sexuality is both endangered and dangerous, sexually active teenagers are seen as both too knowledgeable and lacking knowledge. Kirby and colleagues (1982) suggest that youth have knowledge about sex that they want to hide from their parents; it has been gleaned from peers, the media (Jaccard and Dittus 1993), and from their own sexual experiences. This leads to contradictory claims. For example, Hall (1986) describes a group of African American young women as "quite active sexually" but having little "sex knowledge."

Michelle Fine, a feminist scholar of education, offers insights (1988) that complement the Foucauldian analysis I am developing here. Fine analyzes the absence of a "discourse of female desire" from sex education in schools and the separation of female sexual victimization from female sexual agency. "Discourses of desire" are also missing from social work and social policy literature about "adolescent sexuality." Many scholars assume that sexual activity among youth should be prevented or delayed or see it as dangerous or deviant.[3] None of these authors includes analyses of the pleasures young people seek in exploring sex, their lack of private spaces in which to pursue consensual sex with partners of different genders, and their need for particular types of information about sex and about HIV prevention. I also found an absence of discussion about the role that social policy and social work could play in facilitating the development of sexual agency and autonomy among youth. Only a minority of authors construct sexual feelings as ethically positive (for example, Gochros 1982; Shapiro and Allen-Meares 1986; Chilman 1989; Hacker 1989). These "subjugated" discourses are missing from the social work literature. In a 1976 lecture Foucault used the term "subjugated knowledges" to mean a

> whole set of knowledges that have been disqualified as inadequate to their task or insufficiently elaborated: naive knowledges, located low down on the hierarchy, beneath the required level of cognition or scientificity. . . . These unqualified, or even directly disqualified knowledges (such as that of the psychiatric patient . . . of the delinquent etc.) . . . involve what I would call popular knowledge though it is far from being a general commonsense knowledge. [It] is on the contrary a particular, local, regional knowledge, a differential knowledge incapable of unanimity and which owes its force only to the harshness with which it is opposed by everything surrounding it.   *(Foucault 1980:82)*

Thus in social work literature and practice concerning youth sexuality, subjugated knowledge is the diverse sexual knowledge of young people and the knowledge developed by marginalized communities such as girls who have been sexually abused or lesbians and gay men.[4]

The social work and social policy literature on teenaged pregnancy is also deeply influenced by the discourses of developmental psychology in which youth is constituted as a particular stage that lacks qualities deemed to belong to "adulthood." Some social work scholars construct adolescents as lacking "thinking skills" and having a "sense of invulnerability" (Armstrong 1991:320) or lacking knowledge about sexuality. One author argues that more young people do not use contraceptives because "adolescents (especially the younger ones) have not achieved [a] level of cognitive ability" that would allow them to "connect present with future consequences" (Wodarski 1987:175). I would argue that this discourse draws on ahistorical, and class- and ethnicity-specific conceptions of the abilities of youth. Scholars use the term *adolescents* when the subjects of the discussion are girls and young women; for example, they study girls' rather than boys' use of contraceptives. The literature also suggests that (low-income) African American young women lack knowledge of "reproductive biology" (Chilman 1983; Shifman et al. 1986). One program attempted to impart "correct" terms for "body parts and functions" (Shifman et al. 1986:43) to a largely African American group of low-income teenaged females. The aim was to replace their terminology and beliefs about menstruation, birth control, and teenaged pregnancy with "facts commonly accepted by the orthodox medical system and within the behavioral sciences" (45). Klerman and colleagues (1983) suggest that young (black) women lack skills in "future" planning that would help them avoid pregnancies, complete high school, and build careers. Young African American girls are believed to need "life-planning" (Gibbs 1986) or "future planning" that "combine[s] career and reproductive planning" (Quinn 1986:106). Quinn also argues that these will "address one of the recently-identified root causes of adolescent pregnancy—lack of a future orientation among adolescents, particularly among low-income and minority girls" (1986:108). These authors do not mention the limitations of such interventions in the absence of social, racial, and economic change.

Social work discourses racialize youth sexuality. Authors such as Chilman (1985, 1988), Armstrong (1991), and Plotnick (1993) deploy scientific knowledge to constitute racial differences in childbearing. Hall (1986) negatively describes early childbearing by young women of color as "recidivist." Gibbs (1986), Chilman (1988), and Armstrong (1991) problematize early sexual activities by black girls. African American young women are constructed as lacking expert-authorized knowledge about sex while having a surfeit of experiential knowledge (see Chilman 1983; Klerman et al. 1983; Hall 1986; Shifman et al. 1986). The only males whose "sexual irresponsibility" is discussed are African American (see Resnick et al. 1993), although it would appear from this literature that only African American young women lack "future planning" (see Klerman et al. 1983; Gibbs 1986; Quinn 1986).

In this section I have focused on the relevance to social work scholarship of Foucault's analysis of the pedagogization of children's sexuality. This literature sees youth sexuality as immature, dangerous, and endangered and as requiring the guidance of expert adults. I would argue that social work's role is constituted as preventing sexual activity among young people, especially females, either directly or through strategies aimed at improving parental abilities to regulate their teenagers' sexualities. I found that social work scholars do not discuss young people's sexual desires or ways that social work could respect their sexual knowledge and facilitate youthful sexual expression.

Psychiatrized Homosexuality and Heteronormativity

Foucault's fourth strategic unity is the "psychiatrization of perversions." The particular form of power/knowledge that Foucault terms sexual science developed within medical and psychological research; this research determined that sexual behaviors are rooted in biological instincts and are either within the range of normality or are deemed abnormal or pathological. Within bio-power, intervention at the level of the regulation of populations led, for example, to legal sanctions against homosexuality in many Western societies. Foucault argues that although sodomy was prohibited legally, it was but one of a multitude of unlawful acts outside of certain types of marital sex. With the development of bio-power in the eighteenth and nineteenth centuries emerged a new "specification of individuals. . . . The sodomite had been a temporary aberration; the homosexual was now a species" (1990:42, 43). Foucault also draws on this example to show potential relationships between sexual science, as a form of power/knowledge, and resistance and the formation of subjectivities. Psychiatry and medicine labeled homosexuality a perversion and gave "the homosexual" a case history; this created a space for a form of resistance that Foucault calls a "reverse discourse": "Homosexuality began to speak in its own behalf, to demand that its legitimacy or 'naturality' be acknowledged" (101).

The social work literature I reviewed for this chapter was published between 1980 and 1995; at the beginning of this period some scholars still construct homosexuality as pathological. Strean suggests that "mature sexuality" is marked by "a mutually gratifying relationship with a member of the opposite sex" (1983:26), and he includes homosexuality as one of several "immature forms of love" (27). Striar and Ensor report, without a critical commentary, that when residences for youth are segregated by gender in order to discourage heterosexual activity, "homosexuality can then surface as a problem, creating for some administrators and staff a more disturbing moral and ethical dilemma" (1986:55). Some authors discuss the causes of homosexuality but not those of heterosexuality, thus inscribing homosexuality as abnormal. Strean argues that "homosexual men or women cannot accept and usually fear their own gender" and are "quite terrified of the opposite sex" (1983:29). Drawing on one interpretation of Freudian thought,

Strean posits castration anxiety as a prime cause of male homosexuality, whereas for lesbians "the etiological factors frequently emanate from oedipal conflicts and penis envy" (165). In a similar vein Chilman argues that the causes of homosexuality may be found in overattachment to mothers, failure to "learn appropriate male family roles" (1983:61), and girls' experiences of male violence as a result of which they "adopted distrustful, antagonistic attitudes towards males" (62). Chilman further constitutes homosexuality as pathological by arguing (without citing references) that "it is commonly recognized in the literature that adolescents (especially boys) are often inducted into homosexual behavior through the advances of homosexual adults" (1983:62), and she calls for more research into this "fact." Chilman also calls for research on the influence of single-sex living situations, such as summer camps, on the sexual orientation of children and youth and says that

> It has been the writer's personal observation that pre-adolescent and early adolescent girls often form strong affectional attachments to older campers and counselors. . . . [This] situation has been observed to be heavily affected by the sexual orientation of camp leaders. If some of the stronger ones appear to be committed homosexuals, a group contagion effect can be noted, with a large number of campers pairing off into "loving couples." Considerable anxiety may result, with even younger children becoming overtly aware of a homosexual life-style in the camp. It further has been observed that the great majority of these girls return to their heterosexual orientation soon after they reach home.   *(1983:62–63)*

Chilman thus constructs heterosexuality as natural and endangered and homosexualities as pathological and predatory, although her narrative reassures the reader, who is assumed to be heterosexual, with its "normal" conclusion.

Gilchrist and Schinke depict the "truly homosexual adolescent" (1983: 244) as needing support rather than "conversion to heterosexuality," and they suggest (without any supporting evidence) that most same-sex sexual relations are "rehearsals for intimacy or attempts to fulfill natural needs for warmth, understanding, and assistance or guidance," which do not necessarily confirm "lifelong homosexual preferences" (245).

After the early 1980s I found that the marginalization of nonheterosexual orientations is no longer accomplished through extremely negative representations but takes other forms, such as exclusion or token inclusion. A number of concepts drawn from "queer theory" (deLauretis 1991; J. Butler

1993; Warner 1993; Seidman 1994) were useful in complementing the Foucauldian analysis of sexuality I have developed in this chapter. As Berlant and Warner (1995) argue, queer theory is best conceived of as a newly emerging set of commentaries rather than a coherent school of thought. Among other themes, queer theory seeks to contest the binary opposition between heterosexuality and homosexuality, and "heteronormativity," that is, the power relations that constitute heterosexuality as normative (Warner 1993). Both notions inform the analysis that follows.

I found that, from the mid-1980s, the construction of heteronormativity is accomplished in a number of ways in social work and social welfare publications on youth sexuality. Titles of articles suggest that they are about "adolescent sexuality" in general, whereas the contents are concerned solely with sexual relations between boys and girls; for example: "Adolescent Sexuality and Education" (Scales 1983), "Psychosocial Correlates of Sexual Attitudes and Behaviors in Urban Early Adolescent Females" (Gibbs 1986), "Factors Associated with Sexual Activity in Early Adolescence" (Hall 1986), "Enhancing Adolescents' Sexual Development and Feeling of Self-Worth" (Schultz 1986), and "Adolescent Male Sexuality: 'Boys Will Be Boys?'" (Freeman 1992). Many authors conflate *sexuality* and *heterosexuality*. Chilman argues that "sexuality is the key theme of adolescence," largely because of "preparation for reproduction" (1983:5). Chilman clarifies her implicit assumption regarding sexual orientation when she suggests that greater differentiation between male and female bodies at puberty "creates tensions and attractions between them" (5). She also says, "Both males and females have their special strengths and their special vulnerabilities. The strengths can be uniquely supported and vulnerabilities uniquely assuaged in an enduring intimate love-sex relationship" (101).

Social work and social welfare scholars also conflate *sexual activity* and what they term *coitus* or *sexual intercourse,* by which they mean one type of heterosexual activity. Examples of this way of rendering heterosexuality normative can be found in Chilman (1983, 1989), Gilchrist and Schinke (1983), Klerman and colleagues (1983), Scales (1983), Moyse-Steinberg (1990), and Trad (1993). Other scholars make token references to the existence of homosexuality. Diamond and Diamond's 1986 article on "adolescent sexuality" is concerned with heterosexuality except for one paragraph about transsexuality and homosexuality, which the authors argue are "usually the result of biologically based predispositions" (11) that should receive an empathic response. Hall's 1986 article on "sexual activity in early adolescence" focuses exclusively on heterosexuality, as do Schultz (1986) regarding "adolescents' sexual development," and Shifman and colleagues (1986) concerning "adolescent sexuality education."

From the mid-1980s, apart from a few one-word or one-line references in Hacker (1989), I found that lesbian and gay sexualities completely disappear from social work publications about youth sexuality. I would argue that this is the result of the different discourse that frames this social work literature. In the early and mid-eighties adolescent sexuality and teenage sexuality were the central categories. Even as "lesbian and gay youth" emerged as a marginalized category, the literature became saturated with articles about pregnancy and teenage parenting (see Dore and Dumois 1990; Moyse-Steinberg 1990; Rubenstein et al. 1990; Taylor 1990; Armstrong 1991; A. Butler 1992; Freeman 1992; Carlson et al. 1993; Cervera 1993; Combs-Orme 1993; Jaccard and Dittus 1993; Plotnick 1993; Resnick et al. 1993; Trad 1993; Luker 1994; Meyer 1994; Massat 1995). The categories of adolescent pregnancy and and teen parenting allow even less space for lesbian and gay sexualities and constitute heterosexuality as powerfully normative. Discussions of lesbian, gay, and bisexual youth take place only in articles that focus on that topic, whereas all other articles focus exclusively on heterosexuality. Neither the content nor the bibliographies of the latter literature recognize the existence of a developing body of social work knowledge on nonheterosexual youth.

In publications that focus on nonheterosexual youth, the subject is variously described as "adolescent homosexuality"—by Malyon (1981), Ricketts (1986), and Sullivan and Schneider (1987)—or as "lesbian and gay youth"— by Saperstein (1981), Cates (1987), Hunter and Schaecher (1987), Sullivan and Schneider (1987), Mallon (1992), and Sullivan (1994). Thus within social work discourses about adolescent sexuality and lesbian and gay youth an opposition is constructed between heterosexuality and other sexual orientations. I found that scholars whose work concerns lesbian and gay youth accept and reproduce this binary. The terms of their entry into social work discourse require that authors who focus upon lesbian and gay sexualities situate those sexualities within a gay/straight binary in a heterosexually dominated context and accept their status as a subordinate literature that will not be integrated into the main body of social work knowledge on youth sexuality.

Most authors who focus on lesbian and gay youth contest the marginality of homosexualities by critically analyzing heterosexual dominance and its effect on nonheterosexual youth. I would argue that they should move beyond Foucault's notion of a reverse discourse or the claiming of a stigmatized identity and draw on analyses developed in gay and lesbian social movements to reject the terms of social work discourses and critique social work practices and broader social relations. They epitomize what Foucault called subjugated knowledges.

I found that social work articles about lesbian, gay, and bisexual youth critique the social power of heterosexuality and its effect on lesbian, gay, and bisexual youth (only a 1987 article by Cates lacks this critical framework). Jacobsen (1988) and Tremble (1988) argue that homosexuality is socially constructed as deviant (or stigmatized [Schneider and Tremble 1986]); Hunter and Schaecher (1987) suggest that this leads to the isolation and harassment of, or violence toward, lesbian and gay youth. Jacobsen (1988) and Tremble (1988) critique the assumption that all young people are heterosexual; Ricketts (1986) points to how homosexuality is constituted as a threat to adolescents.

A number of these scholars also draw on the subjugated knowledges of lesbian, gay, and bisexual youth who have been clients of social work and social welfare to develop a critical analysis of the response of social work and other services to these youth. Several authors argue that social workers and other personnel are ill informed and discriminatory (see Saperstein 1981; Vergara 1984; Hunter and Schaecher 1987; Mallon 1992; Sullivan 1994), that agencies lack relevant policies (see Hunter and Schaecher 1987; Mallon 1992), and that child welfare and other youth-serving agencies fail to meet the needs of or provide equal access to lesbian and gay youth (see Saperstein 1981; Vergara 1984; "Alan" 1988; Mercier and Berger 1989; Mallon 1992; Sullivan 1994). Saperstein (1981), "Alan" (1988), and Mallon (1992) suggest that lesbian and gay youth clients face silencing and denial of their sexual orientation by agencies, whereas Vergara (1984) and Mallon (1992) add that these young people are subjected to verbal harassment and physical abuse while in the care of agencies. A shortage of lesbian-positive and gay-positive services for youth is critiqued by Saperstein (1981), "Alan" (1988), Mallon (1992), and Sullivan (1994). These subjugated knowledges of lesbian and gay communities and clients of social services inform the work of scholars who call for gay young people to be provided with support in dealing with "problems at home" with parents and siblings (see Saperstein 1981; Mercier and Berger 1989; Mallon 1992; and Sullivan 1994). Saperstein (1981), Mercier and Berger (1989), and Sullivan (1994) argue that parents and other family members need to change in order to meet the needs of their lesbian or gay children; Saperstein (1981) calls for social workers to help parents to make these changes.

I found that the marginalization of these articles, as in the failure of other social work publications to cite them, was accomplished despite their publication in social work journals such as *Child Welfare, Social Work in Education,* and the *Social Worker.* This suggests that there are processes through which they are constituted as a subordinate form of knowledge.

In summary, I found that Foucault's analysis of psychiatrized homosexuality was useful in understanding this social work literature, particularly when I also drew on queer theory's notion of heteronormativity. In the early 1980s homosexuality was pathologized in the literature; since then two developments have taken place. On the one hand, social work journals have published a growing number of articles that focus on lesbian and gay youth. At the same time same-sex desire has disappeared from the rest of the social work literature on youth sexuality, an exclusion that is reinforced by a focus upon teenaged pregnancy. I would argue that articles concerning lesbian and gay youth have much to offer social work scholarship on youth sexuality because of their critical analyses of relations of power in society and in social work practice.

Social Work Practices

I would now like to draw on my own research (O'Brien 1994; O'Brien, Travers, and Bell 1993) to expand on some of the critical analyses of social work practices provided by the scholars discussed here. This research drew on the knowledge of lesbian, gay, and bisexual clients of youth services to understand how sexualities are constructed in these agencies. The young people's accounts showed how heteronormativity is constituted through social work practices in ways similar to the processes that take place in social work literature.

Although the psychiatrization of lesbian, gay, and bisexual youth does not appear in the literature after the early 1980s, it was still occurring within social work agencies in the early 1990s. In the following quotes young people describe their experiences:

YOUNG WOMAN: How they dealt with the whole issue, I put it together and I went, "Fuck, they can't deal with this. They think it's a sickness. They think it's a psychiatric problem that needs to be balanced by drugs. And, um, I can't address it because of their issues."[5]

C. O'BRIEN: Did they ever offer you counseling about sexual orientation?

YOUNG MAN: Actually, they recommended me to, ah, go to a couple of places. They wanted me to go to [a mental hospital] and I refused. And so they recommended me to go see a psychiatrist over at [a hospital], and I went to that for a while. . . .

C. O'B: How come you didn't want to go to [the mental hospital]?

YOUNG MAN: Just the name scared me. It scared me, made me feel like I was some psychopath or something.

YOUNG WOMAN: They said you have to see Dr. [X] . . . and within the fifteen minutes that I met him until I walked out and told him to fuck himself, he was telling me how sick and, um, disturbed I am because I'm a lesbian. And I must have been sexually molested, and I must have been this, and I must have been that.

This young woman's angry response to the psychiatrist shows that she had access to a discourse that reversed pathologization and claimed lesbian as a positive identity. Dr. X also attempted to find a "cause" for the pathology of lesbianism, suggesting that the client must have been sexually abused as a child. This practice takes place even among social workers who are ostensibly drawing on a gay-positive discourse, as the following example shows:

C. O'B: Did your worker ever raise the topic of sexual orientation?

YOUNG MAN: All the time, talked about it all the time.

C. O'B: And what kinds of things would he say?

YOUNG MAN: Basically, what anybody else told me. He said it was okay to be gay, and he, a lot of the time actually he thought the reason why I was gay was because of me being sexually abused by another male.

Other workers draw on particular psychological theories of homosexuality as an immature phase that must be worked through in order to achieve mature adult heterosexuality:

YOUNG MAN: I talked to [my worker] about what normal teenagers would ask, like . . . "Sleeping with another guy, is that normal?" He said, "Yeah,

everybody has a gay experience, there's nothing really wrong with it."
He goes, "But, you know, everybody goes through that phase."

I found that there were multiple other ways in which lesbian, gay, and
bisexual clients were told that agencies viewed a nonheterosexual orientation
as pathological.

YOUNG WOMAN: Right off the bat, when they did my assessment, it was
pretty clear that, "Hey, no, this is wrong. This cannot carry on in this
house."

YOUNG WOMAN: I wasn't allowed to talk about my homosexuality. I was-
n't allowed to talk about it at all. We used to have group meetings at
night, um, and, like, I was living with these people and when I wanted
to tell them . . . I was basically told, "Don't talk about it, it's not an issue,
it's not to be discussed here." But it was a big part of my life.

YOUNG WOMAN: They discontinued my one-on-one [individual counsel-
ing]. And she was very effective with me, um. I could talk to her, I
trusted her, um. And they told me I couldn't see her again. Because, you
know, they said, one day I got sat down, and they said to me, "Look we
think you like [A]." And I was, like, "Yeah, she's a good-looking woman.
But what's your point?" And they said, "Well, who else do you think is
good-looking on the staff?" So I was, like, "So-and-so and so-and-so."
And they wouldn't let me associate with those people.

YOUNG WOMAN: They always asked me, "Are you sure, are you sure you're
a lesbian? Are you sure?" . . . It really upset me because I was having to
defend myself when I shouldn't.

A Foucauldian analysis is not adequate in explaining all aspects of power
relations regarding these issues. I also found it useful to return to queer theory's concept of heteronormativity. A central way in which heteronormativity is established in social work agencies is through silence about nonheterosexual orientations:

YOUNG WOMAN: They never said anything. They never said anything.
They, everyone assumed that everyone was straight. It wasn't talked
about. It wasn't acknowledged.

YOUNG MAN: I felt like they expect everyone to be straight 'cause you walk in, and they asked me every question in the book except that. I almost expected to be asked that when I went there, you know. And they would have meetings every day about job findings and stuff. But there was never a meeting about anything like that.

Heteronormativity was also constituted by the lack of lesbian, gay, and bisexual staff who were open about their sexual orientation with clients:

YOUNG WOMAN: There was lesbian workers there. They didn't come out and say they were lesbians. They never said anything.

YOUNG WOMAN: I thought there was this one [gay staff member]. I always thought he was a nice man, and after [a dispute about the client's being openly gay] he just stayed right out of it. . . . And I saw him at a bar a year later, and he came up and was talking to me, and I thought, "I don't want you talking to me. Get away from me." 'Cause I needed his help.

Lesbian, gay, and bisexual clients experienced considerable pressures to pass as heterosexual, that is, to hide their sexual orientation from other clients:

YOUNG MAN: I've never actually seen somebody get beat up because they're gay or bisexual or even suspected of it. I've never seen it. All I've heard is a lot of talk about it. And that's enough for me to not say anything.

YOUNG MAN: All those places you have to be so careful. . . . All they do is sit and put down those "fucking faggots" or all those bashings, and it's like, laugh, laugh, laugh.

C. O'B: Did you feel like you had to pretend to be straight?

YOUNG MAN: Yeah, oh yeah. Yeah, for my own protection.

C. O'B: What were you afraid would happen if you didn't?

YOUNG MAN: I was afraid I would get beat up.

YOUNG MAN: [There was] a lot of violence from them, you know, talking about violence. I'm always hearing about how they went to [a park] and, you know, "Beat up a couple of fags," so they say.

YOUNG MAN: You'd hear all the time the boys talk, "fucking faggot." "They think they run the world, fucking fags." Stuff like that. Half the time it wouldn't even make sense what they said, it would be so stupid. But I mean, they said it, so for my own protection I thought it was better to keep quiet about it. And I did.

I found that staff also participated in or incited verbal harassment of young gay clients:

YOUNG MAN: It got to be more the kids, but for me it was the staff who started it. Like you could hear them snickering and making their little comments. . . . Like, if we'd be going on a outing in the car and the staff, like, knew I was bisexual, we'd be driving down the street and one staff, I remember him, he pointed at this guy and said, "That guy looks like a faggot." And then he turned to me and said, "Do you know him?" Stuff like that.

Thus I would argue that, within the everyday practices of social work, heteronormativity is continually constructed and homosexuality patholo-gized.

Youth sexualities are contested within social work and social welfare. I found that much of the academic literature follows the conventions of what Fou-cault has termed sexual science in focusing attention on the "occurrence" and "causes" of young people's sexual activities. Youth sexuality and procre-ation are generally constituted as both natural and as social problems, as dangerous and endangered, although some scholars are positive about young people's sexual expression. I would argue that social work's role is not envi-sioned as developing strategies to encourage sexual agency among young women or to provide gay-positive support to youth exploring nonheterosex-ual sexual orientations. Instead, social work's role is seen as one of prevent-ing teenaged pregnancies or delaying sexual activities. I found that homo-sexuality was constituted as pathological in the early 1980s, and in later years the literature simply ignores it, though practice does not. Foucault's concept of subjugated knowledges proved useful in analyzing the "missing discourse of desire," the marginalized social work literature on lesbian, gay, and bisexual youth, and social work practice with young clients. Thus social work and social welfare literature and practice are far from being socially neutral or limited to technical interventions; they are deeply implicated in the construction of power relations in sexuality.

NOTES

1. I limit my discussion of social work and social welfare literatures on youth sexuality to publications since 1983.

2. The shift in Gibbs's object of analysis, from gender-neutral "teenagers" to girls and young women, is a move characteristic of this deeply gendered discourse. Another example is provided by Hall's essay, "Factors Associated with Sexual Activity in Early Adolescence": "Of every 100 children born to unmarried women in 1981 . . . approximately 40 were born to young women between 15 and 19 years of age. . . . Girls 14 and under are even sexually active. During the five year period between 1971 and 1976 one-half million 13 and 14 year old girls had coital experience annually" (1986:23).

Thus "sexual activity" among "adolescents" comes to mean solely the activities of girls.

3. For examples of authors who assume that sexual activity among youth should be prevented or delayed see: Kirby et al. (1982), Diamond and Diamond (1986), Quinn (1986), Striar and Ensor (1986), Freeman (1989), and Moyse-Steinberg (1990). Authors who depict sexual activity as dangerous include Chilman (1983), Hall (1986), and Shapiro and Allen-Meares (1986). Gibbs (1986) constitutes sex as dangerous.

4. On the intersection of feminist analyses of sexual abuse and Foucault's notion of subjugated knowledge, see Vikki Bell's *Interrogating Incest* (1993).

5. These quotations are drawn from transcripts of in-depth interviews I conducted in Toronto with seventeen former clients of youth residential services in 1992. Complete anonymity was guaranteed to all interviewees, and identifying details have been deleted or changed. For further discussion see O'Brien (1994) and O'Brien, Travers, and Bell (1993).

REFERENCES

"Alan" [pseudonym]. 1988. Without comment. *Social Worker* 56 (2): 75–88.

Armstrong, Bruce. 1991. Adolescent pregnancy. In Alex Gitterman, ed., *Handbook of social work practice with vulnerable populations.* New York: Columbia University Press.

Bergman, A. G. 1988. Pregnant teenagers: Deterrents to service use. *Social Service Review* 62 (4): 694–704.

Bell, Vikki. 1993. *Interrogating incest: Feminism, Foucault, and the law.* London: Routledge.

Berlant, Lauren and Michael Warner. 1995. What does queer theory teach us about X? *PMLA* 110 (3): 343–49.

Butler, A. C. 1992. The changing economic consequences of teenage childbearing. *Social Service Review* 66 (1): 1–31.

Butler, Judith. 1993. Critically queer. *GLQ* 1 (1): 17–32.

Carlson, B. E., S. A. Abagnale, and E. S. Flatow. 1993. Services for at-risk, pregnant, and parenting teenagers: A consortium approach. *Families in Society: The Journal of Contemporary Human Services* 74 (6): 375–80.

Cates, J. A. 1987. Adolescent sexuality: Gay and lesbian issues. *Child Welfare* 66 (4): 353–64.

Cervera, N. J. 1993. Editorial notes: Serving pregnant and parenting teens. *Families in Society* 74 (6): 323.

Chilman, C. S. 1983. *Adolescent sexuality in a changing American society.* New York: Wiley.

———. 1985. Feminist issues in teenage parenting. *Child Welfare* 64 (3): 225–34.

———. 1988. Never-married, single, adolescent parents. In C. S. Chilman, E. W. Nunally, and F. M. Cox, eds., *Variant family forms*, vol. 5 of Families in trouble series. Newbury Park, Calif.: Sage.

———. 1989. Some major issues regarding adolescent sexuality and childbearing in the United States. *Journal of Social Work and Human Sexuality* 8 (1): 3–25.

Combs-Orme, Terri. 1993. Health effects of adolescent pregnancy: Implications for social workers. *Families in Society* 74 (6): 344–54.

deLauretis, Teresa. 1991. Queer theory: Lesbian and gay sexualities, an introduction. *differences* 3 (2): iii–xviii.

Diamond, Milton and G. H. Diamond. 1986. Adolescent sexuality: Biosocial aspects and intervention strategies. In Paula Allen-Meares and D. A. Shore, eds., *Adolescent Sexualities: Overviews and Principles of Intervention.* New York: Haworth.

Donaldson, P. E., M. H. Whalen, and J. W. Anastas. 1989. Teen pregnancy and sexual abuse: Exploring the connection. *Smith College Studies in Social Work* 59 (3): 289–300.

Dore, M. M. and A. O. Dumois. 1990. Cultural differences in the meaning of adolescent pregnancy. *Families in Society* 71 (2):93–101.

Fine, Michelle. 1988. Sexuality, schooling, and adolescent females: The missing discourse of desire. *Harvard Educational Review* 58 (1): 29–53.

Foucault, Michel. 1972. *The archaeology of knowledge* and *The discourse on language.* Translated by A. M. Sheridan Smith. New York: Harper.

———. 1980. *Power/Knowledge: Selected interviews and other writings, 1972–77.* Edited and translated by Colin Gordon. New York: Pantheon.

———. 1990. *Introduction*, vol. 1 of *The history of sexuality.* Translated by Robert Hurley. 1978. Reprint, New York: Pantheon.

Freeman, Edith M. 1989. Adolescent fathers in urban communities: Exploring their needs and role in preventing pregnancy. *Journal of Social Work and Human Sexuality* 8 (1): 113–31.

———. 1992. Adolescent male sexuality: "Boys will be boys"? *Social Work in Education* 14 (4): 235–38.

Gibbs, J. T. 1986. Psychosocial correlates of sexual attitudes and behaviors in urban early adolescent females: Implications for intervention. In Paula Allen-Meares and D. A. Shore, eds., *Adolescent sexualities: Overviews and principles of intervention*. New York: Haworth.

Gilchrist, L. D. and S. P. Schinke. 1983. Counseling with adolescents about their sexuality. In C. S. Chilman, *Adolescent sexuality in a changing American society*. New York: Wiley.

Gochros, H. L. 1982. Social work and the sexual oppression of youth. In J. R. Conte and D. A. Shore, eds., *Social work and child sexual abuse*. New York: Haworth.

Hacker, S. S. 1989. AIDS education is sex education: Rural and urban challenges. *Journal of Social Work and Human Sexuality* 8 (1): 155–70.

Hall, E. H. 1986. Factors associated with sexual activity in early adolescence. In Paula Allen-Meares and D. A. Shore, eds., *Adolescent sexualities: Overviews and principles of intervention*. New York: Haworth.

Hunter, Joyce and Robert Schaecher. 1987. Stresses on lesbian and gay adolescents in schools. *Social Work in Education* 9 (3): 180–90.

Jaccard, James and Patricia Dittus. 1993. Parent-adolescent communications about premarital pregnancy. *Families in Society* 74 (6): 329–43.

Jacobsen, E. E. 1988. Lesbian and gay adolescents: A social work approach. *Social Worker* 56 (2): 65–67.

Kirby, Douglas, Lynn Peterson, and Jean G. Brown. 1982. A joint parent-child sex-education program. *Child Welfare* 61 (2): 105–20.

Klerman, L. V., J. F. Jekel, and C. S. Chilman. 1983. The service needs of pregnant and parenting adolescents. In C. S. Chilman, *Adolescent sexuality in a changing American society*. New York: Wiley.

Luker, Kristin. 1994. No. [Debate 7: Preventing teenage pregnancy—Should public policy be directed toward preventing teenage pregnancy?] In M. A. Mason and Evelyn Gambrill, eds., *Debating children's lives: Current controversies*. Thousand Oaks, Calif.: Sage.

Mallon, Gary. 1992. Gay and no place to go: Assessing the needs of gay and lesbian adolescents in out-of-home care settings. *Child Welfare* 71 (6): 547–56.

Malyon, A. K. 1981. The homosexual adolescent: Developmental issues and social bias. *Child Welfare* 60 (5): 321–30.

Massat, C. R. 1995. Is older better? Adolescent parenthood and maltreatment. *Child Welfare* 74 (2): 325–36.

Mercier, L. R. and R. M. Berger. 1989. Social service needs of lesbian and gay adolescents: Telling it their way. *Journal of Social Work and Human Sexuality* 8 (1): 75–95.

Meyer, C. H. 1994. Editorial: Little girls with big problems. *Affilia* 9 (4): 334–37.

Moyse-Steinberg, Dominique. 1990. A model for adolescent pregnancy prevention through the use of small groups. *Social Work with Groups* 13 (2).

O'Brien, Carol-Anne. 1994. The social organization of the treatment of lesbian, gay, and bisexual youth in group homes and youth shelters. *Canadian Review of Social Policy* 34 (Winter): 37–57.

O'Brien, Carol-Anne, Robb Travers, and Laurie Bell. 1993. *No safe bed: Lesbian, gay, and bisexual youth in residential services.* Toronto: Central Toronto Youth Services.

Plotnick, R. D. 1993. The effect of social policies on teenage pregnancy and childbearing. *Families in Society* 74 (6): 324–28.

Quinn, J. A. 1986. Rooted in research: Effective adolescent pregnancy prevention programs. In Paula Allen-Meares and D. A. Shore, eds., *Adolescent sexualities: Overviews and principles of intervention.* New York: Haworth.

Resnick, M. D., S. A. Chambliss, and R. W. Blum. 1993. Health and risk behaviors of urban adolescent males involved in pregnancy. *Families in Society* 74 (6): 366–74.

Ricketts, Wendell. 1986. Homosexuality in adolescence: The reification of sexual personalities. In Paula Allen-Meares and D. A. Shore, eds., *Adolescent sexualities: Overviews and principles of intervention.* New York: Haworth.

Rubenstein, Elaine, Susan Panzarine, and Patricia Lanning. 1990. Peer counseling with adolescent mothers: A pilot program. *Families in Society* 71 (3): 136–41.

Saperstein, Sue. 1981. Lesbian and gay adolescents: The need for family support. *Catalyst* 3 (4): 61–70.

Scales, Peter. 1983. Adolescent sexuality and education: Principles, approaches, and resources. In C. S. Chilman, *Adolescent sexuality in a changing American society.* New York: Wiley.

Schneider, Margaret and Bob Tremble. 1986. Gay or straight? Working with the confused adolescent. In James Gripton and Mary Valentich, eds., *Social work practice in sexual problems.* New York: Haworth.

Schultz, L. G. 1986. Enhancing adolescents' sexual development and feelings of self-worth. In Paula Allen-Meares and D. A. Shore, eds., *Adolescent sexualities: Overviews and principles of intervention.* New York: Haworth.

Seidman, Steven. 1994. Queer-ing sociology, sociologizing queer theory: An introduction. *Sociological Theory* 12 (2): 166–79.

Shapiro, C. H. and Paula Allen-Meares. 1986. Foreword. *Journal of Social Work and Human Sexuality* 8 (1): 3–25.

Shifman, Lydia, Clarissa S. Scott, Nancy Fawcett, and Lavdena Orr. 1986. Utilizing a game for both needs assessment and learning in adolescent sexuality education. *Social Work with Groups* 9 (2).

Stafford, J. M. 1987. Accounting for the persistence of teenage pregnancy. *Social Casework* 68 (8): 471–76.

Strean, Herbert. 1983. *The sexual dimension: A guide for the helping professional.* New York: Free Press.

Striar, S. L. and P. G. Ensor. 1986. Therapeutic responses to adolescent psychiatric patients' sexual expression: Beyond a restriction/permission stance. In Paula Allen-Meares and D. A. Shore, eds., *Adolescent sexualities: Overviews and principles of intervention.* New York: Haworth.

Sullivan, Terrance and Margaret Schneider. 1987. Development and identity issues in adolescent homosexuality. *Child and Adolescent Social Work* 4 (1): 13–24.

Sullivan, T. R. 1994. Obstacles to effective child welfare service with gay and lesbian youths. *Child Welfare* 73 (4): 291–304.

Taylor, Linda. 1990. Adolescent parents: An intervention strategy. *Social Worker* 58 (2): 77–81.

Trad, P. V. 1993. Abortion and pregnant adolescents. *Families in Society* 74 (7): 397–409.

Tremble, Bob. 1988. Reference points: A qualitative examination of gay and lesbian adolescence. *Social Worker* 56 (2): 68–70.

Vergara, T. L. 1984. Meeting the needs of sexual minority youth: One program's response. In Robert Schoenberg and Richard S. Goldberg, eds., *Homosexuality and social work*. New York: Haworth.

Warner, Michael. 1993. Introduction. In Michael Warner, ed., *Fear of a queer planet: Queer politics and social theory*. Minneapolis: University of Minnesota Press.

Weatherley, R. A. and V. G. Cartoof. 1988. Helping single adolescent parents. In C. S. Chilman, E. W. Nunnally, and F. M. Cox, eds., *Variant family forms*, vol. 5 of Families in trouble series. Newbury Park, Calif.: Sage.

Weeks, Jeffrey. 1991. Against nature. *Essays on history, sexuality, and identity*. London: Rivers Oram Press.

Wodarski, J. D. 1987. *Social work practice with children and adolescents*. Springfield, Ill.: Charles C. Thomas.

Wood, D. William and Sandy Nuttall. 1987. Single adolescent mothers: Selected aspects of unscheduled parenting in Ontario. *Social Worker* 55 (4): 160–64.

CHAPTER 7

Foucault and Therapy: The Disciplining of Grief

Catherine E. Foote and Arthur W. Frank

Therapy After Foucault[1]

Can therapy retain its good name after Foucault? Once therapists have understood and even partially accepted Foucault's ideas of power, normalization, surveillance, and the disciplining of subjects, can they continue in good conscience? This chapter shows how a Foucauldian critique affects the conceptualization of the therapeutic task in the particular field of grief counseling. Our point is not to render therapy impossible but to extend therapists' sense of how problematic their work is. We hope to effect a Foucauldian reconstruction of the therapeutic that reverses our opening question. Rather than ask whether therapy is possible after Foucault, we suggest that it could never realize its possibilities before him. How has grief come to be "disciplined"? In the 1917 paper that is the *locus classicus* of therapeutic attention to grief, "Mourning and Melancholia," Freud seeks to forestall applying labels of pathology to grief: "Although mourning involves grave departures from the normal attitude to life, it never occurs to us to regard it as a pathological condition and to refer it to medical treatment. We rely on its being overcome after a certain lapse of time, and we look upon any interference with it as useless or even harmful" (1984:252).

Freud then provides a graphic evocation of mourning that is all the more striking because of his denial of its basis in pathology:

> The distinguishing mental features . . . are a profoundly painful dejection, cessation of interest in the outside world, loss of the capacity to love, [and] inhibition of all activity. . . . It is easy to see that this inhi-

bition and circumscription of the ego is the expression of an exclusive devotion to mourning which *leaves nothing over* for other purposes or other interests. It is really only because we know so well how to explain it that this attitude does not seem to us pathological.

(1984:252; emphasis added)

Contrast Freud's insistence on the nonpathological nature of mourning with the following statement by a leading therapist and researcher of bereavement today, Therese Rando:

A significant proportion of the bereaved experience complications. There are approximately 2 million deaths per year in the United States, with each individual death affecting from 8 to 10 family members, for a total of 16 to 20 million new mourners each year. After exhaustively studying the literature, Raphael [1983] estimates that as many as one in three bereavements result in "morbid outcome or pathological patterns of grief." If Raphael's statistic is applied, the potential exists for 5 to 6 million new cases of complicated mourning each year.

In fact, these figures may be misleadingly low because they fail to account for other individuals affected by the death, such as neighbors, friends, coworkers, students, former in-laws, or others outside of the family system who are vulnerable to complications.

(1993:5; citations omitted)

The contrast between Freud and Rando involves not only the pathologizing of grief but the demographic extension of the bereaved. Those "who are vulnerable" expands to become virtually universal: within any decade, almost within any year, who could be omitted?

Freud hardly averts his eyes from the derangement of bereavement, but he regards this as a part of life, not a cause for therapeutic intervention. Rando advocates "improved diagnostic categories for uncomplicated and complicated bereavement in the psychiatric nomenclature and subsequent revisions of the *Diagnostic and Statistical Manual.* Inclusion of these diagnoses will indicate an appropriate awareness of the need to focus research and intervention on grief and mourning" (1993:14). How does Foucault help us, first, to understand the shift from Freud to Rando, and then to imagine what might be an appropriate role for therapy in bereavement? The first question must be resolved before we can address the latter.

The next section outlines the relation that Foucault posits between power, truth, and the self. The third section details a Foucauldian understanding of how grief became pathologized, establishing the grieving self as an object of power. We then consider the experience of bereaved people and describe their ways of grieving—not as pathology but as resistance.

As an orientation and epigram to these sections, we quote Foucault on the most general parameters of his project of critique:

> It seems to me . . . that the real political task in a society such as ours is to criticize the working of institutions which appear to be both neutral and independent; to criticize them in such a manner that the political violence which has always exercised itself obscurely through them will be unmasked, so that one can fight them.
>
> *(quoted in Rabinow 1984:6)*

We understand therapy as such an institution: apparently benign and outside relations of power yet a strategy by which power shapes the self in ways that do violence to that self. It is all the more difficult to unmask, and to fight, because of what we will understand later in the chapter as therapy's commitment to *truth*. A claim to truth at this point in Western civilization is perceived to be neutral and independent, and thus for Foucault power functions most potently when it presents itself as claims to truth. Let us reiterate that we offer the following critique not to proclaim the end of the therapeutic but rather to show, in the final section of this chapter, possibilities for the reconstruction of therapy along lines that account for Foucault's insights.

Power, Truth, and the Self

For Foucault, following Nietzsche, nothing is ever "above" power; on the contrary, that which presents itself as beyond matters of power is precisely what must be examined as a site of power. Claims to be beyond power are made in the name of truth: power is temporal, truth eternal; power reflects interests, truth is disinterested; power is wielded for self-interest, truth simply *is*. Thus Foucault writes, "My problem is to see how men govern (themselves and others) by the production of truth" (1991:79).

Although the implications of Foucault's investigations are profoundly sociological, Foucault says that his general theme is not society but "the discourse of true and false" (1991:85). The therapeutic is such a discourse in at least two senses. First, it claims truth for its "findings": consider Rando's references to statistical rates of prevalence and "exhaustive" searches of "the literature." Such a discourse presents not only its own truth but claims to be a kind of truth of truths, a metatruth. Second, just as the categories of true and false divide the world into a hierarchy, so do the categories of normal and pathological.

The therapeutic, then, is a prime example of what Foucault calls "a code which rules ways of doing things" (1991:79). The things that are done include—but are hardly limited to—talking cures, provision of disability benefits, administration of drugs, and hospitalization. Foucault perpetually calls our attention to how "doing things" depends on "a production of true discourses which serve to found, justify and provide reasons and principles for these ways of doing things" (1991:79). The practice of therapy depends on a "true discourse," which, whether it is called psychiatry or mental health or clinical social work, has at its core the possibility—indeed the imperative—of a "true" division of the normal from the pathological.

Of course, the exact terms of this division—who is placed on which side of the divide—will always be subject to some contest. In the case of the *Diagnostic and Statistical Manual,* the most famous such contest was over the inclusion of a diagnostic label for homosexuality (see Bayer 1981). But Foucault's point is that, although the exact terms of the division are contested, the general principle of division is one of those practices that are "accepted by both sides as absolutely self-evident" (1988a:96–97). Gays who protested being labeled did not protest the principle of psychiatric diagnosis itself. Truth becomes a form of power (107) precisely because it is accepted as self-evident.

Thus for Foucault the unmasking of power requires "the political history of the production of 'truth'" (112). The quotation from Rando exemplifies a discourse that has truth as its function and thus attains "specific powers" (112). "This has always been my problem," Foucault writes, "the effects of power and the production of truth. . . . My problem is the politics of truth" (118). The problem of this chapter is how bereavement counseling is both an effect of truth and a production of more truth. We understand grief therapy as an effect of power and a means of perpetuating power, and we ask whether there is any way out of this circle. But that question depends on a further Foucauldian move: showing how the concept of the self developed within the discourses of truth, and how power is effected through the self's seeking its own truth.

Students of social control have long recognized that power can be maintained by external force only within circumscribed situations. Coercive power (what Foucault also calls "domination" [1988c:3, 12]) is the limit, not the rule, in societies. Most power, most of the time, must be effected by those who are "being" controlled. The internalization-of-power argument posits that those being ruled either accept the demands of those in power as legitimate or fear that "they"—those who have power—may be watching. Foucault's early work on power (for example, *Discipline and Punish* in 1979), with its emphasis on surveillance, struggles with this opposition between those who guard through surveillance and those who are guarded. His later work (for example, *Technologies of the Self* in 1988) affords decreasing attention to the guards. Instead, he understands power as effected through knowledge of the self and what he calls "technologies" of the self.

Foucault describes the human sciences, including social work, as "truth games" through which human subjects aspire to know the truth of their selves and are enjoined to seek this truth through practices of care. Truth games are related to specific technologies, and most significant are the technologies of the self. Foucault's description of technologies of the self is readable as a generic definition of therapy: "Technologies of the self . . . permit individuals to effect by their own means or with the help of others a certain number of operations on their own bodies and souls, thoughts, conduct, and way of being, so as to transform themselves in order to attain a certain state of happiness, purity, wisdom, perfection, or immortality" (1988b:18).

At the end of the twentieth century, technologies that operate on bodies include exercise regimes, diets, designer drugs, and cosmetic surgery; those that affect the psyche include self-help books, talk shows, recovery programs, and counseling. Much of what is now encompassed by the terms *alternative medicine* and *New Age* practices are technologies that transform both body and psyche.

What is at stake in technologies of the self is "how an individual acts upon himself" (1988b:19). Foucault perceives an increasing breakdown of any distinction between "the technologies of the domination of others" and those of the self acting upon itself (see also 1988c:2). The "contact between" these two forms of domination is what he calls "governmentality" (1988b:19). Through governmentality the "management of individuals" is made possible by discourses claiming, again, truth—the truth of the self, or the "self-knowledge" that Western civilization from the Greek oracle to Freud has held up as its ultimate prize (19ff).

Therapy is the most prevalent form of those practices that Foucault calls "ascetical." He describes these practices as exercises "of self upon self by which one tries to work out, to transform one's self and to attain a certain mode of being" (1988c:2). Ascetical practices become the way that care of the self is practiced (1988b:22; 1988c:4–5): to know the self is to care for the self, and to care for the self is to transform the self through self-knowledge. "And why do we care for ourselves, only through the care for truth?" Foucault asks (1988c:15). Foucault never lived to answer the global question—"What caused all Western culture to begin to turn around this obligation of truth?" (1988c:15)—but he creates new possibilities for unmasking specific practices, and perhaps Foucault was always more comfortable with the local inquiry than the global.

A final note on technologies of the self, most germane to therapy: although such technologies depend on individuals acting upon themselves, individuals do not act alone. Individuals do not invent particular truth games by themselves—even a Freud develops a truth game begun before him—and they do not play these games by themselves. Truth games generally, and technologies of the self specifically, always are played out in relationships. For Foucault power is always *relational*, as the following statement specifies: "I hardly ever use the word 'power' and if I do sometimes, it is always a short cut to the expression I always use: the relationships of power. . . . I mean that in human relations . . . power is always present: I mean the relationships in which one wishes to direct the behavior of another" (1988c:11).

This statement, particularly when read out of context, requires qualification. When Foucault writes of one's wishing to direct the behavior of another, he does not mean that this one—the confessor, prison guard, social worker, or public health official—has power *over* the other. Rather, he means that within the truth game that they are *both* playing, they share the common goal of the one's being directed toward some self-truth by the other. The nature of the game is to convince both parties that they are mutually engaged in a production of truth. Thus, to return again to the Rando quotation, the Foucauldian critique does not suggest that she seeks to wield therapeutic power over those she classifies as pathological in their grief. Rather, Rando seeks to care for the bereaved by directing them toward the truth of their grief and of their selves. This truth is the *mutual obligation* of both the therapist and client, doctor and patient, observer and observed. Within their relationship the one directs the other, but this direction is not *having* power. Rather, providing direction is the role one plays in the relation of power that encompasses both.

The "unmasking" of any technology of power, such as therapy, is directed toward both parties in that relationship of power, and the potential to fight against the violence of that power is open to both. Having written all this, we should reaffirm that the Foucauldian critique does not deny imbalances, including the practical advantage enjoyed by one party in this relationship over the other, and the disparity of resources available to each. But if the theorist is to grasp what makes this advantage or disparity not only possible but in many cases what makes it self-evident, power must be understood as more than "power over." Power, as we understand Foucault's use of the term, represents the bedrock cultural assumptions of truth and goodness that, when embodied in specific codes of knowledge and practice, give some people immediate practical power over others. This practical power involves not only the ability to direct that other but the willingness—even gratitude—of the other to be directed.

Grief as a Technology of the Self

Grief—like madness (1973), medicine (1975), prisons (1979), and sexuality (1980) for Foucault—is a site of disciplinary power: each of these social institutions directs the exercises of a self working upon the self.[2] The objective of this work is to produce the self required by the institution. Grief invokes relations of power that create the bereaved as individual subjects who are "docile" in the dual Foucauldian sense of being (a) objects of knowledge, and (b) minds and bodies to be shaped by the practical application of that knowledge. The bereaved are to be known by therapy and to be shaped by therapeutic knowledge.

A Foucauldian critique seeks the dominant discourse of grief: the therapeutic discourse through which "the grievers" are produced as an object of professional knowledge *and* as a subject for themselves. Therapy, as a technology of the self, requires both: a professional knowledge of certain types of selves and a personal commitment to know the self. This dominant discourse of grief is created and reproduced in the therapeutic practices described here. The object of each practice is not to impose upon "the griever" externally but to colonize from within, so that those who are objects of this discourse see themselves as proper objects. The goal is to shape the subjectivity of the bereaved, and this shaping of subjectivity is what Foucault means by "discipline."

Normalization

The "self-evident" premise of therapeutic intervention in bereavement is that there are normal and abnormal responses to death and loss. This division must exist in order to demarcate the "abnormal" as the legitimate object of therapeutic intervention: therapy becomes self-evident because the abnormal or pathological is self-evident. Abnormal is what can be brought back to normal by means of therapeutic fixing. None of this implies that the therapeutic professions have created grieving or that grieving is not an immensely painful, preoccupying, and even lifelong condition; recall Freud's description of "mourning which leaves nothing over for other purposes or other interests." What the therapeutic professions do is interpret an increasing proportion of grieving as pathological and in need of being brought back to normal.

Freud's description of the person in grief is rich in the specificity of its description: "profoundly painful dejection, cessation of interest in the outside world, loss of the capacity to love, [and] inhibition of all activity." By contrast, Rando's description of what she calls "complicated mourning" is phrased in clinical labels that lack specificity of reference to behavior: "morbid, atypical, pathological, neurotic, unresolved . . . distorted, abnormal, deviant, or dysfunctional" (1993:11; emphasis omitted).

People have these labels attached to them when there is "some disturbance of the normal progress towards resolution" (Rando 1984:59). *Normal* is defined in terms of *progress*, and abnormal is its opposite, the failure to "accommodate" to the loss (1993:40, 149). Thus abnormal is described variously as absent grief, delayed grief, inhibited grief, distorted or exaggerated grief, conflicted grief, unanticipated grief, chronic or prolonged grief, and abbreviated grief (1984:59–62; 1993:156). In sum, complicated mourning either lasts too long (prolonged or chronic) or not long enough (abbreviated). It is either expressed too demonstrably (exaggerated, distorted, conflicted) or not demonstrably enough (absent, inhibited, delayed). What is left over—as normal or "uncomplicated" mourning—becomes difficult to imagine.

As a strategy of power, the normalization of grieving works in two stages. First, the abnormal is defined in contrast to a supposed category of the normal. Second, the clinical criteria for candidacy in the abnormal are expanded until the normal is defined out of existence or at least relegated to the margins. The normal remains less as a reality than as the therapeutic ideal, the objective of a technology of the self. Normalization becomes the self-evident ideal that supports a technology, and the technology self-evidently requires therapeutic assistance. We thus move to the complementary processes of medicalization, totalization, and individualization.

Medicalization

Despite what Freud says about grief's not being pathological and therapy not only uncalled for but potentially harmful, "Mourning and Melancholia" suggests the differentiation of normal and pathological responses to grief and thus lays the groundwork for the medicalization of grief.

In his sociological study of death practices, Lindsay Prior writes that in the nineteenth century, even though grief was sometimes seen as a cause of insanity, it was "never interpreted as itself pathological. Grief, if anything, was a condition of the human spirit or soul rather than of the body and in that sense it could neither be normalised or medicalised" (1989:135). Prior describes the progressive formulation of grief as a "disease" within the psychoanalytic literature. He quotes the influential psychiatrist Colin Murray Parkes (who wrote in 1975): "On the whole, grief resembles a physical injury more closely than any other type of illness. . . . But occasionally . . . abnormal forms arise, which may even be complicated by the onset of other types of illness" (Prior 1989:136).

In equating grief to physical injury, Parkes removes it from the realm of psychopathology but leaves it well within the sphere of illness. His next sentence suggests that infrequently "abnormal forms arise" and reaffirms grieving as a potential nexus of "other types of illness." Prior summarizes the essential shift that this passage illustrates: "Grief was something in the body which could be measured and assessed. The intensity and duration of grief were factors whose origins could be located in the biochemistry of the body or in the infantile history of the subject" (136). Grief becomes a disordered state with somatic and psychological symptoms.

Prior is especially insightful in noting that the medicalization of grief both requires and asserts a developmental metaphor: "Human behaviour is seen to involve an unfolding of human potential towards an ultimate stage of stability or 'reintegration'" (136). Grief is expected to be an ordered, limited process that moves by identifiable steps toward "recovery": restored happiness, adaptation to the absence of the deceased, reestablished engagement with the everyday world. Among the various "stage theories" that Prior cites as examples of such thinking, the best known is certainly Elisabeth Kübler-Ross's five-stage theory of dying (1969), which, even if we take seriously her injunction that the stages need not occur sequentially, does require culmination in the final stage of "acceptance." Standard clinical usage refers to whether patients (not necessarily dying) have *reached acceptance* in their illness, and this vocabulary of resolution has been extended to the bereaved as well. To fail to reach acceptance is constructed as pathological and thus susceptible to treatment and cure.

Individualization

The developmental metaphor can appear self-evident now, yet its "victory" was over a competing view of grieving, most famously put foreword by Emile Durkheim in *The Elementary Forms of the Religious Life* (1915). Prior describes the Durkheimian view: "The intensity of grief was not the product of some inner unfolding, but of social processes which tended to channel grief in some directions whilst deflecting it away from others" (1989:137). Prior goes on to cite several more recent studies that examine grief as socially structured rather than as an embodied manifestation of inner states with idiosyncratic meanings.

The work of sociologists such as Deborah Lupton on body management and control (1995:7–13) and Arlie Hochschild on "feeling rules" (1983:63–68) exemplifies the road not taken in the understanding of bereavement. Hochschild specifically sets out the fairly strict expectations and boundaries that society allows for the expression of grief emotions. Following the work of Erving Goffman (1972:Appendix), Hochschild's account reveals the "pathological" as a label that results from failing to manage one's emotions according to appropriate feeling rules: showing too much emotion in one place or not enough in another. The fate of Meursault in Albert Camus's *The Stranger* (1946) epitomizes Hochschild's view: Meursault's shooting a man under ambiguous circumstances is judged to be murder rather than self-defense, based largely on testimony about his earlier lack of demonstrated emotion following his mother's death. Meursault's conviction is for failing to follow society's feeling rules properly. He is, in effect, executed for "absent grief."

To depict grieving as following or refusing to follow socially prescribed feeling rules would place grieving in a social context, thus undercutting the opportunity for medicalized therapy to separate out individuals as patients whose social context is less important than their inner states. The biomedical premise of therapy is that the patient can be treated in isolation from the context, and some resolution—if not full cure—can be achieved without challenging the social group within which the person lives and, in this case, grieves. Individualization means treating *only* the patient, once medicalization has rendered the person in grief as a patient. In Foucauldian terms power requires an individual subject to become the object of its normalizing discourses, and grief becomes the privatized, subjectivized experience of individuals (Mellor 1993).

Totalization

But if medicalized psychotherapy treats only the individual patient, the corollary is that anyone can, and perhaps everyone should, be a patient. Power must be able to extend itself throughout a population, and because everyone dies, most people will grieve, sooner than later. Grief, like sexuality, is a rich site for power because anyone becomes a potential subject for disciplined grief.

Kenneth Doka's concept of "disenfranchised grief" (1989), while resting on solid sociological observation, helps to produce an even more inclusive category of grievers. Disenfranchised grief is experienced when a person incurs "a loss that is not or cannot be openly acknowledged, publicly mourned, or socially supported" (1989:4). The grief is "disenfranchised" because the relationship to the deceased is not recognized (for example, a former spouse or an extramarital lover dies), the loss is not recognized (the death of a pet or the loss of a valued possession or property), and/or the griever is not recognized (the very young, the very old, or the mentally disabled) (4–7).

Although Doka underscores the existence of fairly specific social feeling rules about who can grieve for whom (or what), the concept of disenfranchised grief also renders far more people candidates for "grief work." Bereavement need no longer be the result of death only: every sort of loss must now be grieved, and these losses become describable in clinical terms. The effect of such descriptions is twofold. First, the person in "mourning" becomes a candidate for a therapeutic technology of the self, and, second, even if a social process caused the loss (for example, an economic recession that created loss of jobs), that phenomenon is still individualized as one person's "grief."

"Grief Work"

When grief is conceptualized as a personal problem to be overcome, clinical responses to bereavement (whether individual psychotherapy, group counseling, or workshops) take on a metaphor of "grief work" (see, for example, Worden 1991). The description suggests that individuals have *work* that they need to do, that therapy *is* work, and that in doing this work bereaved people display themselves as doing what society expects of its members.

Other connotations of work are also present: that grieving is a task to be mastered and finally accomplished, that such accomplishment is productive, and that grief work has a continuity with other socially acceptable work. The distance from the clinic to the workplace is reduced; each becomes an extension of the other. For Foucault power works precisely through such a network of connections: the productive subject—the worker—is reproduced at each site in this network.

Grief work is practiced within a "bereaved role" analogous to Talcott Parsons's sick-role theory (Parsons 1951; Frank 1991, 1995). Parsons argues that being sick places the individual within a role defined by certain socially structured expectations. These are, first, that illness is not the sick person's fault; second, that the sick person is excused from normal responsibilities; and third, that the sick person has an obligation to seek medical treatment, comply with that treatment, and get well. Treatment returns the sick person to health and, with health, to normal social responsibilities. The sick role was never so much an experienced reality as it was a description, and a brilliant one, of the dominant discourse of illness. The interest and the longevity of Parsons's concept lie in his expression of the social ideal of illness behavior. We propose the "bereaved role" as capturing several dimensions of the dominant discourse of the social ideal of bereavement.

First, the bereavement role is to be temporary. The developmental metaphor for grief culminates in the accepted wisdom that "time heals" (though for many people it heals neither soon enough nor well enough to exclude the need for clinical intervention). The normal expectation that grief will follow a time-limited linear progression from disorientation to accommodation is expressed in Rando's concept of "STUGs" or "subsequent temporary upsurges of grief" (1993:64–77). STUGs may be brought on by an anniversary, a life-cycle transition, coming across a memento of the deceased person, or any other association with the absence and loss. Rando introduces STUGs as a residual category that explains deviations from the usual linear course of "time heals." The formulation of this concept reinforces the expectation that initial grief, as well as later upsurges of grief, will be short term and will not pervade the griever's life.

Second, while grieving, a person occupies an excluded class that carries some benefits (for example, bereavement leave from a job) but implies other obligations. People are supposed to engage in grief work, and this work is supposed to progress and have an end, marked by returning to real work. While doing this grief work, some ways of behaving are appropriate and others are pathological.

Such bereavement leaves as are offered by the workplace attempt not only to allow the bereaved person to forget job responsibilities for awhile but to keep the demonstrable grief out of the work site. Extensive interview data gathered by Foote clearly reflect the workplace expectation that once such a brief leave is over, the grief is over as well. If mourning then continues, it is "complicated" and requires therapeutic intervention.

Third, professionals are entitled to intervene in grief, principally by demarcating what is appropriate and what is pathological. As described earlier, any grieving can be judged pathological in its excess or its absence, its length or its brevity. Professional intervention will probably occur second-hand: for most people what we have called clinical intervention will not be individual psychotherapy but will take place through the increasingly professional permeation of what the medical sociologist Eliot Freidson once called the "lay culture" of medicine (1988). Where once the lay culture was truly lay—kitchen table talk comparing friends and family who had been treated in what way for which symptoms—lay talk, and lay thinking, increasingly is saturated with professional opinion offered through television and radio, self-help books, workshops, and support groups.

As we were writing this chapter, Frank spoke at a large hospital-sponsored conference for families of children with cancer. Rando's *Treatment of Complicated Mourning* (1993) was prominent among the books being offered for sale by the conference organizers to the group's members. Although written for professionals, the book is very much a part of the popular culture of bereavement, shaping people's expectations of how they should grieve. Selling the book not only made professional advice available but carried a message that such advice is necessary.

Policing Boundaries

Any society puts boundaries not only around dying and the dead but around mourning as an extension of dying. The observation is commonplace that contemporary Western society seeks to cloister death in hospitals. Although hospice care, either in homes or in freestanding facilities, is once again allowing people to participate in their loved ones' dying, one impetus of the right-to-die movement—a movement that enjoys considerable popular support—is the desire to die before going through the extremes of dying.

The ideal of a "deathless death" (Kastenbaum 1993:83)—whether this is the ideal of the perfectly pain-controlled hospital death or of euthanasia—is reproduced in the cultural message that grief ought to be private and controlled: clean, quiet, and quick. Grief should be sequestered: contained, confined, not allowed to flood or overwhelm lives. Thus "complicated mourning" is defined as pathological, instead of being understood as reflecting all the complications of lives and relationships, filled as they are with irresolutions, unfinished business, haunting images of suffering, regrets, missed opportunities, and the grieving person's fear of dying the same way. These are the normal complications of dying and bereavement—personal tragedies for those who go through them but no more pathological for that.

Society polices mourning—mourning is kept within certain boundaries—because death must be kept within certain boundaries. The sociologist Anthony Giddens describes death as the "point zero at which control lapses" (1991:203). For both Giddens and Zygmunt Bauman (1992), death is the scandal within the modernist project of rational, technical control over life and living. Modernist discourse celebrates youth, health, choice, self-improvement, productivity, and consuming (Riches and Dawson 1996:4). If aging is undeniable, the aged can still be portrayed as athletic, engaged in leisure, and sexually active. Realities such as watching one's group of friends dwindle owing to death are rarely depicted in images of aging.

Undoubtedly, the greatest influence on popular and professional thinking about dying in the last thirty years has been Kübler-Ross's five stages of dying (1969): denial and isolation, anger, bargaining, depression, and acceptance. For our purposes the importance of this theory is in what it excludes, or the boundary it polices. By focusing exclusively on the dying person's movement between psychological attitudes toward dying, and the need for caregivers to be responsive to the stage the dying person is in, Kübler-Ross provides a "consensually certified distractor" (Kastenbaum 1993:82) from the physical changes and deterioration the dying person is experiencing. The embodiment of death is obscured by exclusive emphasis on the psychology of dying.

Grief, like death itself, is undisciplined, risky, wild. That society seeks to discipline grief, as part of its policing of the border between life and death, is predictable, and it is equally predictable that modern society would medicalize grief as the means of policing.

In discussing normalization, medicalization, individualization, totalization, grief work, and policing boundaries, we have made little direct reference to Foucault. What Foucault adds to the other theorists we have cited is an understanding of all these processes as the workings of power. Power relations are enacted at the interface between the normal and the pathological, in the interest of moving the subject from the latter to the former. But normal is a mirage. The resolution of complicated grief turns into the need for intervention in whatever else remains complicated: one's sexuality, workplace participation, family relationships, and the list—the web of power relations holding the subject within some technology of the self—goes on. We all remain, all the time, "vulnerable to complications," as Rando so well evokes the psy view of life.

Power lives off complications, because each is an occasion for disciplining the self. Each complication renders the person a candidate for some technology of the self that promises to find the truth of the present complication and restore the person to the "normal" trajectory toward the truth of his or her being. That these truths are a good thing is self-evident; thus the institutions of truth seeking appear both neutral and independent.

What, then, does Foucault mean when he writes in the passage quoted at the beginning of this chapter of the "political violence" exercised obscurely through these institutions? To unmask these violences we must view complicated mourning from another perspective: no longer as individualized and pathological but as social resistance to a dominant discourse. This in turn generates our final question: If complicated mourning represents a refusal to become the kind of person that appropriate grieving, as a technology of the self, requires one to be, does some space still exist for a therapeutic response to complicated mourning, and what might such a therapy look like?

Complicated Mourning as Resistance

Foucault describes any power relationship as "nothing other than the instant photograph of multiple struggles continuously in transformation" (1989:188). In the last section we provided one snapshot of the bereaved person caught up in a therapeutic governmentality: labeled by psychotherapy, individualized, normalized, and medicalized. Such a person's participation in a technology of the self—producing appropriate grief by her or his own means or with the help of others, such as a grief counselor—thus appears as a kind of false consciousness, and Foucault's theoretical intervention then seems to parallel Marx's project of demystifying workers' understanding of capitalism so that they would revolt, seize power, and end domination. Foucault, however, is far more attentive than Marx to the subtle workings of power. For Foucault power is not the same as domination. To explore Foucault's distinction of power from domination, we juxtapose the photograph of the bereaved person as victim of clinical intervention with an image of the mourner as resister of the dominant discourse of grieving.

The last section presented a series of social practices, some overlapping and others disconnected. Taken together, these practices circumscribe what we call the dominant discourse of grief. The fundamental narrative of this discourse is that "normal" grieving is short term and follows a linear trajectory from acute to moderate to a thing of the past. Even during the most intense periods of grieving, mourners are expected to restrain their displays of grieving to appropriate times and places. In the developmental metaphor time is expected to heal. When people are not healed after a "reasonable" period of time (Rando 1993:149), the mourning is judged to be "complicated" and pathologized. When individuals cannot display proper "resolution" of complicated mourning, they are at minimum expected to participate in some technology of the self that is designed to bring about this resolution. These technologies range from individual or family psychotherapy to participating in support groups and reading self-help books. The technology of the self is thus the fallback discipline for those who have initially failed to discipline themselves within the dominant discourse's expectations of normality.

Foucault imagines society as a network of interlocking dominant discourses, all having to do with the production of selves. Thus the dominant discourse of mourning overlaps with discourses of marriage, parenthood and childhood, sexuality, work and health, friendship and group participation, and cultural and ethnic membership, and these discourses overlap with still others. Discourses demand and produce real effects on people, particularly on people's bodies, but they are not hegemonic. In his earlier work Foucault presents resistance to the dominant discourse almost as a residual category— a limiting possibility rather than an ongoing, constitutive part of social process. His later work, especially his interviews, brings resistance into his theory—not as what happens at the margins of power but as the reciprocal and inherent complement of power. "I am not positing a substance of resistance versus a substance of power," Foucault says, "I am just saying: as soon as there is a power relation, there is a possibility of resistance. We can never be ensnared by power: we can always modify its grip in determinate conditions and according to a precise strategy" (1988a:123).

Foucault is more explicit about the mutual interplay of power and resistance when he speaks of how "power relationships open up a space in the middle of which the struggles develop" (1989:187). Resistance is the hole in power, and only power/resistance can form a whole; again, resistance is not marginal to power but constitutive of power.

Foucault differentiates power from domination by giving resistance a constitutive site within power. The following statement clearly distinguishes power from domination, showing the place of resistance in the former:

> This analysis of relations of power constitutes a very complex field; it sometimes meets what we can call facts or states of domination, in which the relations of power, instead of being variable and allowing different partners a strategy which alters them, find themselves firmly set and congealed. When an individual or a social group manages to block a field of relations of power, to render them impassive and invariable and to prevent all reversibility of movement—by means of instruments which can be economic as well as political or military— we are facing what can be called a state of domination.   *(1988 :3)*

We quote this passage in full because of the importance of the distinction Foucault is making between "congealed" domination, against which resistance can be only marginal, and power, which is a mobile, variable interplay of the dominant discourse and resistance to it. Foucault describes power in the following statement:

> These relations of power are then changeable, reversible and unstable. One must observe also that there cannot be relations of power unless the subjects are free. If one or the other were completely at the disposition of the other and became his thing, an object on which he can exercise an infinite and unlimited violence, there would not be relations of power. In order to exercise a relation of power, there must be on both sides at least a certain form of liberty. . . . That means that in the relations of power, there is necessarily the possibility of resistance, for if there were no possibility of resistance—of violent resistance, of escape, of ruse, of strategies that reverse the situation—there would be no relations of power.   *(1988 :12)*

Again we quote at length because this passage represents a considerable clarification, and perhaps modification, of Foucault's presentation of power in some of his earlier books. The core of this clarification is that the necessity of resistance is what differentiates relations of power from domination.

> The characteristic feature of power is that some men can more or less entirely determine other men's conduct—but never exhaustively or

coercively. A man who is chained up and beaten is subject to force
being exerted over him. Not power. But if he can be induced to speak,
when his ultimate recourse could have been to hold his tongue . . . then
he has been caused to behave in a certain way. His freedom has been
subjected to power.   *(1988a:83–84)*

Inducing speech when the other could remain silent, therapy is power
but not domination. The situation is certainly inequitable in terms of
resources: therapists have on their side the professional credentials, an office,
and a title, perhaps the ability to mandate further treatment and even to
order involuntary commitment. Most of all, therapists present themselves
within the assumptions of the dominant discourse: they are the arbiter of
normal, and their patient/client is abnormal. But these imbalances are not
immutable differences; they give rise to counterstrategies of resistance: refut-
ing the therapist's interpretations, missing appointments, dropping out of
therapy, continuing to display "symptoms," or organizing countertherapy
support groups under the generic title of "victims of psychotherapy."

A convenient example of the layering of power and resistance played out
one night on the radio, as a sexuality therapist responded to listeners' letters.
One young woman was complaining of pain during intercourse. The radio
therapist offered some practical advice but then stopped to comment on
another aspect of the listener's letter. "This woman has a problem," the therapist said. "She has a psychiatrist." The therapist went on to describe sexist
comments the psychiatrist had made when the listener took her problem to
him, and the radio therapist recommended that the woman tell the psychiatrist that she objected to what he had said. Here we see the interweaving of
power and resistance. The radio therapist exemplifies the dominant discourse of sexuality: her work is about normalization and totalization; using
mass media, she recreates sexuality as a technology of the self. But woven
into that exercise of power is resistance to another aspect of the dominant
discourse. As the radio therapist criticized the sexism of the psychiatrist, she
counseled resistance to psychiatric power. We quickly appreciate how serious
Foucault was in calling relations of power "a very complex field."

Foucault's critique of power cannot demystify power, because relationships of power already include resistances that do the ongoing work of
demystification. His critique, unlike Marxist critiques of power, does not
have to conclude with "this then is what needs to be done" (Foucault
1991:84), because in practices of resistance "this" is already being done.
Moreover, resistance is not a countertheory: "It doesn't have to lay down the

law for the law," Foucault writes. "It is a challenge directed to what is" (1991:84).

Just as power is directed first and foremost toward the body, so resistance begins in the body: "One is not radical because one pronounces a few words; no, the essence of being radical is physical; the essence of being radical is the radicalness of existence itself" (Foucault 1989:191). We thus propose to understand complicated mourning as one instance of such a *physical* radicalness. People engaged in complicated mourning present no countertheory of their condition. Instead, these people use their bodies to disrupt normal expectations, including emotional restraint, diet, sexuality, and work. Unlike the dominant discourse, those who resist "lay down no law," but in their embodied refusal of what the dominant discourse demands, they "challenge what is."

The attempt of therapy to extend itself to "cover" complicated mourning is predictable. Grief counseling is another technology of the self. In this therapy the body of the griever is rendered docile; it is the stuff that therapy seeks to reform and conform. Most important, clients or patients are expected to be the instrument of their own conformation. As quoted earlier, Foucault defines technologies of the self as practices that "*permit* individuals to effect by their own means or with the help of others a certain number of operations on their own bodies and souls, thoughts, conduct, and way of being, so as to transform themselves in order to attain a certain state of happiness, purity, wisdom, perfection, or immortality" (1988b:18; emphasis added). Foucault characterizes the helping professions as presenting "a formidable trap":

> What they are saying, roughly, is this: ". . . So, come to us, tell us, show us all that, confide in us your unhappy secrets." . . .
>
> This type of discourse is, indeed, a formidable tool of control and power. As always, it uses what people say, feel, and hope for. It exploits their temptation to believe that to be happy, it is enough to cross the threshold of discourse and to remove a few prohibitions. (1988a:114)

At the beginning of this chapter we quoted, as a kind of epigram, Foucault's reference to the "political violence" perpetrated by such a discourse. We now present this violence in its more complex dimensions.

The violence done to the bereaved is to tell them that what Freud calls their "grave departures from the normal attitude to life" are not, in a moral sense, right. If, as Freud observes, the bereaved feel a profoundly painful dejection, if they lose interest in the outside world, if they lose their capacity to love, if they are unable to act, if their mourning *leaves nothing over,* then, according to post-Freudian therapy, they must confide their unhappy secrets to some agent of the therapeutic. They must engage in a remedial technology of the self until they have attained, once again, a certain state of happiness. The imperative character of these injunctions is backed by a more formidable tool than police. What instigates compliance is people's temptation to believe that they ought to be happy and that a technology of the self can deliver them to this happiness if only they will apply that technology to themselves, for themselves, with all diligence. If only, in other words, they will become docile bodies available to be shaped by this technology.

People can resist this normalizing discourse, and if resistance were not possible, the situation would be one of domination, not relationships of power. Yet an inequality of the dominant discourse and embodied resistance remains. Resistance is possible, but resistance compounds the wounds that complicated mourning already bears. To the wounds of real grief the dominant discourse adds the wounds of telling people that their grief is their abnormality, that it—that they—are wrong, misdirected, out of place. They are wrong in the sense that they are insults to the truth of human happiness. Resistance generically attempts to claim what the dominant discourse calls wrong and redefine it as right. But to resist one must place oneself further outside, effecting yet another "grave departure from the normal attitude to life." Resistance is a compounding of mourning, because it also can "leave nothing over for other purposes or interests."

Power does not simply provide for resistance; power instigates and requires resistance, and the price paid by those who resist must never be underestimated. Resistance may be the possibility left open by power—the hole in its center—but the cost of resistance is no less an extension of the violence inflicted by power.

How, then, can therapy cease to be an instrument of the dominant discourse, inflicting violence, and instead become not only a modality of resistance but a means of healing the wounds caused by the violences of power? We seek to make the case for such a therapy-of-resistance, but we need to remain mindful, and keep the reader mindful, that our attempt may be yet another ruse of power as it perpetually incorporates—literally swallows up— resistances into the dominant discourse. Thus we emphasize the need to keep open the question of whether any reformulation of the therapeutic does more than extend the dominant discourse by means of creating "resistance" as a new technology of the self, depending on its own truth and disciplining subjects in the search for this new truth.

Yet Foucault encourages us not to become lost in a theoretical maze of our own creation. "It is the reality of possible struggles that I wish to bring to light," he says, referring to "points of resistance and the possible points of attack" (1989:189). Power is not hegemonic; resistance and attack remain real possibilities.

Therapy as Resistance

Since the late 1980s some practitioners of family therapy have become especially knowledgeable about Foucault and innovative in their attempts to apply Foucault's critique of the therapeutic to their work. The Australian social worker and family therapist Michael White set the agenda for this movement. Although we do not wish to minimize others' contributions (see, for example, de Shazer 1991; Fish 1993; Flaskas and Humphreys 1993; Frosh 1995; Hare-Mustin 1994; Hindmarsh 1993; Laird 1991; Larner 1994, 1995; Luepnitz 1992; Madigan 1992; Paré 1995; Parry and Doan 1994; Pocock 1995; Redekop 1995), we take White as our exemplar of attempts at Foucauldian therapy (White 1993; White and Epston 1990; Wood 1991; see Weedon 1987, chap. 5, for a feminist anticipation of the core of White's critique).

White begins with the uncontroversial premise that life is constituted by attributing meaning to experience. He then follows a considerable body of literature (cf. Frank 1995, chap. 3) that subsumes these meanings under the rubric of narrative. The narrative is the primary frame for making meaning; through narratives people make sense of their experiences. Experience is thus "storied" in a dual sense: people ascribe meaning to experiences by telling them in certain stories, and the stories people have available to tell determine the range of interpretations they can ascribe to an experience.

White follows Foucault in suggesting that most people's stories draw on the dominant discourse. People have their stories set in place for them by a society that is structured through the availability of "tellable" stories. The social availability of preferred stories, and the assimilation of experience to these narratives, is how power works. The power of the dominant discourse is to include some stories as tellable and to exclude others as marginal and abnormal. All of us will find that some part of our experience cannot be told within acceptable stories—what White (following Erving Goffman) calls "unique outcomes." For any of us there are always gaps, inconsistencies, and contradictions between the story that arises, unavoidably and spontaneously, from our lived experience and what we know are socially acceptable narratives. Thus any of us lives between stories that can be told—that fit into the narratives of the dominant discourse—and stories that remain half articulated, more sensed than spoken, because the dominant discourse has no narrative for such experiences or for such interpretations of experiences.

People enter therapy when the gap becomes intolerable between the story they sense they are living and the story that the dominant discourse offers for giving meaning to their lives. White's idea here seems parallel to the sociologist Dorothy Smith's concept of a "line of fault" (1987), specifically, between the experience of women and the male-oriented narratives within which women are expected to interpret and tell their experience. Women's experiences that refuse to fit male narratives thus appear, from the perspective of those narratives, as what Rando calls "complicated." Traditional therapy then offers to reinterpret women's experiences to them, so that they do become tellable within male narratives, thus remedying the line of fault.

The personal problems that people bring to therapy, according to White, are, above all, problems of fit between their lived experience and the story that the dominant discourse imposes on these experiences. White's therapy seeks to "externalize" the story that the dominant discourse imposes, including the labeling of clients' problems as their own pathology. In a reversal of the conventional premise of psychopathology, the problem is no longer understood as emanating from within the client's psyche but rather as being external, in the social-cultural story that is being imposed on the client.

As White does therapy, the client's experience is not wrong; the story imposed on that experience is wrong. This story must be objectified as a social product or construct, held up as a thing to be examined and critiqued, so that the client can be separated from the totalizing, individualizing discourse that subjugates through normalizing judgments. Whereas most therapy derives its power from affirming these judgments as "diagnoses," White criticizes diagnoses as cultural productions that create and sustain relations of power: relationships between clients and their family, friends, and coworkers; relationships between client and therapist; and relationships between client and social institutions.

The therapeutic task is to open a discursive space in which clients can develop their own interpretive story—a story that affords meaning to their experiences—and to recognize how the dominant discourse works to deny this story. Thus the therapist becomes a partner in resistance, providing precisely the "consensual validation" that earlier functionalist students of the therapeutic, such as Talcott Parsons (1951), maintain that therapists are to avoid providing. Parsons understands therapy as the normalizing effort to bring deviation back within the dominant discourse; White understands therapy as nurturing resistance to the dominant discourse.

Therapy becomes a space within which suppressed meanings of experience can be performed. Such performances are deviant, and therapy is political—White claims no neutrality for his work. Unmasking power and giving voice to marginalized experience must go beyond resistance to transformation. As feminist theorist Nancy Hartsock argues:

> We need to . . . build an account of the world as seen from the margins, an account which can expose the falseness of the view from the top and can transform the margins as well as the center. The point is to develop an account of the world which treats our perspectives not as subjugated or disruptive knowledges, but as primary and constitutive of a different world.
>
> (1990:171)

Clients' symptoms or problems are first honored as a form of resistance to practices of power that are impoverishing their life. Rather than using therapy as a technology of the self, the therapist helps clients to recognize those technologies of the self in which they are already enmeshed: how are they being recruited to police their own life? How are those thoughts and behaviors labeled as "crazy" understandable as resistances to that policing? Through these questions both client and therapist are liberated from the self-evidence of the dominant discourse and its local politics. The client is then freed to create alternative stories, although, as we understand such therapeutic practice, any ideal of ever arriving at some final "authentic" story must remain suspect. The ideal, rather, is to learn to keep stories responsive to experience and to recognize for what they are those lines of fault that continue to emerge. Resistance is no end state where one can be; rather, it is a perpetual process of arrival.

Once a "symptom" or "problem" has been externalized as an imposition of the dominant discourse on the client's experience, a decision can be made about whether that particular strategy of resistance is the most useful and desirable. Some forms of resistance may be self-destructive; eating disorders, alcoholism, violence, drug abuse, and promiscuity are obvious examples. White recognizes that the therapist inescapably has certain values—physical self-preservation is a baseline for most of us—but says that therapists should not become the expert who claims some truth for clients and works to move clients toward that truth. For changes in clients' lives to be lasting, clients themselves must write a new story with a better fit to lived experience. The old story of the person-before-therapy who "had problems" is reinterpreted as an effect of the dominant discourse's exercising its power over the client's life. This story is part of an injustice that the therapist must join in naming for what it is and working against. Through this work the client develops a sense of personal agency.

What, then, is complicated mourning, if we interpolate from White's therapeutic model? Complicated mourning begins in a tension between the bereaved person's physical and emotional feelings and the social and cultural messages about how that person is supposed to feel. Time is supposed to heal, but what if the bereaved person feels worse over time? In therapy-as-resistance these feelings are understood as complicated but not in the sense of being reflections of the person's abnormality; rather, the complication is the line of fault between the person's feelings and the dominant discourse of grief.

If sociologists such as Bauman and Giddens are correct—that death does threaten a rational controlled world with the chaos of the uncontrollable—the objective of traditional therapy is to discipline grief in order to keep life safe from this chaos. Therapy-as-resistance accepts the chaos. Using the terms proposed by Frank (1995), the therapeutic objective is no longer restitution but acceptance of the legitimacy of chaos, while holding out the possibility of understanding mourning as an ongoing quest. "Chaos" is no longer the condition of being "totally disabled" by grief (Riches and Dawson 1996:14); rather, chaos is the necessary beginning of allowing oneself to experience the full magnitude of the loss that the person has suffered. The "quest" is no search for a "super-self" (14) but, rather, acceptance of lifelong processes of seeking to find the meaning of the deceased person in one's life while resisting the demand to relegate that death to the past and "get on with" a life that excludes the presence of the deceased.

Because self-help or support groups are a common recommendation by counselors to the bereaved, we should add a note about our ambivalence toward the role of such groups in therapy-as-resistance. We have observed the work of support groups in which members' comments to each other reproduce and reinforce what the dominant discourse demands, and we have seen them become places where those experiencing similar disempowerments can develop a consensual understanding of their social-cultural-political context and what this context does to them (Gorman 1993:250). Sometimes support groups police resistance, and other times they foster resistance. Just as Foucault teaches that the objective of the "carceral society" is to render the prison guard unnecessary as people become the agents of their own subjection, so the objective of a therapeutic society is to render the presence of the certified therapist unnecessary, as clients reassert for themselves the demands of the dominant discourse as the story that they each must live. On other occasions, when the guard is gone, people break free.

What might Foucault have said about White's work and the idea of therapy-as-resistance that we have presented? His first observation might be that the idea of how much anyone can rewrite his or her story must be qualified. Foucault is clear that any practices by which subjects reinvent themselves "are nevertheless not something that the individual invents by himself. They are patterns that he finds in his culture and which are proposed, suggested and imposed on him by his culture, his society and his social group" (1988c:11). However true this may be, it leaves considerable freedom regarding *which* patterns—which stories, in White's sense—the individual chooses. The point of therapy-as-resistance is not to invent a new story but to give the person the fullest choice among all potential stories, including those derived from Foucault himself, whose stories of resistance are now part of the common store from which people can choose.

A more serious issue is whether, within the Western tradition, anyone can ever define a strategy exterior to the obligation to truth. Does not resistance seek to tell the truth of the power relationships supported by the dominant discourse? And so long as we are playing any truth games, are we not caught in another technology of the self, seeking to produce better versions of ourselves and disciplining ourselves in this cause of truth? Is not the unmasking of "truth" only another level of seeking truth?

If resistance were solely a theoretical project, the search for a strategy outside truth games might be impossible, but the Foucauldian point, reasserted throughout his writing, is that his work—and our analysis here— seeks not to produce a theory but to show possibilities of practice. "The problem, you see, is one for the subject who acts—the subject of action through which the real is transformed" (Foucault 1991:84). Speaking of penal reform, Foucault leaves no doubt that any transformation that occurs "won't be because a plan of reform has found its way into the heads of the social workers" (82–85). Instead, transformation can come only from those who "have come into collision with each other and with themselves, run into dead-ends, problems and impossibilities, been through conflicts and confrontations." Transformation will occur only when "critique has been played out in the real, not when reformers have realized their ideas" (84–85). The point is not to achieve any theoretical resolution in academic essays such as this one, but discussions such as this can show directions of practice where resistance can be "played out in the real."

We want to emphasize here that, for Foucault, the "real" is not solely a social construction. Foucault asserts he does *not* say "that there is nothing there and that everything comes out of somebody's head" (1988c:17). He goes on to clarify this assertion, using his work on madness as an example:

> Some draw the conclusion that I said that nothing existed—I have been made to say that madness does not exist, although the problem was quite the contrary. It was a question of knowing how madness, under the various definitions that we could give it, could be at a certain moment, integrated in an institutional field which considered it a mental illness, occupying a certain place alongside other illnesses.
>
> *(1988c:17)*

Foucault is also clear that for all he sought to unmask truth games such as psychiatry, the connection of this practice to relationships of power "in no way impairs the scientific validity of the therapeutic efficacy of psychiatry" (1988c:16). This passage shows particularly clearly how different Foucault's interest was from that of the "antipsychiatry" movement of the 1960s, associated with such theorists as Thomas Szasz and R. D. Laing. For Foucault the issue is not to abolish or even delimit psychotherapeutic practice but to sever such practice from the self-evidence gained by its insinuation in claims to truth. And even on this point Foucault qualifies himself with a double negative that is worth untangling: "one can in no way say that the games of truth are nothing else than games of power" (1988c:16). To those who portray Foucault as a relativist, this statement is a good response. Games of power certainly are played out through truth claims, but not all games of truth are only games of power.

"There is always a possibility, in a given game of truth," Foucault says, "to discover something else and to more or less change such and such a rule and sometimes even the totality of the game of truth" (1988c:17). Elsewhere he is fairly specific about what such a change might sound like in therapy. Writing with reference to the pathologizing of homosexuality, Foucault describes how the dominant discourse can be turned into resistance: "But taking such discourses literally, and thereby turning them around, we see responses arising in the form of defiance: 'All right, we are the same as you, by nature sick or perverse, whichever you want. And so if we are, let us be so, and if you want to know what we are, we can tell you better than you can'" (1988a:115). And then referring to feminists' response of defiance to the pathologizing of women: "Are we sex by nature? Well then, let us be so but in its singularity, in its irreducible specificity. Let us draw the consequences and reinvent our own type of existence" (115). In the imagination of grief that this passage provides, the bereaved person might say, "Yes, my mourning is certainly 'complicated,' but let *my* voice speak these complications; do not assimilate them and trivialize them by your labels that say nothing of my experience. I live these complications in my body, while you only watch them. Let me be the expression of my own complications."'

How might a counselor respond to such speech? As we pursue this line of interpolation from Foucault, we imagine the therapist in two concurrent and overlapping roles. One is that of witness who is willing to hear and to see what the dominant discourse seeks to invalidate, to set apart, to silence. The other role is to remind the bereaved person—and these reminders will have to be repeated over considerable time and through many variations—that the dominant discourse demands *its* story, tied to its truth game and relationships of power, and that anyone who accepts these games as reality invites injury.

In the end the therapist must follow Foucault when he writes that he won't tell those who seek reform "what is to be done" or give them advice or instructions; such advice would only tie them down or immobilize them. Instead, Foucault's project is "precisely to bring it about that they 'no longer know what to do', so that the acts, gestures, discourses which up until then had seemed to go without saying become problematic, difficult, dangerous" (1991:84). Dominant discourses tell people what to do, and people who have been told then bring to therapy their chaos that what they are being told to do isn't right for them. The objective of counseling is not to make it right for them, as does traditional therapy in seeking ways to "reframe" social demands and thus assimilate its clients to these demands (Epstein 1994). The objective is to witness this chaos and accept it while showing the client how it works: how dominant discourse necessarily creates lines of fault, and how the client has had the strength of conviction not to assimilate her or his experience to the dominant discourse. When the client is thus placed outside dominant discourses and no longer knows "what is to be done," when any sense of "what is to be done" is understood as an external imposition that creates another line of fault, the person has reached that "true" position of strength and possibility that Foucault calls "no longer knowing what to do." That position is no more difficult and dangerous than life already is.

Foucault's Ethic

Foucault accepted his academic stardom, but he refused "to take a prophetic stance, that is, the one of saying to people: here is what you must do—and also: this is good and this is not" (1989:190). Here is the role he imagined for himself:

> For a rather long period, people have asked me to tell them what will happen and to give them a program for the future. We know very well that, even with the best intentions, those programs become a tool, an instrument of oppression. . . . My role . . . is to show people that they are much freer than they feel, that people accept as truth, as evidence, some themes which have been built up at a certain moment during history, and that this so-called evidence can be criticized and destroyed. To change something in the minds of people—that's the role of an intellectual.
>
> *(1988d:10)*

And, we would add, the role of a therapist as well.

People come to counselors asking what will happen and wanting a program for the future. The tougher therapists—Freud, Lacan, Laing, among others—resisted these demands, knowing that the person's problem was one of already having too many voices in her or his head saying what to do. Foucault's critiques ground such ethical practice. Clinicians must abandon their "old prophetic function" (Foucault 1988a:124), and because power can never disappear from the therapeutic relationship, the therapist must play the games of power "with a minimum of domination" (18).

The therapeutic role is to show people that they are much freer than they feel they are. The claims on their thoughts and behaviors that they have accepted as truth only represent what their social and cultural milieu demands from them, and these demands say more about that society's fantasies of what will destroy it than they say about the well-being of the individual. Our present historical moment has the fantasy that it will be destroyed if it accepts the reality of death. That fantasy demands the disciplining of grief, because uncontrolled mourning threatens to unmask the fantasy for what it is. Denial of death is society's fantasy, but it need not be any individual's story. The dominant discourse can be criticized and even destroyed. Therapy can change something in the minds of people and in the stories that give meaning to their experience.

NOTES

1. Throughout this chapter we use *therapy* as a generic term (see Epstein 1994) that includes any of the counseling practices carried out by clinical social workers.

2. For another application of Foucault, see Foote 1986 on an understanding of family law as a site of disciplinary power.

REFERENCES

Bauman, Zygmunt. 1992. *Mortality, immortality, and other life strategies.* Palo Alto, Calif.: Stanford University Press.

Bayer, Ronald. 1981. *Homosexuality and American psychiatry: The politics of diagnosis.* New York: Basic Books.

Camus, Albert. 1946. *The stranger.* Translated by Stuart Gilbert. New York: Vintage.

de Shazer, Steve. 1991. *Putting difference to work.* New York: Norton.

Doka, Kenneth J., ed. 1989. *Disenfranchised grief: Recognizing hidden sorrow.* Lexington, Mass.: Lexington Books.

Durkheim, Emile. 1965. *The elementary forms of the religious life.* Translated by Joseph Ward Swain. 1915. Reprint, New York: Free Press.

Epstein, Laura. 1994. The therapeutic idea in contemporary society. In Adrienne S. Chambon and Allan Irving, eds., *Essays on postmodernism and social work,* pp. 3–18. Toronto: Canadian Scholars' Press.

Fish, Vincent. 1993. Poststructuralism in family therapy: Interrogating the narrative/conversational mode. *Journal of Marital and Family Therapy* 19, no. 3 (July): 221–32.

Flaskas, Carmel and Catherine Humphreys. 1993. Theorizing about power: Intersecting the ideas of Foucault with the "problem" of power in family therapy. *Family Process* 32, no. 1 (March): 35–47.

Foote, Catherine E. 1986. *Toward a new understanding of the problem of spousal and child support after separation and divorce through Michel Foucault's analytics of power.* Publication series: Working Papers on Social Welfare in Canada. Toronto: University of Toronto Faculty of Social Work.

Foucault, Michel. 1973. *Madness and civilization: A history of insanity in the Age of Reason.* Translated by Richard Howard. New York: Vintage.

——. 1975. *The birth of the clinic: An archaeology of medical perception.* Translated by A. M. Sheridan Smith. New York: Vintage.

——. 1979. *Discipline and punish: The birth of the prison.* Translated by Alan Sheridan. New York: Vintage.

——. 1980. *An introduction,* vol. 1 of *The history of sexuality.* Translated by Robert Hurley. New York: Vintage.

——. 1988a. *Politics, philosophy, culture: Interviews and other writings, 1977–84.* Edited by Lawrence D. Kritzman. New York: Routledge.

——. 1988b. Technologies of the Self. In Luther H. Martin, Huck Gutman, and Patrick H. Hutton, eds., *Technologies of the self: A seminar with Michel Foucault,* pp. 16–49. Amherst: University of Massachusetts Press.

——. 1988c. The ethic of care for the self as a practice of freedom. In James Bernauer and David Rasmussen, eds., *The final Foucault,* pp. 1–20. Cambridge, Mass.: MIT Press.

———. 1988d. Truth, power, self: An interview with Michel Foucault. In Luther H. Martin, Huck Gutman, and Patrick H. Hutton, eds., *Technologies of the self: A seminar with Michel Foucault*, pp. 9–15. Amherst: University of Massachusetts Press.

———. 1989. *Foucault live (Interviews, 1966–84)*. Edited by Sylvère Lotringer and translated by John Johnston. New York: Semiotext(e).

———. 1991. *The Foucault effect: Studies in governmentality*. Edited by Graham Burchell, Colin Gordon, and Peter Miller. London: Harvester Wheatsheaf.

Frank, Arthur W. 1991. From sick role to health role: Deconstructing Parsons. In Roland Robertson and Bryan S. Turner, eds., *Talcott Parsons: Theorist of modernity*, pp. 205–16. London: Sage.

———. 1995. *The wounded storyteller: Body, illness, and ethics*. Chicago: University of Chicago Press.

Freidson, Eliot. 1988. *Profession of medicine: A study of the sociology of applied knowledge*. 2d ed. Chicago: University of Chicago Press.

Freud, Sigmund. 1984. Mourning and melancholia. In Angela Richards, ed., and James Strachey, trans., *On metapsychology: The theory of psychoanalysis*, pp. 245–68, vol. 11 of *The Pelican Freud library*. 1917. Reprint, Harmondsworth, Middlesex, U.K.: Penguin.

Frosh, Stephen. 1995. Postmodernism versus psychotherapy. *Journal of Family Therapy* 17, no. 2 (May): 175–90.

Giddens, Anthony. 1991. *Modernity and self-identity: Self and society in the late modern age*. Palo Alto, Calif.: Stanford University Press.

Goffman, Erving. 1972. *Relations in public: Microstudies of the public order*. New York: Harper Colophon.

Gorman, Jane. 1993. Postmodernism and the conduct of inquiry in social work. *Affilia* 8, no. 3 (Fall): 247–64.

Hare-Mustin, Rachel T. 1994. Discourses in the mirrored room: A postmodern analysis of therapy. *Family Process* 33, no. 1 (March): 19–35.

Hartsock, Nancy. 1990. Foucault on power: A theory for women? In Linda J. Nicholson, ed., *Feminism/Postmodernism*, pp. 157–75. New York: Routledge.

Hindmarsh, Jennie Harré. 1993. Alternative family therapy discourses: It is time to reflect (critically). *Journal of Feminist Family Therapy* 5 (2): 5–28.

Hochschild, Arlie Russell. 1983. *The managed heart: Commercialization of human feeling*. Berkeley: University of California Press.

Kastenbaum, Robert. 1993. Reconstructing death in postmodern society. *Omega* 27 (1): 75–89.

Kübler-Ross, Elisabeth. 1969. *On death and dying*. New York: Macmillan.

Laird, Joan. 1991. Enactments of power through ritual. *Journal of Feminist Family Therapy* 3 (1&2): 99–122.

Larner, Glenn. 1994. Paramodern family therapy: Deconstructing postmodernism. *Australian and New Zealand Journal of Family Therapy* 15, no. 1 (March): 11–16.

———. 1995. The real as illusion: Deconstructing power in family therapy. *Journal of Family Therapy* 17, no. 2 (May): 191–217.

Luepnitz, Deborah Anna. 1992. Nothing in common but their first names: The case of Foucault and White. *Journal of Family Therapy* 14, no. 3 (August): 281–84.

Lupton, Deborah. 1995. *The imperative of health: Public health and the regulated body.* London: Sage.

Madigan, Stephen Patrick. 1992. The application of Michel Foucault's philosophy in the problem externalizing discourse of Michael White. *Journal of Family Therapy* 14, no. 3 (August): 265–79.

Mellor, Philip A. 1993. Death in high modernity: The contemporary presence and absence of death. *Sociological Review* 41 (1): 11–30.

Morris, Meaghan and Paul Patton, eds. 1979. *Michel Foucault: Power, truth, strategy.* Sydney: Feral.

Paré, David A. 1995. Of families and other cultures: The shifting paradigm of family therapy. *Family Process* 34, no. 1 (March): 1–19.

Parry, Alan and Robert E. Doan. 1994. *Story revisions: Narrative therapy in the postmodern world.* New York: Guilford.

Parsons, Talcott. 1951. *The social system.* New York: Free Press.

Pocock, David. 1995. Searching for a better story: Harnessing modern and postmodern positions in family therapy. *Journal of Family Therapy* 17, no. 2 (May): 149–73.

Prior, Lindsay. 1989. *The social organization of death: Medical discourse and social practices in Belfast.* London: Macmillan.

Rabinow, Paul, ed. 1984. *The Foucault reader.* New York: Pantheon.

Rando, Therese A. 1984. *Grief, dying, and death: Clinical interventions for caregivers.* Champaign, Ill.: Research Press.

——. 1993. *Treatment of complicated mourning.* Champaign, Ill.: Research Press.

Raphael, Beverley. 1983. *The anatomy of bereavement.* New York: Basic.

Redekop, Fred. 1995. The "problem" of Michael White and Michel Foucault. *Journal of Marital and Family Therapy* 21, no. 3 (July): 309–18.

Riches, Gordon and Pamela Dawson. 1996. "An intimate loneliness": Evaluating the impact of a child's death on parental self-identity and marital relationships. *Journal of Family Therapy* 18, no. 1 (February): 1–22.

Smith, Dorothy E. 1987. *The everyday world as problematic: A feminist sociology.* Toronto: University of Toronto Press.

Weedon, Chris. 1987. *Feminist practice and poststructuralist theory.* Oxford: Basil Blackwell.

White, Michael. 1993. Deconstruction and therapy. In Stephen Gilligan and Reese Price, eds., *Therapeutic conversations*, pp. 22–61. New York: Norton.

White, Michael and David Epston. 1990. *Narrative means to therapeutic ends.* New York: Norton.

Wood, Andrew. 1991. Outside expert knowledge: An interview with Michael White. *Australian and New Zealand Journal of Family Therapy* 12, no. 4 (December): 207–14.

Worden, J. William. 1991. *Grief counseling and grief therapy: A handbook for the mental health practitioner.* 2d ed. New York: Springer.

CHAPTER 8

Resistance and Old Age: The Subject Behind the American Seniors' Movement

Frank T. Y. Wang

A critical question at stake in political discourse is the creation of a collective identity. In addressing the question "What shall we do?" the "we" is not a certainty but must be constantly negotiated. Whenever we engage in action and political discourse, we are engaging in the construction of our collective identity. The process of identity construction is never given once and for all, and is never unproblematic.

Although youth and productivity are constructed as "the essential self" of American culture, the image of old age is inevitably associated with dependency and uselessness as the Other. Old age is devalued, and older people have almost no substantial and meaningful role. The negative public image of the elderly has emerged as a norm, organizing all levels of social life for both the young as well as the old and pathologizing old age as a "social problem." However, the negative image of older people also provides a focal point of resistance for the American seniors' movement. As the aging population has been constructed as a "social problem" in need of public intervention, older Americans have played the role not of passive but of active participants, if not dominant players, in shaping, reformulating, and transforming the representation of the elderly in public discourse. The American seniors' movement illustrates the dialectic relationship between power and resistance, agent and structure, subject and object, that is embedded in constant and never-ending struggles portrayed in Foucault's model of power/subject/resistance (Foucault 1982). The aim of this chapter is to illuminate Foucault's notions of subject and resistance by drawing examples from the historical construction of the subject behind the American seniors' movement. By centering the subject in a web of power/resistance, Foucault proposes a dialectic relationship between power and resistance. Neither side has total control over the other. Individuals are neither as free in exercising their individual will as liberalism suggests, nor are their actions totally determined and constrained by their locations within the broader social relations as suggested in neo-Marxist structuralist thinking.

My analysis demonstrates how the identities and strategies of seniors' groups are shaped by the socioeconomic and political conditions in specific historical periods and how the resistance and struggles of these groups transformed the external structures, in turn giving rise to new seniors' groups and forms of existence. The purpose of this chapter is not to provide a comprehensive examination of the history of the seniors' movement or to present new historical evidence but to describe Foucault's notion of power and resistance through a reinterpretation of selected literature on the seniors' movement.

I have two rationales for choosing this topic. First, Foucault's concept of disciplinary power is well known and tends to be used in a way that reinforces the notion that the control of disciplinary power is total, which leads to a conclusion that escape is impossible and society can never be free from power and oppression (see, for example, Baar 1991; Hartsock 1990). What has been neglected is Foucault's notion of resistance and subjectivity, which is indispensable for fully understanding his model of the exercise of power: power is exercised through constructing individuals as subjects. Neglecting his notions of resistance and subjectivity inevitably leaves Foucault's critical project incomplete and distorted. The overemphasis on power and neglecting the subjectivity of Foucault's concepts of power tend to lead to the conclusion that disciplinary power produces social control. This reduces Foucault's approach to a simple functionalist and instrumentalist account of modern institutions. What has been overlooked are the productive and positive aspects of power that maximize the lives of people. Simplistic use of Foucault's notions of power denies us access to an appreciation of the local experiences and struggles of people around us and denies us chances to learn from Foucault so that we can explore new strategies for social changes.[1]

Second, Cohen (1985) identifies two paradigms of analysis of social movement, the strategy oriented and the identity oriented. The former focuses on the instrumental and strategic rationality of collective action and stresses objective variables such as organization, interests, resources, opportunities, and strategies to account for large-scale mobilization. The school of resource mobilization, which prevails in American studies of social movements, is representative of the strategy-oriented paradigm. Major studies of that analysis of the seniors' movement also follow the resource mobilization school (Coombs and Holladay 1995; Pratt 1976, 1993; Holtzman 1963; Williamson, Evans, and Powell 1982; Wallace and Williamson 1992). On the other hand, the identity-oriented paradigm seeks to understand subjective experiences of social movements, such as the origin and logic of group solidarity and their search for identity, autonomy, and recognition. Indeed, the formation of collective identity in a social movement is decisive for later interpretations of individual and collective interests and potential strategies for mobilizing the public. Though both types of analysis investigate the vital aspects of social movements, they tend to be mutually exclusive (Cohen 1985). Foucault's notion of subjectivity and power (1982), establishing a dialectic relationship and thus blurring the distinction between agent and structure, offers an alternative analytical framework that is sensitive to the complexity of their reflexive relationship and offers the possibility of closing the gap between the two different paradigms for the study of social movements.

Foucault's Concepts of Power, Subject, and Resistance

One of Foucault's major contributions is his placing of subjectivity in the center of power technology. Power has long been viewed as operating exclusively through the repression of an essential subjectivity. Crushing subjectivity has been assumed as necessary for power to operate. In contrast to orthodox interpretations of power, Foucault portrays a new form of power, which he suggests is also the most effective mechanism of power, operating in precisely the opposed direction, not by repressing subjectivity but by promoting, cultivating, and nurturing it (Miller 1987). Foucault describes the productive nature of power as follows: "What gives power its hold, what makes it accepted, is quite simply the fact that it does not simply weigh like a force which says no, but that it runs through, and it produces, things, it induces pleasure, it forms knowledge, it produces discourse; it must be considered as a productive network which runs through the entire social body much more than as a negative instance whose function is repression" (Foucault 1979:36).

In Foucault's view power functions best not by directly imposing force on people but by indirectly constituting the subjectivity of the individuals. Power can influence people's behavior because it shapes the ways people understand and interpret reality and knowledge. Power reaches its effect because it produces "truths" for people—not because it hides "the Truth" from people.

Power maximizes life because it provides subjectivities for people to assume in their daily lives instead of depriving people of their subjectivities. This new form of power is what Foucault called disciplinary power (1977), which is in contrast to coercive forms of power such as physical violence.

Foucault's model of power develops from his observation of an essential trait of Western societies since the nineteenth century, "that the force relationships which for a long time had found expression in war, in every form of warfare, gradually became invested in the order of political power" (1977:102). During conflict and antagonism the old form of power seeks to dominate the actions of the others through the use of force in the form of "war"; however, the new form of power actively influences the thought and choices available to others in the form of "politics." The old form of power is characterized by its use of force to achieve ultimate domination. The result is determined in that specific moment of confrontation: total subordination or being eliminated. The power relationship ends when the force is applied, the domination is attained, and possibilities of resistance are destroyed. The new form of power never achieves total domination. Power operates through constructing our subjectivities, shaping our identities, regulating our views of the world. This can be completed only when we actively assume the subjectivity that is offered through power relations. What power can do is induce us to participate. Power depends on our active participation in the discourse offered and regulated by it to maximize its effect and minimize alternative outcomes. The need for our engagement implies that power has a relational character. Our total or partial refusal to participate or to participate in a way that is not expected by power is a sign of resistance. Therefore, power is not something to be possessed; instead, it is a phenomenon that is exercised in social relations. Foucault uses the relational character of power to develop his notion of resistance and argues against the possibility of total control through power. He formulates the relationship between resistance and power as follows: "Where there is power, there is resistance, and yet . . . this resistance is never in a position of exteriority in relation to power. Should it be said that one is always 'inside' power, there is no 'escaping' it. . . . This would be to misunderstand the strictly relational character of power relationships" (Foucault 1978:95).

Foucault's model of power offers a critique of Enlightenment thinking. As we celebrate the progress of our civilization in dealing with conflict through democratic procedures of politics, instead of the violent confrontation of wars, Foucault warns us that power did not disappear; instead, it has become more subtle and delicate. In *Discipline and Punish* (1977) he deconstructs the notion that the modern prison is the rational and humanist solution to the barbaric system of punishment preceding it. Similarly, the institutionalization of modern democratic politics does not represent an equal distribution of political power but in fact a transformation of forms of power from the physical armed force of premodern wars to the disciplinary power of the modern state. The source of power no longer comes from the feudal king who claims sovereignty but from the capacity to represent the well-being of the whole society. This form of power does not take the form of war, a confrontation of absolute force. Instead, this form of power takes the form of politics, which seeks to maximize its effects and minimize alternative outcomes by inciting individuals to participate in its discourse. Foucault's work thus is interested in how individuals are constructed as subjects. The subject, not power, is the center of Foucault's project (Foucault 1982). The object of his works on punishment, madness, medicine, and sexuality, then, is to create a history of the different modes by which human beings are made subjects.

Contrary to the portrayal of the free subject in liberal thinking, the human subject is not a given but is constituted through discursive practices. A regulated subjectivity always emerges from the daily social practices that have produced individuals as subjects. To understand how power operates, it is necessary to understand Foucault's conception of discourse and discursive formation. Foucault views discourses as media of power relations. Only through discourses can we understand who we are and what is real. All discourses are partial and selective representations. Power operates through discourses because of their partial representation of all. Some are included exactly because others are excluded, and some are normalized because others are marginalized in a discourse. Foucault emphasizes the social aspect of discourse by asking that we "not treat[ing] discourse as groups of signs (signifying elements referring to contents or representations) but as practices that systematically form the objects of which they speak" (Foucault 1977:49). He sees discourse as a practice embedded in social relations rather than as groups of statements circulating in our daily language. Power is everywhere—dispersed and tolerable because it is hidden—and operates through our daily use of language in our every social encounter.

Because one relation involves two parties, a reverse relation is always possible. Discourse works in two directions. "Discourse transmits and produces power; it reinforces it, but also undermines and exposes it, renders it fragile and makes it possible to thwart it" (Foucault 1978:101). His work on sexuality illustrates the double-sided effect of discourse. He constitutes homosexuality as a subject for understanding in the discourse of sexuality, but Foucault also sees that homosexuality provides a subject, the homosexual, so that homosexual people struggle to find their voices, to speak for themselves. The birth of the seniors' movement provides another example.

The Elderly as the Dependent and Frail

If we use Foucault's notion of power and subject to understand the issue of old age, we begin to ask questions about how elderly people are represented, how public discourse shapes our understanding of being old, and how the process of aging is understood—that is, the evolution of discourses about old age. Old age, then, is a dynamic concept shaped and reshaped over time by competing and often contradictory claims, not a static definition with a fixed interpretation. The category of old age and the elderly becomes a political field, open for competing claims by various social actors. Becoming old is no longer an individual biological phenomenon. Rather, old age is culturally and socially given. The aging experiences of the elderly are a product of social interactions.

Though social historians have no consensus on when the social status of the elderly began to fall or whether it did indeed fall, they do agree that at the beginning of the twentieth century, old age was increasingly stigmatized and the elderly were negatively viewed and represented, a result of changing values that emphasized achievement rather than traditional authority (Fischer 1977). The rise of the capitalist economy provided the context for a reinterpretation of old age. The elderly were devalued because their diminishing physical strength meant labor that was less profitable for capitalism. Retirement became the key market mechanism that ensured a constant supply of fresh and young labor for the market. In an environment in which occupation is the overriding determinant of status, the often involuntary exclusion of the elderly from the labor market produced in them a sense of marginality (Pratt 1976:82). Retirement became the social institution that produced the meaning of old age as lack of economic security and loss of social status. In the context of an increasingly established and expanding capitalist economy, old age began to be understood as a social problem (Conrad 1992). Although the negative discourse on old age permeated the views of the public and formed the core of various forms of ageism (Butler 1975), it also made old age an object to be discussed and a subject for the elderly themselves to address and redefine (see table 8.1). The presence of this negative public discourse on old age gave birth to the American seniors' movement.[3]

Multiple Functions of the Negative Discourse on Old Age

Power produces discourses, and discourses are both enabling and constraining. As Foucault describes the multiple functions of discourses in the exercise of power, "discourses are tactical elements or blocks operating in the field of force relations; there can exist different and even contradictory discourses within the same strategy" (Foucault 1978:101–102). Similarly, the same discourse can also exist through different strategies. Responding to the negative discourse of old age as frail and dependent, the California Institute of Social Welfare (CISW) and the Townsend group in the first-generation seniors' movement of the Great Depression developed two different strategies for improving the economic security of the elderly.

CISW, led by George McLain, represented a group that confessed to the negative image of old age by acknowledging their frailness and dependency in order to win support for higher levels of public assistance.[4] McLain, the host of a radio show, used his program to organize CISW; he was a younger man who said he would take care of his older supporters. As their "Uncle George," McLain sent members inspiration, counsel, and reports of his efforts during his daily show and in a monthly newspaper. In return, the members sent money to finance the office, radio shows, and lobbying (Keith 1982). CISW's greatest success, an action that conformed to the public image of the dependent elderly, was getting initiative proposals on the California ballot for more public assistance for the elderly and fewer humiliating bureaucratic hurdles to get the money (Keith, 1982).

Although Dr. Francis Townsend, a physician and social reformer, accepted the view that the elderly were dependent, he reinterpreted old age with positive meaning; Keith would say Townsend emphasized old age. Townsend, a contemporary of McLain's, proposed to give every old person $200 a month, which had to be spent within that month, thereby stimulating production, providing jobs, and leading the recovery of the economy. He not only emphasized the legitimacy of the elderly as recipients of assistance but also claimed that pensions would help end the depression by boosting the demand for goods and services (Townsend 1943). More than just a pension proposal, the plan aimed to end the depression by giving buying power to the elderly. In response to the dependent and nonproductive image of the elderly, Townsend prescribed a positive role for them as saviors of the economy for American society. Support for Townsend became loud and strong. The Townsend movement mushroomed into a mass crusade with a dues-paying membership in the hundreds of thousands. Arthur Schlesinger Jr.

TABLE 8.1 Stages of American Seniors' Movement

Stage	Period	Representative Groups	Group Leader	Organization Structure	Group Identity and Appeals
Rise and fall of the first-generation seniors' movement	1930s (Great Depression) and 1940s	California Institute of Social Welfare	George McLain (a middle-aged radio show host)	Charismatic leader	Confesses to the negative image of old age in order to win support for higher level of public assistance.
		Townsend movement	Francis Townsend (a skillful public speaker and writer)	Charismatic leaders	Emphasizes old age and reinterprets it with positive meaning. Claims that the pensions would help end the depression by boosting the demand for goods and services.
Rise of the second-generation seniors' movement	1950s and 1960s	American Association of Retired People (AARP)	Ethel Percy Andrus (a retired school principal)	Started with Charismatic leader and moved to grassroots organization.	Replaces the negative image of old age as dependent and frail with the image of retired worker as independent and self-sufficient.
		National Council of Senior Citizens (NCSC)	Aime Forand (a retired member of Congress)	"Created by organized labor with an activist, partisan political orientation"	Emphasizes old age as a basis for rights claiming.
Growth and institutionalization of the second-generation seniors' movement	1970s and 1980s	Gray Panthers	Maggie Kuhn (an activist associated with church)	Started with charismatic leader and moved to grassroots organization	Emphasizes common discrimination toward the young and the old from those powerful middle-agers and emphasizes radical social change and excludes group from incrementalist politics.

		AARP	Attracted massive participation and became the largest seniors' group	Emphasizes old age and increased its lobbying and influence in politics with a stress on a more positive image for the old.
		NCSC	Remained the second-largest seniors group	Emphasizes old age and lobbies for issues of specific material benefit to the elderly.
The established seniors' movement under attack	1980s and 1990s Welfare state crisis	AARP	Remains the largest seniors' group with grassroots network	Emphasizes old age but is forced to defend itself against the image of "wealthy and greedy pensioners draining the young taxpayers through their voting power." Coping strategy has been protecting its past gains.

called the Townsend movement "the most striking political phenomenon of 1935" (cited in Pratt 1976:24).

However, each discourse is simultaneously enabling and limiting. It is enabling because discourses grant human beings new subjectivity in each specific discursive practice; it is limiting because at the same time discourses turn human beings into objects constrained by the logic and norms associated with each discourse. The breakdown of the first-generation seniors' groups offers an illustration. The elderly people who participated in CISW accepted the negative image of old age in order to establish their deserving status, which in turn set up limits for the growth of CISW. In 1948, when CISW demanded that California's first state welfare director be a CISW trustee, business groups and newspapers were outraged. If old people were so dependent and needy, the illogic of their acquiring power led to the conclusion that their leader was power hungry. McLain was soon labeled as using the elderly for his own gains. The public called for protecting the elderly against George McLain and discredited CISW (Keith 1982). In other words, CISW crossed the boundary it had set up for itself when it assumed a subjectivity as a group of frail and dependent elderly people.

Similarly, Townsend redefined old age and transformed the needy and dependent elderly into the solution to the depression. The Townsend movement reached its limits when the Townsend Plan was replaced by the Social Security Act (SSA) in 1935. The one-man office of the Townsend movement did not live up to its positive image of old age. The movement was so identified with Townsend in name, origin, ownership, and control that its adherents became virtually synonymous with him (Holtzman 1963:203). The organization's structure did not reflect its belief in the positive role of the elderly person. Scholars later identified its lack of a grassroots structure to encourage its members' participation as a major reason for the failure of the Townsend movement (Pratt 1993; Holtzman 1963). One month after the U.S. House of Representatives defeated the Townsend Plan bill sponsored by John S. McGroarty (D-Calif.), it approved a congressional investigation of Townsend. When the top-down nature of the Townsend movement was clearly exposed, it was not difficult to attribute the old people's unbecoming demands to their leader. The public discourse—that the founder and cofounder of the movement had benefited financially from it—undermined faith and confidence in the whole movement.

The negative discourse of the elderly as dependent and frail has been the major reason that the seniors' movement has gained public support for its claims, and some gerontologists see it as the primary source of legitimacy for the seniors' movement, distinguishing it from other social movements (Wallace and Williamson 1992). While the seniors' movement draws public support through adopting the negative discourse on old age, it is also regulated by the logic associated with that discourse. When other social movements tend to disrupt the normal functioning of social institutions through actions such as work strikes to create pressure, the seniors' movement is notable for its generally nondisruptive tactics (Wallace and Williamson 1992). The latter reflect not only the elderly's lack of effective means to threaten key functions of society but also that the negative discourse on old age prevents the seniors' movement from using militant approaches—the public expects the elderly to assume an inferior status instead of a powerful one, and a powerful one would undermine the legitimacy of the claims for assistance by the seniors' movement.

Although it is true that Foucault emphasizes the analysis of discursive practices as a major mechanism of power, he also emphasizes the analysis of nondiscursive practices, the conditions that make the shifts of discursive practices possible. What, then, were the conditions that made the seniors' movement possible in the 1930s? As Keith points out, it was the depression-born desperation "guaranteeing almost any messiah at least a temporary audience" (1982:96). The large number of poor elderly during the depression helped solidify the view that their poverty was not their fault and provided a fertile ground for the first-generation seniors' movement. The issue of the old poor came to public attention because the dramatic economic recession meant that large numbers of the elderly were facing immediate and personal danger (Holtzman 1963). Under those circumstances Townsend's radical plan of providing a universal pension to all elderly people was intelligible and made possible the positive role of the elderly as saviors of American society.

Passage of the SSA in 1935 made the Townsend Plan moot and eventually resulted in the failure of the Townsend movement (Holtzman 1963). The demise of the Townsend movement had important effects on the way discourse developed in the seniors' movement. The Social Security program has become an important social institution for old age by producing an increasing number of pensioners and bringing retirement into the everyday experiences of the American elderly. Through the implementation of the old age pension program emerged a new subjectivity, pensioner, which laid the basis for the second-generation seniors' movement. The unwavering essential that the Townsend Plan put forward for public debate was that old age should be defined as an age category with rights to income and a right to participate in social change. The legislation accepted the former part of the message by using age as the borderline between work and retirement but rejected the notion of age as the sole basis for claiming rights. The subject constructed and signaled by the legislation is a retired worker, mostly male, with a long history of involvement in the paid labor market.

The SSA excludes women's unpaid caring work at home because their labor does not earn them economic security for their old age. The gendered nature of SSA, which forms the backbone of American social welfare, is well explored by feminists. Fraser (1989) describes the American welfare state as a two-tiered system constructed along gender lines with social insurance for male workers and public assistance for female dependents. With the establishment of Social Security, inequalities in the labor market, such as levels of payment and length of labor participation—which themselves are the results of the social positioning of gender, race, and class—were translated into an universal measurement, the level of pension. The role of Social Security, which becomes increasingly indispensable in the lives of contemporary American elderly, reinforces the value of work and the inequalities inherent in the labor market, thus continuing to penetrate individuals' lives in old age.

Older Person as Retired Worker: An Alternative Subject

It was, then, no coincidence that the major groups of the second-generation seniors' movement in the 1950s organized themselves around their experiences as retired workers. They sought to transform the public discourse of old age, not through confessing or emphasizing old age as in the 1930s but through erasing it. The names of the emerging seniors' groups, such as the National Association of Retired Civil Employees (NARCE) and the National Retired Teachers Association (NRTA), announced a cautious new beginning, where age was not even allowed to stand alone as a principle of recruitment (Keith 1982:100).

This shift of discourse on old age was possible because of the establishment of the Social Security program, a result of the seniors' movement in the 1930s. This shift of group identity from older person to retired worker illustrates the reflexive relation of power and resistance as well as agent and structure. The seniors' movement in the 1930s struggled for public provision of income security to elderly people and gave birth to the Social Security Act. The result of their resistance later provided the conditions for the subsequent seniors' movement to grow. With the increasing number of pension-ers, the seniors' movement in the 1950s gained its momentum around the newly emerging social identity of retired workers.

Similarly, although the Townsend Plan failed, the Townsend movement paved the way for the second-generation seniors' movement to emphasize old age as positive. "The Townsend movement fashioned a self-conscious-ness among many of the elderly and proved that the mobilization of the elderly population is possible, which prepared American society to include the elderly into a part of its pluralist politics" (Holtzman 1963:208). The rad-icalism represented by the Townsend movement may have made the more moderate approaches adopted by the emerging seniors' groups, such as the American Association of Retired Persons (AARP), National Council of Seniors Citizens (NCSC), or even the Gray Panthers (the most vocal group in the American seniors' movement), more acceptable by contrast.

The birth of NRTA, which later expanded and became the AARP, demonstrates the characteristics of the emergent seniors' groups. Its founder, Ethel Percy Andrus, was a retired principal who was angered by the low level of pensions received by retired teachers and, through forming a national mass organization, sought legislative changes to improve retirement income. Andrus had a dual purpose in mind when she established NRTA: on the one hand, she recognized the greatest fear of retirees among the elderly was ill-ness or accident; on the other hand, she aimed to establish "a new way of feeling about themselves [the elderly], a new role to play in the society they had helped build, a new framework in which they could find ways to help themselves and each other" (cited in Pratt 1976:51). Unlike the California Institute of Social Welfare or the Townsend movement, NRTA not only responded to the material needs of its members but also aimed to provide a new and positive definition of old age through a mutual help approach among the elderly. Their identity as retired workers was designed to erase the image of old person as dependent and frail and to challenge the contempo-rary cultural production of identity in old age. The determination to chal-lenge the representation of old age led AARP into the struggle for identity and transformed the American seniors' movement into what Cohen (1985) calls "new social movements," which are characterized by their targeting of cultural practices of identity, instead of public policies, and their focus on civil society instead of the state or economy. The search for one's own claim to identity directly questions current practices of knowledge formation and challenges the privileges of knowledge, in which Foucault sees claims to truth as the center of modern disciplinary power. The politics of identity is one of the major characteristics of contemporary struggles against domination. The seniors' movement is no exception.

The subject cannot exist in abstract thinking but must be embodied in practices. The vision of an independent old age became real when Andrus persuaded a private insurance company to provide NRTA members a non-cancelable and inexpensive group health insurance plan with monthly payments and no physical examination, which no other company offered an elderly person in 1955. The retired teachers found that by assuming the role of "retired" instead of "old" as a group identity, they could get what they wanted from society. The retired worker provided an alternative subject that allowed the elderly to communicate to the wider society that self-sufficiency in old age was possible.[5]

It is worth noting that, although women's issues were not the focus of NRTA, the establishment of NRTA can be seen as women's collective resistance against the penetration of gender discrimination in the labor market into their old age. Given that teaching is one of the marginalized and female-dominated occupations, it was through the collective experience of marginalization as teachers that the founder of NRTA was able to establish the subject for group solidarity. In other words, the women's experiences of being marginalized in the labor market became the basis for initiation of the NRTA in 1947. When Andrus was angry at her first pension check, her immediate reaction was to find an effective counterposition. As a middle-class and well-educated professional, she knew mass organization was the only strategy available for gaining a voice in American pluralist politics; she also was aware of the stigmatized image of the elderly and the highly valued independence symbolized by the image of worker. The unavailability of feminist discourse as an effective counterdiscourse in her struggle might have framed her strategy. The key is not her understanding of the issue as a women's issue but the discourses available to her in her efforts to communicate with outsiders. Her choice of subjectivity was limited by the structures, such as pluralist politics, the capitalist economy, and the work-achievement–oriented welfare state in which she was located. Foucault notes that "the aim of struggles is the power effects as such" and people "do not look for the 'chief enemy,' but for the immediate enemy" (Foucault 1982:211). For Andrus the "immediate enemy" was the low level of pension for retired teachers, not the gendered nature of the labor market, though the "chief enemy" might be the patriarchal relations in the labor market. Exactly because existing studies fail to explore the relationship between women and the development of the seniors' movement, which renders women invisible in the American seniors' movement, further studies are needed to reconstruct the history of the seniors' movement from the women's viewpoint in order to make women a subject in our understanding.

The development of seniors' groups like NRTA/AARP has laid the foundations for another, far more successful round of militant seniors' groups. A group that tries to erase old age by identifying its members as workers tends to make old age more visible (Keith 1982:102). The successful testimony of AARP in demonstrating that old age could be a rewarding segment of life affected not only outsiders' views of old age but transformed insiders' attitudes toward old age from erasing old age to recognizing it. This unexpected development built a good foundation for a type of association that emphasizes the common identity, old age. Once again, militant old people emerged as leaders, but this time they were backed up by participatory organizations addressing a wider society apparently more ready to accept the old as activists (102).

The Politicization of Seniors' Groups

The 1970s and 1980s were a period of stability for the seniors' groups that eventually led them to achieve a higher political status in influencing public policies. A major characteristic of this stage was that seniors' groups demanded a positive recognition of old age by society, which resulted in the politicization of existing seniors' groups and the emergence of militant seniors' groups. A crucial factor was the massive number of American elderly participating in the seniors' groups. The establishment of the Social Security program significantly reduced the poverty rate among the elderly and provided stable income security for retired people in their old age. The 1950 Social Security Act amendments dramatically expanded its clientele base, increasing its coverage from 60 percent to 80 percent of all workers (Pratt 1993:81). Most of all, the expansion in coverage led to a pronounced shift toward the middle class in the clientele base of Old Age Security Insurance by recruiting self-employed business and professional people and state and local government employees. Pratt notes that "the 1950 amendments enlarged significantly the ranks of the more easily mobilized elderly, thereby indirectly enhancing the potential for successful organizing efforts" among the American elderly (82). This new class of well-educated, high social status, and wealthy elderly people were the major participants in the seniors' groups.

The Gray Panthers are the most vocal of the senior groups that empha-size old age. They first gained attention in 1970 by picketing with banners and signs to protest abuses in nursing homes (Pratt 1979). However, what these militant seniors emphasize is not the distinction between the old and the young but common discrimination against both groups from those pow-erful middle-agers. When Maggie Kuhn, the founder of the Gray Panthers, started the group of about one hundred people with such a militant name, she worked to make it intergenerational in focus and membership while retaining its character as a seniors' movement organization (Wallace and Williamson 1992). Its early organizational ethos incorporated much of the spirit and organizational thinking embraced by the social movements of the 1960s. The Gray Panthers emphasized its grassroots character and the need to foster networks of autonomous local affiliates. It viewed existing federal programs for the aged as destructive of seniors' dignity and self-respect and as a way to legitimize the oppression of elderly people. The Panthers empha-size radical social change and exclude themselves from the incrementalist politics embraced by most mainstream seniors' groups, such as AARP and NCSC. Panthers demonstrate, picket, and lobby for better health care for the elderly; fairer representation of old people by the media; adequate hous-ing through rent control and regulation of condominium conversion; and abolishment of mandatory retirement (Keith 1982:104). Kuhn differed from the leaders of the 1930s by appealing more to the general social conditions of the elderly than by proposing a specific popular program, which led Bin-stock to comment that the Panthers were "the only organization working to solve the problems of human beings rather than those of the profession and the industry" (1974, cited in Powell, Branco, and Williamson 1996:137).

On the other hand, AARP continues to grow. With an increasingly bureaucratic administrative system and steady revenues from selling mem-bers all kinds of services, such as insurance, travel, and drugs, the seniors' groups such as AARP became powerful grassroots organizations with large memberships with high status and sophisticated organization (Pratt 1976). By the 1970s the seniors' movement was ready to secure a voice for itself in American pluralist politics. The persona the seniors assumed was no longer purely that of retired workers but mixed that identity with that of elderly people. With increasing recognition of old age as a positive experience, the seniors' groups were ready to demand to be treated in distinctive ways based on old age and have a positive and permanent place in society.

Changes within AARP itself illustrated this shift. AARP conducted no government lobbying until 1967 because Ethel Percy Andrus was committed to free-enterprise solutions to social problems. Its determination to provide an alternative and positive conception of old age focused on the social domain of civil society, not the economy or state. However, AARP began to increase its lobbying and building linkages with government agencies and legislators in the 1970s. The shift began with its lobbying for the passage of a resolution declaring mandatory retirement to be in violation of rights guaranteed under the U.S. Constitution. Yet, compared with other seniors' groups, AARP was still a moderate association that made no effort to change the structure of society. AARP attracted mostly middle-class and professional retirees, and the services to its membership were still the mainstay of its recruiting and financial base. Much of its lobbying and provision of information to decision makers continued to stress a more positive image for the old rather than specific material benefits.

As the second-generation seniors' movement found its political entree through its members' status as retired workers instead of elderly people, seniors' groups tended to mass along occupational lines. While AARP attracts mostly middle- and upper-class people and professionals, the National Council of Senior Citizens (NCSC) is a working-class seniors' group with a strong association with the union movement. Although its easy membership terms have helped AARP grow—it now has more than 28 million members and is the largest seniors' group—NCSC is the second largest with 4.5 million members. The differences between AARP and NCSC are significant and reflect the social classes of their membership. If the goal of AARP is individual uplift and social betterment, NCSC tends to orient itself to the political goals of changing social structure and modes of resource allocation (Pratt 1976:89). AARP pays more attention to member services, whereas NCSC focuses its resources on lobbying. Furthermore, the focus of NCSC's lobbying is more practical than symbolic, with particular stress on improved income levels. NCSC is also consistently more willing than AARP to demand deeper social changes to provide more financial security for old people.

Leaders of seniors' groups have managed to gain greater levels of generalized acceptance in Washington, because their constituents have a well-documented basis for making claims on society and because the leaders have learned to present their case in a manner that appeals to politicians (Pratt 1976:198). The seniors' movement has gained adherents largely because millions of aging people have come to identify with its objectives. Politicians at all levels are increasingly aware of elderly voters as an electoral constituency and actively seek to support issues of aging. Legislators and administrative personnel cite seniors' interest groups as important sources of information for decision making. Groups like AARP and NCSC testify regularly before Congress (Pratt 1983). Coombs and Holladay (1995) contend that the American seniors' groups have the power to routinely use all channels of access to influence policy making. These established seniors' groups have become part of the decision-making process in federal government, which Pratt calls an "old-age policy system" (1976:208) with a triangular alliance—officials in the executive branch, leaders in Congress, and leaders of major seniors' groups— that is a major actor at all stages of policy making in regard to old age.

Intergenerational Conflict

The seniors' movement had dramatic success in achieving recognition that old age is and should be a positive and permanent category in the population and on the political scene. In the 1980s this success led to an era of intergenerational conflict and placed the seniors' movement in a position to protect rather than to seek expansion of its status. Although the American elderly have not yet reached a privileged status, their great gains in financial support, symbolic recognition, and political access to decision making are now being portrayed as threatening to its members who are not old.

The persistent image of a physically frail and dependent elderly person in need of assistance has been significantly altered by debates in which intergenerational conflict figure strongly. Younger generations now see the elderly as a rapidly growing population of greedy, relatively affluent people whose voting power means that their collective dependence is straining the economy while sustaining their self-interest and sacrificing the young (Coombs and Holladay 1995; Katz 1992). The intergenerational conflict tends to frame policy issues in terms of older generations versus younger generations (Walker 1990; Quadagno 1989; Johnson 1995). Moreover, this backlash is intensified by the portrayal of the elderly as an all-powerful political machine that will engage in bloc voting to defeat any threat to its benefits (Wallace Williamson 1992). As a result, the long-standing public view of elderly people as a deprived and especially deserving group has begun to erode and be replaced with fiscal concern (Estes 1989). As a leading British gerontologist, Allan Walker, points out, "A significant shift has begun to occur in the long-standing consensus about the deprived status of elderly persons, and, to some extent, about their position as the most deserving minority groups" (1986:194).

The media tend to exaggerate the power of senior citizens. Although the seniors' groups establish their political influence through their huge membership, their effectiveness is reduced by the diversity of the elderly population. The dramatic increase in the number of seniors' groups has weakened their influence because of competition and discord among them (Pratt 1993). However, media misrepresentations of senior power contribute to fears about the strength of the "gray vote" and to debates related to issues of intergenerational equity. For example, beginning in the mid-1970s, the neoconservatives vividly recast the elderly in the mass media as "greedy geezers" and "savage grannies" whose powerful "geriatric juggernaut" in Washington shamelessly protected their gains at the expense of the needs of the rest of American society, especially children. The classic expression of this redefined image appeared on the March 28, 1988, cover of the *New Republic,* which depicts approaching hordes of sinister-looking "greedy geezers," armed with golf clubs, bearing down on the reader. The titles of articles in *Forbes* magazine, such as "The Monster That's Eating Our Future" in 1981 and "Can We Afford Them?" in 1980, demonstrate the shifting image of elders as the cause of the social security crisis.[6]

Again, we see the tactical use of discourses in different strategies. The intergenerational conflict is partly the result of the positive image of the elderly at a time when generations are competing for limited public resources. This image is behind both the mutual help approach adopted by AARP and the intergenerational debate. The latter is possible only because of the success of the seniors' groups in the 1970s and 1980s. The debate also draws on the socially constructed reality of an era of fiscal constraint, which has haunted social policy debates in Western countries since the 1980s. Thus the rise of intergenerational conflict should be understood as part of the "welfare state crisis" (Mishra 1984) and the retreat of the state in the social provision of welfare launched by neoconservatives who came into power in the 1980s. As various writers have suggested (Walker 1990; Quadagno 1989; Johnson 1995), the idea of intergenerational conflict is socially constructed by the media, politicians, and economists to divert attention from demands for government responsibility and universal entitlement programs. The rhetoric of intergenerational conflict legitimates antiwelfare state policies and faults the family for failing to take responsibility for their elders. By framing aging issues as a conflict between the young and the old, the role of the state disappears, and the once public responsibility of social care for the elderly is reprivatized. Despite the negative portrayal of the elderly as "greedy geezers," opinion polls seem to suggest that the elderly are perceived as deserving of continued public support (Gilliland and Havir 1990; Coombs and Holladay 1995). Although intergenerational conflict has not marginalized the needs of the elderly, lawmakers may no longer assume the needs and legitimacy of the elderly, or, at a minimum, their needs may become secondary to budgetary concerns (Estes 1989).

Within this process of defending its past achievements the class-based nature of the American seniors' movement becomes clear. While working-, middle-, and upper-class elderly find ways to represent their interests through AARP and NCSC, the more disadvantaged elderly, such as the poor, women, and minority elderly, are still underrepresented politically. Although the major age-based groups have a firm presence in public policy, they have not chosen to pursue policy objectives that would address the most fundamental problems confronting much of the older population. Rather, the groups have worked out mutual understandings and managed to arrive at "a fairly stable pattern of reward distribution and accommodation" (Hudson and Binstock 1976:386). These seniors' groups fail to address the economic and social conditions of the severely disadvantaged aged.

In the era of fiscal constraint the American seniors' movement has reached its limits. The elderly are split into different sectors and are forced to pit themselves against each other. With the older population growing, representation by the American seniors' movement becomes increasingly difficult. The battle over the Medicare Catastrophic Coverage Act of 1988 illustrates how the elderly's interests are divided along advantaged-disadvantaged lines. The legislation represented the largest expansion of Medicare since the program was established in 1965 and was designed to protect beneficiaries from having their life saving wiped out by huge medical bills. After seniors paid a modest annual deductible, Medicare would cover all their remaining hospital costs. However, because Congress set aside no public revenue for implementing the act, the funding of expanded benefits had to come from the beneficiaries themselves, which meant the wealthy elderly would pay a larger share. Because the act would have benefited an estimated thirty-three million elderly and disabled Americans, AARP was a strong early supporter of the legislation. However, after the act was passed, the advantaged elderly organized and fought against it and finally got it repealed because they did not perceive that they needed the coverage (Coombs and Holladay 1995:329).

While we see that the elderly are active agents in resisting the effects of the negative image of old age by constructing counterdiscourses, we also see how the structure constrains their freedom of choice in their formation of group identity. It was no coincidence that the first-generation seniors' groups all emphasized the lifelong hard work done by the poor elderly, and most second-generation seniors' groups were formed around their identity as retired workers. Work, which means paid employment exclusively, is so deeply cultivated into our ways of evaluating others as well as ourselves that the elderly saw it as the only viable way to defend their deserving status. As soon as the second-generation seniors' movement was constructed as a movement of retired workers, the factor that split the elderly according to their access to paid employment opportunities became encoded in the fate of the seniors' movement. Each discourse is simultaneously enabling and limiting. The elderly with less access to paid employment were excluded from the seniors' movement as soon as the seniors' movement assumed the subject of retired worker. The dilemma is that to form a politics of aging, the subject must be defined, and that very definition inevitably excludes someone. Under Schattschneider's definition of political organization as the mobilization of bias (1960), the naive assumption of a universal political project dies because no subject is all inclusive. There is no single Truth but multiple partial truths. Instead of searching for a universal political project to free all, Schattschneider proposes a series of never-ending specific struggles to replace the universal one-time struggle.

Universal Versus Specific Struggles

The tendency to pursue one's own interests leads gerontologists to debate whether seniors' groups should be seen as interest groups or as a social movement (Hudson and Binstock 1976). Behind this debate is the wish that we tend to hold for participants of a social movement: that people will not organize in pursuit of their self-interest. Because of that wish we tend to search for a pure identity based upon old age, which would form a universal identity to unite all the elderly, serve to transcend the self-interest motive of the participants, and inform the seniors' movement on behalf of the elderly as a whole. But the fact is that old people, like everyone else, are shaped by individual experience, social location, and cultural background; they have many social identities, each of which may gain priority for political action at various times; and these identities, such as age, gender, ethnicity, and occupation, are likely to become sources for constructing group identity by various recruitment patterns of formal associations.

In sharp contrast to the Marxist approach of seeking a universal strategy of revolution through collective action by the oppressed, Foucault rejects the possibility of universal transformation; instead, he urges us to explore multiple sites of struggles in their local and historical locations. "Their (power) existence depends on a multiplicity of points of resistance. These points of resistance are present everywhere in the power network. Hence there is no single locus of great Refusal. . . . Instead there is a plurality of resistance, each of them a special case" (1978:95). Although the seniors' movement fails to act toward transforming the fundamental social structure and promoting the well-being of the elderly as a whole at a time of fiscal constraint, we have witnessed the seniors' movement's successful transformation of the negative discourse on aging through assuming the identity of workers and providing the possibility for political participation for the elderly. Yet at the same time the movement is constrained and split because the worker identity excludes nonworker elderly and is vulnerable to the various hierarchical division of occupations. Instead of viewing the seniors' movement as the only and one-time struggle, we should see it as a constant and never-ending struggle in which what has been established as a counterdiscourse in this round usually becomes the central discourse of the next round.

Embedded Resistance: Suicide of Elderly Chinese Women

Although the seniors' movement has been the major focus of this chapter as an illustration of the collective forms of resistance among the elderly, I do not intend to say that individual forms of resistance are less important or meaningful. On the contrary, I want to point out that the desire to gain control over one's life is equally strong and meaningful in both forms of resistance. I argue that the patterns of resistance are culturally dependent. In a liberal democratic capitalist society like the United States, forming organized groups as special interests in a pluralist politics is the legitimate way to seek political change and thus the normative form of resistance. That is, the strategy of mass organization is intelligible to American elderly people only in the context of American democratic and pluralist politics. However, the form of resistance is also hierarchically distributed. Access to this form of resistance is limited to certain groups of elders and is distributed along power relations. Immigrant elders, for instance, often are people who emigrated from societies without histories of civil participation and thus are not socialized into civil organizing. Furthermore, these marginalized groups of elderly tend to have less wealth, professional expertise, verbal ability, and time to engage in organizing groups. The proof of this is that minority elderly, female elderly, and poor elderly are marginal actors in the American seniors' movement.

Foucault looked at power in all social relations, and his model of power expands the domain of political struggles to everyday social relations, which validates all forms of resistance at local sites. In this sense other forms of resistance by older people are no less significant than civil organizing in terms of changing power relations. Yet these forms of resistance—such as suicide and mental illness—tend to be labeled as abnormal or deviant behaviors under the professional gaze. For example, the act of a Chinese elderly woman who commits suicide is no less meaningful in terms of her desire to initiate changes in the power relations in her daily life than an older American man's participation in the Gray Panthers. The meaning of resistance can be fully appreciated only in its local and historical contexts.

Unlike the common Western view of suicide as personal behavior that expresses interpersonal anger and conflict and that is a mental health problem (Osgood and McInstoch 1986), in Chinese society committing suicide has a strong social and collective character. The state promoted suicide as a proper response for gentry women whose honor had been tampered with, even accidentally, through awarding the victim a "tablet of honor" in the Ching dynasty of the late nineteenth and early twentieth centuries (Wolf 1975). Ernest Alabaster summarizes a case in which the woman was posthumously awarded such a tablet: "An elderly unmarried women killed herself after discovering that a drunken man, mistaking her bed for that of a friend, had fallen asleep on it" (cited in Wolf 1975:111). In this case, women's beds were a symbol of their loyalty to their husbands and untouchable by other men. Suicide was promoted as an acceptable and appropriate response for women's resistance. Suicide for Chinese women was and still is a socially acceptable solution to a variety of problems that offer no other solution. Although the problem facing each woman varies, the options available to women have been collectively regulated through the practices of the state—the public ritual of awarding tablets to some women who committed suicide. As Foucault (1977) points out, any tool of power must involve the issue of representation. Through the power of naming, the state was able to normalize certain behaviors and marginalize others. The effects of awarding the tablets were not targeted at the deceased but the living. The tablets make the behavior of suicide visible to other women and serve as a "model" to discipline the whole social body.

Jumping to the conclusion that awarding the tablet of honor to women was the Chinese imperial state's way of regulating women's sexual behavior insulates us from examining the experiences of Chinese women who commit suicide. The state-promoted discourse of suicide offers a subject for Chinese women and a real tool in their struggle to change power relations. For these women, committing suicide was not a "hegemony" that showed that they were cheated or hidden from the truth but a real choice that could grant them not only termination of their suffering but also the power, the means, to punish others. In the context of Chinese culture, which emphasizes the unconditional responsibility of adult children to care for their elderly, the act of senior suicide itself convicts children, especially sons and daughters-in-law, of the most immoral crimes, unfilial behavior (Wolf 1975). Chinese women can replicate the discourse of suicide not because they are deceived from identifying the "real" source of their oppression, the patriarchal Chinese family system, but because the discourse produces a subject that can dramatically alter the power relations.

Using the dominant professional view, which deems suicide a symptom of mental illness, would alienate and pathologize the elderly by decontextualizing their subjective experience. The term *suicide* is an impersonal and objectified form of knowledge that represents a variety of lived experiences, deprived of their particularity as if they have homogeneous meaning (Smith 1990). Our professional training, based mainly on this objectified form of knowledge, tends to prohibit us from understanding the culturally embedded meaning of the struggles in which the elderly are engaged. Thus we lose the ability to construct a dialectic relationship with the elderly and to transform the power relations.

Similarly, the seniors' movement as a form of resistance is embedded in American pluralist politics (Estes 1979), which is based on the assumption that citizens are free to associate in order to compete for limited political resources. In this political context the seniors' movement takes its form and gains access to decision making, although it is constrained by the political context at the same time. The development of civil society, regulated by the rule of pluralist interest-group politics, sets the stage for the politics of identity of the elderly for the seniors' movement.

Genealogy as a Form of Resistance

What is important is our capacity to reject or subvert the subject offered by power relations. Butler (1992) proposes that the way to deconstruct the essentialist usage of certain concepts and to destabilize terms such as *old age* that have been used as an instrument of oppressive power relations, is "not to censure its usage, but, on the contrary, to release the term into a future of multiple signification by continuing to use them, to repeat them subversively, and to displace them from the context in which the term has been deployed" (17). The process is a permanent contest for democratization to give voices to subjugated subjects. When the elderly are represented only by the discourse of a retired worker, for example, an elderly woman's experience as lifelong housewife, a minority's experience as illegal worker, and the experience of a part-time worker are excluded from that usage; these experiences need to be revealed and heard in a public discourse to fully deessentialize the term old age. This is what Rattansi (1994) recognizes as one of two approaches for undertaking the project of deessentializing the subject— exposing the many "sites" of resistance and variance that serve to fragment the subject. The other approach is by constructing genealogies of subject formation. *Genealogy* here means a history from the perspective of a person or a group of people instead of a history for all, and the goal of this genealogy is to construct "a historical awareness of our present circumstance" (Foucault 1982:209). The search for genealogy forces us to question our daily discursive practices and scrutinize the subjectivity we assume. By using a genealogical critique, we are able to distance ourselves from the discourses in which we participate every day. Through that self-distancing we are able to see more clearly the local practices of power and thus pave the way for a vision of old age as a space of fluid boundaries that provides room for diverse and even conflicting understandings of old age and aging.

Only through a full understanding of the historical context of struggles does it become possible for us to destabilize the established knowledge and to reconstruct the subjugated voices. By using genealogical critique to provide that new capacity of self-denial and reconstruction of "our history of the present," we are able to participate in the struggles and thus to transform the underlying power relations. Searching for a universal strategy and a criterion for effective resistance will only further marginalize and alienate other forms of resistance by older people and exclude the possibilities of participating in their struggles. Instead, Foucault replaces the universal revolutionary project of Marxism with a set of genealogical projects of various struggles in local settings. His hope is that the capacity of human beings to reject the subjectivity or to subversively assume the regulated subjectivity will grow by examining from a distance the historical process in which we are constructed as subjects in our located social field. Focusing attention on specific situations would lead to a better understanding of how the power relations operate locally, which would enable us to identify points and patterns of resistance in constructing alternative discourses in our strategies for struggles.

Implications for Social Work Practices

The emphasis on locality has important implications for social workers because most social work practices encounter individuals, families, and communities directly. The nature of local practices places social workers in the most appropriate position to participate, observe, and intervene in the operation of power relations. Daily contacts with clients offer social workers first-hand information on the sources and forms of resistance and thus the potential sources and forms of counterdiscourses. Foucault's work on the locality and historicity of resistance thus contributes to the linkage of the microlevel and the macrolevel practices.

I argue that social workers for the elderly need to understand their resistance in the context of their social positioning and associated discourses in order to effectively engage and assist the elderly. Foucault expects professionals to be specific intellectuals rather than universal intellectuals by engaging in local struggles. He especially emphasizes historical awareness. The ability to create a genealogy to revive the subjugated voices is what Foucault expects for professionals. Genealogy, then, is a form of resistance. The practice of genealogical knowledge should not be limited to professionals but needs to extend to individuals, especially oppressed ones.

As a social work profession, we are trained to speak in a universal language to interpret our practice. Foucault's notions of specific intellectual and genealogical critique imply that we should stop interpreting, perpetuating, and pathologizing the lives of the older people who seek help from us by dropping our impersonal professional categories, which eliminate and exclude the diversity of their lived experiences. What Foucault asked of us is to listen to the lived experience, the struggle and resistance of the elderly, and to foster their capacity as well as ours to resist the subjugation of subjectivity to the dominant discourse of old age. It is true that the experience of the seniors' movement shows that the diversity among the elderly constitutes an obstacle to forming a cohesive consciousness among the elderly. However, the diversity becomes an obstacle only when we define political struggle in the domain of interest-group politics; if we define every social encounter embedded in all social relations as political struggle, diversity then becomes a resource of resistance, and our daily practices could list a variety of potential focal points of resistance.

NOTES

1. For a critique of the undue emphasis on power in the application of Foucault's concepts, see Lacombe (1996).

2. Foucault rejects the notion of a truth for all but maintains there are multiple truths.

3. The historical review of the American seniors' movement that follows draws heavily on Keith (1982), Pratt (1976, 1993), and Wallace and Williamson (1992).

4. Here I borrow the division developed by Keith (1982) to distinguish different attitudes among seniors' groups toward the boundary of old age. She used the terms *confess, emphasize,* and *erase* in her description of the attitude of seniors' groups toward old age.

5. The plan proved to be so immensely popular that retirees outside the teaching profession tried to smuggle their way into the NRTA (Keith 1982). Andrus decided to respond to these nonteacher retirees by forming the American Association of Retired Persons in 1958 to make group insurance available to anyone older than fifty-five.

6. For a rich collection of examples of representation of the American elderly in mass media, see Powell, Branco, and Williamson (1996:173–83).

REFERENCES

Baar, Jan. 1991. The challenge of critical gerontology: The problem of social construction. *Journal of Aging Studies* 5 (3): 216–43.

Binstock, R. H. 1981. The politics of aging interest groups:Interest group liberalism and the politics of aging. In R. B. Hudson, ed., *The aging in politics: Process and policy*, pp. 47–73. Springfield, Ill.: Charles C. Thomas.

Butler, Judy. 1992. Contingent foundations: Feminism and the question of "postmodernism." In Judy Butler and Joan Scott, eds., *Feminists theorize the political*, pp. 3–21. New York and London: Routledge.

Butler, R. N. 1975. *Why survive? Being old in America.* New York: Harper and Row.

Cohen, Jean. 1985. Strategy or identity: New theoretical paradigms and contemporary social movements. *Social Research* 52 (4): 663–716.

Conrad, Christoph. 1992. Old age in the modern and postmodern Western world. In T. R. Cole, D. D. Van Tassel, and Robert Kastenbaum, eds., *Handbook of the humanities and aging*, pp. 62–95. New York: Springer.

Coombs, W. T. and S. J. Holladay. 1995. The emerging political power of the elderly. In J. F. Nussbaum and Justine Coupland, eds., *Handbook of communication and aging research*, pp. 317–42. Hove, U.K.: Lawrence Erlbaum.

Estes, C. L. 1979. *The aging enterprise.* San Francisco: Jossey-Bass.

———. 1989. Aging, health, and social policy: Crisis and crossroads. *Journal of Aging and Social Policy* 1 (1/2): 17–32.

Fischer, D. H. 1977. *Growing old in America.* New York: Oxford University Press.

Foucault, Michel. 1977. *Discipline and punish: The birth of the prison.* New York: Vintage.

———. 1978. *The history of sexuality.* New York: Vintage.

———. 1979. Truth and power. In Meaghan Morris and Paul Patton, eds., *Michel Foucault: Power, truth, strategy,* pp. 29–48. Sydney: Feral Publications.

———. 1982. The subject and power. In H. L. Dreyfus and Paul Rabinow, eds., *Michel Foucault: Beyond structuralism and hermeneutics,* pp. 208–26. Chicago: University of Chicago Press.

Fraser, Nancy. 1989. *Unruly practices: Power, discourse, and gender in contemporary social theory.* Minneapolis: University of Minnesota Press.

Gilliland, Nancy and Linda Havir. 1990. Public opinion and long-term care policy. In D. E. Biegel and Arthur Blum, eds., *Aging and caregiving: Theory, research, and policy,* pp. 242–53. Newbury Park, Calif.: Sage.

Hartsock, Nancy. 1990. Foucault on power: A theory for women? In Linda Nicholson, ed., *Feminism/postmodernism,* pp. 157–75. New York: Routledge.

Holtzman, Abraham. 1963. *The Townsend movement: A political study.* New York: Octagon.

Hudson, Robert and Robert Binstock. 1976. Political system and aging. In Robert Binstock and Ethel Shanas, eds., *Handbook of aging and the social sciences.* New York: Van Nostrand Reinhold.

Johnson, Malcolm. 1995. Interdependency and the generational compact. *Aging and Society* 15: 243–65.

Katz, Stephen. 1992. Alarmist demography: Power, knowledge, and the elderly population. *Journal of Aging Studies* 6 (3): 203–25.

Keith, Jennie. 1982. *Old people as people.* Boston: Little, Brown.

Lacombe, Dany. 1996. Reforming Foucault: A critique of the social control thesis. *British Journal of Sociology* 47 (2): 332–52.

Miller, Peter. 1987. *Domination and power.* London: Routledge and Kegan Paul.

Mishra, Ramesh. 1984. *The welfare state in crisis: Social thought and social change.* 2d ed. Brighton, Sussex, U.K.: Wheatsheaf Books.

Osgood, Nancy and John McInstoch. 1986. *Suicide and the elderly.* New York: Greenwood.

Powell, Lawrence, Kenneth Branco, and John Williamson. 1996. *The senior rights movement.* New York: Twayne.

Pratt, H. J. 1976. *The gray lobby.* Chicago: University of Chicago Press.

———. 1983. National interest groups among the elderly: Consolidation and constraint. In W. P. Browne and L. K. Olson, eds., *Aging and public policy: The politics of growing old in America,* pp. 145–79. Westport, Conn.: Greenwood.

———. 1993. *Gray agendas: Interest groups and public pensions in Canada, Britain, and the United States.* Ann Arbor: University of Michigan Press.

Quadragno, J. S. 1989. Generational equity and the politics of the welfare state. *Politics and Society* 17 (3): 353–76.

Rattansi, Ali. 1994. "Western" racisms, ethnicities, and identities in a "postmodern" frame. In Ali Rattansi and Sallie Westwood, eds., *Racism, modernity, and identity on the Western front,* pp. 15–86. Cambridge, U.K.: Polity Press.

Schattschneider, Elmer E. 1960. *The semisovereign people: A realist's view of democracy in America.* Hinsdale, Ill.: Dryden.

Smith, Dorothy. 1990. *The conceptual practices of power.* Toronto: University of Toronto Press.

Townsend, Francis. 1943. *New horizons.* Chicago: J. L. Publishing.

Walker, Alan. 1990. The economic "burden" of aging and the prospect of intergenerational conflict. *Aging and Society* 10: 377–96.

Wallace, S. P. and J. B. Williamson. 1992. *The senior movement: References and resources.* New York: G. K. Hall.

Williamson, J. B., Linda Evans, and L. A. Powell. 1982. *The politics of aging: Power and policy.* Springfield, Ill.: Charles C. Thomas.

Wolf, Margery. 1975. Women and suicide in China. In Margery Wolf and Roxane Witke, eds., *Women in Chinese society,* pp. 111–41. Palo Alto, Calif.: Stanford University Press.

CHAPTER 9

Surveillance and Government of the Welfare Recipient

Ken Moffatt

Increasingly, matters of personal and social welfare are being addressed within a global economic context. In this context neoliberal ideologies are widespread and market-driven relations are tantamount. Social relationships based on the person as consumer rather than the person as citizen infiltrate both private sector and public sector institutions. The emphasis has shifted from public responsibility to private personal responsibility for addressing need (Teeple 1995).

Within this shifting economic and social context social workers continue to make vital and important decisions about the access to resources that affect the health of people in need. Foucault (1988c) challenges us to look at the differing rationalities that influence these decisions. He argues that it is necessary to shift the analysis of social welfare decisions from the perspective of ideological presuppositions to one that explores the specifics of how choices are made with respect to people's well-being as well as the rationalities behind and justifications for those decisions. A great silence surrounds the type of provisional and flexible arbitration that occurs between the social worker and the person in need. Furthermore, Foucault suggests that we have averted our gaze from the technical aspects of decision making and from particular material power relations in health and welfare matters. To begin to unveil the techniques of material relations and the choices made by workers could well create a scandal, he argues, because we are likely to be exposed to matters that are morally unbearable.

In this chapter I unveil the mechanisms of power within the social assistance office. By focusing on the role of the social worker I describe some of the differing rationalities and the "techne" associated with the delivery of welfare. In the first section I reveal the economy of power within the social assistance office and argue that the office operates as a mechanism for disciplinary power. In the second section I situate the power relations of the social assistance office within the broader network of capitalist liberal relations. Finally, I consider how the combination of techniques, data collection, and knowledge creation particular to the social assistance office governs the worker and the client. The rationality associated with this governance relies on the creation of a social category known as the "welfare cheat." Welfare recipients are constituted as beings according to whether they are capable of becoming conscious of their government by others or as "welfare cheats"— those people who do not fit within the network of relations in the social assistance office.

A number of rationalities can function at once within any social welfare agency. It cannot be assumed, however, that they are constructed according to a master plan nor that they create a cumulative effect. But an interplay does exist between the various technologies related to the exercise of power within the social assistance office. At times the result is likely to be surprising in terms of the fluidity of the relationships. At other times the interplay between the rationalities creates power relations that are problematic because of the onerous effect they have on both client and worker.

I conducted in-depth interviews with welfare workers from a large social assistance office in the heart of a major North American metropolitan area. The administrative infrastructure of the office was also explored by reading forms, policy and procedure manuals, directives, and written communications. The welfare workers describe the office as "very urban." The neighborhood in which it is located has a disproportionate number of hostels, homeless shelters, and large poorly planned state housing projects. In fact, welfare workers characterized the entire neighborhood as a "welfare neighborhood." A majority of the residents within the office's catchment area are poor.

The Tapestry of Power Relations in the Social Assistance Office

Contemporary North American power relations are influenced by eighteenth-century European reforms of the nature of punishment. Before the eighteenth century, punishment was public spectacle; the purpose of the public event, such as torture or hanging, was to make obvious the revenge of the sovereign against a criminal. However, a new economy of power was created in the eighteenth century. Within this economy of power, power was distributed more widely rather than concentrated at points of privilege. The reforms allowed for power to operate "everywhere in a continuous way" (Foucault 1979:80). Power was rearranged so that it became constant, regular, and very specific in its effects. This new form of power was advantageous because it could be induced at the smallest element of the social body—at the point of microinterventions. For example, professionals could use it when intervening with their clients. Furthermore, economic and political costs were minimized, whereas the effectiveness of the exercise of power was enhanced; the exercise of power became more efficient and less wasteful (Foucault 1979; Foucault 1980d).

Power is not a principle of individual character. Neither is power an unfathomable property or substance that one possesses (Foucault 1988b). Because power does not exist in a substantive form, neither does it exist in the form of an institution or social structure (Gordon 1980). According to Foucault, power is simply a "certain type of relation between individuals" (Foucault 1988b:83). Every relationship is also a relationship of power. In a broader context power is the complex strategy of relations within a society. Each power relation and strategic maneuver is neither inherently good or bad, but each is dangerous (Foucault 1988c; Gordon 1980; Kritzman 1988).

Power of this sort is deeply entrenched within the social body. Within this economy of power technicians of discipline develop and expand the various techniques and procedures that are useful for the coercion of people's bodies (Foucault 1979). The techniques of power are elaborated so that they are continuous and uninterrupted but at the same time adaptable and individualized (Foucault 1980d). These procedures enhance atomization and docility at the personal level and contribute to the development of meticulous methods for ensuring the inmate or client fits within the social machinery (Foucault 1979).

Discipline operates as an economy of power. According to Foucault, discipline is a means of distinguishing, separating out, and sorting individual bodies from the mass of humanity. Discipline is "the specific technique of power that regards individuals both as objects and as instruments of its exercise" (Foucault 1979:170). The success of disciplinary power is that it is operational through simple techniques. Discipline operates through minor procedures and modest methodologies that in total function as a calculated economy of power (Foucault 1979).

The examination, a technology central to the function of the social assistance office, is an instrument of disciplinary power. The examination, distinguished by its simplicity and effectiveness, combines hierarchical observation with normalizing judgment. Foucault elaborates the character of the examination: "It is a normalizing gaze, a surveillance that makes it possible to qualify, to classify and to punish. It establishes over individuals a visibility through which one differentiates them and judges them" (Foucault 1979:184).

The effect of the examination is the subjection of interrogated people so that they become objects of measurement and study. Within this simple technique lies a profound interrelationship of knowledge and power. The examination makes it possible to collect and constitute knowledge at the point of interaction. The specific details of the micropractice create the possibility of knowledge; in this manner practice and knowledge take on a political nature. The examination implies an entire domain of knowledge related to a specific exercise of power (Foucault 1979).

The examination introduces a type of power in which the economy of visibility is transformed. The disciplinary power that was once visible in public spectacle is invisible in the examination. Those people who are subjected to the interrogation of the examiner are subjected to "a principle of compulsory visibility" (Foucault 1979:187). The visibility of the subjected people ensures the exercise of power. Because the people are constantly under the purview of others, the people remain disciplined in their subjection (Foucault 1979).

The interrogation of clients in order to make them visible is the principle prerogative of the welfare worker. The signing of "consent to disclose" forms by the client is an especially profound moment in the exercise of power by the worker. By signing the form, the client legally and symbolically grants the worker permission to both interrogate the client and to collect collateral evidence to corroborate the truth of the client's answers. As a welfare worker I interviewed explained, the exercise of power within the social assistance office is quite simple—if the client refuses to give information to the worker, the client is not eligible for assistance. A client who will not provide information cannot enter the economy of power within the social assistance office. Of course, the client can refuse to engage in the particular system of knowledge creation that exists within the social assistance office, but with this refusal the client serves no purpose within the system of power relations.

Central to the examination within the social assistance office is the imperative that the client sign any number of forms. At that point the client is made to act as an individual. A welfare worker explains: "You're actually making someone do something that's individual. That is what identifies you [the client] as, as who you [the client] are saying you [the client] are." Documentation through examination begins with the signatures of the client. The signatures are essential to the early stages of the social work assessment. These signatures atomize clients and their problems and fix a client's location for future coding. The client must first be made visible through identification and individualization in order to become engaged within the disciplinary mechanism of the welfare office.

The examination creates an individual for documentation. These individuals—the clients in the social assistance office—are situated both within a field of surveillance and within a system of documentation. The various codes that are used for documentation are a means of formalizing the person within the power relation (Foucault, 1979).

When asked to elaborate on the nature of power within her office, a welfare worker speaks to the power associated with observation that is implicit in the examination:

> Well, I think as a welfare worker, just getting all that information from people—having them disclose their bank accounts or identification— then signing a consent form so that the welfare worker can check their story—to make sure they're telling me the truth. The power base is established right there.

She continues her discussion of power within the social assistance office by explaining eligibility requirements as normalizing judgment. Both the worker and the client are locked in a relationship defined by the examination so long as eligibility requirements are paramount. Every interaction between the welfare worker and the client is one in which the worker sits in judgment of the client's eligibility:

> In order for you to receive assistance I have to determine your eligibility. And, even if it's ongoing, every time you come to see me, I have the right to verify your information—your banking, your education, where you live, your rent, who you're living with, how you're living with them, and so on. So there's the particular dynamic.

The examination is central to determining each individual client in her or his particular specificity. Through the examination the individual is given a status and then linked to any number of markers and measurements meant to characterize each individual client. Finally, the individual is reconstituted as the case. The individual case is the result as well as the object of power.

The individual case is the result as well as the object of knowledge (Foucault 1979).

Eligibility for assistance provides the rationale for measurement and the re-creation of the person as the "case" in the social assistance office. The preoccupation with eligibility does not end with the initial assessment or intake interview. Eligibility of the client drives most interactions throughout the life of the case within the social assistance office. The worker is defined as the watchdog, while the client is the suspect. Both parties are constrained in their roles by the necessity of ongoing surveillance.

The exercise of power in the social assistance office is part of an intricate tapestry that is akin to a complex system. Panopticon, a mechanism of surveillance, is interwoven with the examination to create a combination of disciplinary techniques within the office. Because these technologies of power are not situated within a master schematic of technology, their expression is neither tidy nor is it part of a continuum of techniques (Foucault 1980a, 1980c).

Jeremy Bentham defined the *panopticon* in an architectural form as a jail or place of punishment in which the exercise of power would be both more economical and effective. The panopticon has two main features: the central tower and a peripheral building that surrounds the tower. The tower is constructed so that windows face the inner ring of the peripheral building. The peripheral building is divided into cells that extend the width of the building. At either end of the cell is a window; the interior window is situated so that it is in line with the windows in the tower.

A supervisor is placed within the central tower, and those who are to be supervised are placed individually in each cell. The people to be supervised might be criminals, patients, workers, or paupers. The window on the outside of the cell allows for light to cross the cell. The cell is backlit by light from outside the building. With the aid of the backlighting, the supervisor can observe the movement of the inmate to the smallest detail and with the greatest precision.

Each person who is under supervision within a panoptic structure is constantly visible to the supervisor. Furthermore, by virtue of being located in their individual cells, the inmates are thoroughly individualized. The surveillance of the supervisor is both constant and immediate. The people are not only trapped by virtue of isolation, but they are also trapped by virtue of their visibility. The panopticon is a mechanism that ensures the efficient expression of power relations (Foucault 1979).

In the contemporary social assistance office the client is supervised within the panoptic device. Indeed, the design of the interview rooms within the social assistance office is suggestive of the panopticon. Within the office the interaction between the worker and the client is almost exclusively restricted to the interview room. Many rooms are only as wide as the worker's desk, which divides the room in half. A worker describes the design of the interview room:

> Um, it is fairly small—very, very small. More like a booth. And a desk separates the two people and there is a door [for the worker] to exit from behind [the desk]. The client and the door into the office are at the other end of the room. There is a button, an alarm button, if there is any trouble. . . . There is a desk phone down below on the worker's side. So basically it is, uh, you are not in a room, you are in a booth and you [worker and client] are divided.
>
> So once you are in a little booth with a client, you sort of preassess whether your client is safe or not and, if you think you are possibly at risk, you go into a booth that has Plexiglas and perhaps several inches under the Plexi [through] which you can exchange documents. If you are comfortable, or have a family, they have a couple of large booths where you can actually shake hands when they come in the door, or greet them [laughter].

The design of the office assumes that the worker will take on the role of supervisor and interrogator. A central principle of panopticon is that power should itself be visible but at the same time unverifiable. The mechanism is designed so that the inmates of panopticon are constantly aware of the presence of the central tower from which they are watched. Vital to the functioning of panopticon is that the inmate anticipates that the surveillance could be both continuous and constant. Although the inmates know they are being watched, they do not know precisely at what time, by whom, or in what manner. Foucault explains: "In the peripheric ring, one is totally seen without ever seeing; in the central tower one sees everything without ever being seen" (Foucault 1979:202).

Metaphorically, the clients within the social assistance office are forced into a position within the peripheric zone, while the worker exercises a power from the tower that is both visible and inscrutable. The constant preoccupation with the eligibility of the client creates a dynamic whereby the surveillance by the worker is continuous and constant. The preoccupation with eligibility, furthermore, situates workers in the economy of power so that they are also located within a peripheric zone. Because the data that workers collect on clients are under constant review, workers too are being watched from a central location within the social assistance office.

The dyad of worker and client is imbalanced—the worker is constantly seeing while the client is being seen. One means of maintaining the imbalance in the dyad is through the "forms-driven" interview, coupled with a preoccupation with efficiency. A worker explains that within the interview room the interaction is driven by forms; the forms are linked to the determination of eligibility:

> Everything is based on the clock. . . . We used to joke around in the office sometimes on how quickly you could do an interview. . . . You have a "present condition report" which is just a, just a little piece of paper with some of them reprinted with the information. You have to go and you would ask the customer: Okay, you still living at the same address?—Got any income?—nah, nah, nah—You just go on through the list as quickly as possible. Right, I'm outta here in five minutes [laughter].
>
> . . . It's just like the applications too. [It is] like a joke to see how quickly you can do it. You go in and you sit down and say, "I'm going to ask you some questions. I just want you to answer these questions. I don't want you to ask me any questions until we're finished the form." And then, when you've finished the form, you'd walk out before they had a chance to ask you questions because you were in such a hurry to get them done so you wouldn't fall behind.

Similarly, another worker explains how inscrutable yet visible is the power of the worker as a data collector. At the same time clients must mark themselves with identification so that they are clearly visible to the worker:

> If you're doing six intakes, which have to be completed by the end of the day, and every piece of information completed, a worker essentially can get by with filling the forms, um, writing three or four lines in the write-up, and then just verifying all the information in terms of assets and income—and whether they're eligible—having lived in the city— these are the issues which determine eligibility—appropriate I.D. So speed could be of the essence. . . . The "worst" intakes [occur] where there is minimal eye contact, or none. Uh, the first that the worker would say is: "Could I see your I.D?" Because there is no use continuing if they don't have appropriate I.D. . . . The idea is to get it done. To get the paperwork done, and then you would have time for lunch

and then your afternoon to verify information, assets, income, and so on. So it has little to do with counseling, or helping individuals.

The worker echoes the previous worker's description of an efficient interaction structured by forms. The forms workers are required to complete function as a method of panopticon. The forms are constructed to serve the logic of a particular political rationality of the social assistance office. In practice, the forms structure the interview so that it is drained of any existential value beyond absurdity. The forms also function as techniques of control, which create a dissonance in the relationship that protects against the creation of intersubjective meaning between the worker and client. A welfare worker complains:

> It just seems absurd. It seems like during the interview the goal is to get the forms filled out, and then if you have enough time after the forms, you spend a little time talking. But you're checking your watch because you've got another appointment every half hour. And if you're running late you may only have fifteen minutes. So, basically, uh, I think I lost my sense of priority in a welfare office. You become functional. It's the paper. . . . Hoping that you keep everyone happy or you're going to have your voice mail full.

The tapestry of interrelationships that constitutes the economy of power within the social assistance office is evident. The client is individualized as the case through questions of identification and residence and then is verified by the workers to be a "true" case. The eligibility of the client to remain as a case creates a need for power relations between the worker and the client based on examination and surveillance. The worker is driven by an urgency derived from expectations, such as the number of intakes per day and the appropriate length of an interview; these expectations are defined external to the client/worker dyad. Forms are used to structure the nature of the interaction between worker and client. The verification of the case and the eligibility of the clients in a worker's caseload provide the mechanism for supervision of the worker. Even while the worker is watching the client, the worker is being watched. Efficient interaction provides the justification for these power relations.

The primary effect of panopticon is the internalization of a conscious state of permanent visibility by the inmate or client. Consciousness of visibility by the inmate or client ensures that power functions automatically; power need not be proclaimed or enacted as a public spectacle. Surveillance is permanent in its results because it is exercised at multiple points throughout the agency. The inmates or clients become engaged in the power situation to the point that they exercise their own subjection (Foucault 1979). The welfare worker's feeling of losing a personal sense of priorities suggests that the internalization of permanent visibility is true for the worker as well.

Power is a particular contrived distribution of surfaces, design, and architecture such as the interview booth in the social assistance office. Furthermore, the principles of power are defined by the distribution of bodies such as the calculated separation between the welfare worker and the client. Finally, in the social assistance office, power is circumscribed by a particular gaze that is both inscrutable and constant; power is defined by the lack of eye contact, the efficiency of the interrogation, the abrupt ending to an interview, the intrusiveness of the questions, and the "form-driven" contact. The overall effect of the distribution and arrangement of these mechanisms is a consciousness by the client of disequilibrium and a sense of difference or marginalization.

A primary function of panopticon is to differentiate individuals from the clamoring masses. Each individual is constituted so that the common interests of clients are minimized. In the architecture of the panopticon, walls separate the inmates so that they cannot communicate laterally. At the same time the client is seen but does not see; a client is the object of data collection but not the active subject of communication or decision making (Foucault 1979).

A welfare worker complains about the constitution of the economy of power in her place of employment. She argues that those who create the techniques of intervention and who create the policies and guidelines that direct the worker's judgment with respect to a client's need are naive about the nature of poverty. The decision makers have spent little time in the office. She says: "Let's face it, poverty is not nice to listen to. It is angry, it is usually whining. . . . It's desperate. So it's not appealing." Her description sounds closer to the desperate howling masses of a Goya painting than the efficient machine of panopticon.

It may be, however, that the policy makers who share the responsibility of formalizing and generalizing methodologies and the means to make judgments within the social assistance office are operating on the basis of a particular type of rationality. At the heart of this rationality is a refusal to conceptualize the welfare recipient as a member of a genuine community in which multiple exchanges occur. The policy makers actively create techniques to avoid the "contagion" of anger or desperation and constantly work toward constructing recipients in their solitary individuality (Foucault 1979).

In the idealized version of the panopticon, power is automatic and disengaged from the person who exercises it. Foucault argues that the machinery of panopticon (the gazes, architecture, mechanisms) can function regardless of who exercises the power. Any person can be randomly placed in a position within this great machine, and the efficiency and effectiveness of the exercise of power will not be compromised (Foucault 1979).

The welfare workers in my study insist that there are as many different ways to be a welfare worker as there are workers within the system. They declare that despite all the checks and balances within the social assistance office a great deal of personal judgment is used to determine eligibility. At the same time, they acknowledge, they are part of what one worker characterizes as a "large machine." Another worker explains that just as there are some clients who are remarkable and other clients who are monstrous, some welfare workers are remarkable and others are monstrous.

The welfare workers develop their own strategies of power. At times the workers develop strategies meant to counterbalance the effect of the panopticon, and such resistance is integral to the strategy of power relations exercised by some workers. A welfare worker gave as an example of a strategy of power a social worker's judgment of mental competency of a client. The worker could make a judgment that served the sole purpose of disqualifying the individual or could even characterize the client as a cheat by ignoring the person's competence to comply with the agency's requirements for being constructed as a case. Some workers clearly ignore the competency of clients when they disqualify them from assistance. Other workers may make a personal judgment that a person is not competent to act in a manner that meets agency requirements and processes the application with sensitivity to this judgment. The worker may choose to act as an advocate of the client in order to make sure the incompetent client receives assistance.

Workers also engage in acts that they consider to be subversive. One of the most subversive acts in which a welfare worker can engage is the refusal to listen to client disclosure. In short, the worker can refuse to act as an agent of surveillance. The following welfare worker characterizes subversion as the refusal to interrogate:

> Well, what you can do is, well—what you do is, just sort of not listen. There was one worker, one worker we had, that just went into the interview booth and you know, "the less I know, the better it is for you.

Answer the questions that I ask you," and when the person started going on about work they'd done or anything like that—he just sort of put his head down and [pause] just not listen to it.

Refusing to listen as a subversive act is corroborated by this female welfare worker:

But you, let's say, at Christmas you got a single mom, she's saying you know, like, "My ex-boyfriend gave me two hundred bucks for the kids." Well, theoretically you're supposed to pay attention. A subversive act would be not to hear it. . . . In other words, don't document it. Give the woman a break.

A welfare worker tells the story of a client who had been in prison for most of his adult life. The worker characterized the man as "real bad, like a tough man." The worker made a judgment call to change the circumstances of their interaction by leaving the interview booth:

I just said to him, "Okay, well, I'm going for coffee now. I'll buy you a coffee. Meet me out front. I'll come around [out of the interview booth]." . . . You could just see he was all excited just standing out in front of the office. And he was telling people: "My worker's taking me out for coffee."

This worker changes the nature of the relationship. The worker frames a differing rationality, which requires the collection of a different type of information. In the process he creates a new form of knowledge about the client:

"Well," I told him, "I'm going for coffee right now—come with me and I'll talk to you." And that was the best thing for him, you know. He was walking back to the office with his arm around me, saying: "I've never gone out for a coffee with my worker before." [Laughter.] You know, that made me feel good about it. It turns out he lives, er, his parents live down by where my parents live and he raises pigeons. It gives a real human face to this guy.

In each of these circumstances the workers attempt to exit the panopticon. There seems to be liberating potential in recognizing the many rationalities that exist in the social assistance office. Certainly, we need to better understand how strategies of subversion fit into the tapestry of power relations within the social assistance office.

Client Independence in a Postindustrial Liberal Society

Disciplinary power is not exclusive to the domain of the social assistance office, nor is it restricted to state mechanisms within bureaucracies. Power of this sort is deeply entrenched within the social body as a whole; the social assistance office is simply one location of its expression. The art of discipline and punishment becomes part of everyday action; punishment is subtle, and it operates at multiple points throughout the social body (Foucault 1980b, 1988a; Rose and Miller 1992).

The wide exercise of the disciplinary function within the social body affects the creation of knowledge. The logic of such punishment becomes the protection of the social body as a whole rather than the protection of a sovereign state. The "monster" who is judged to be in need of punishment and subjected to the exercise of power is that person who is perceived to be a threat to the social body. Those who are judged to be "outside of nature" are to be embedded in an exercise of power with its own specific economic rationality based on meticulous calculations (Foucault 1979).

To protect the distribution of wealth and the nature of the system, a hostility must be created that is directed toward those who threaten this system from within. Foucault documents the hostility that was constructed between delinquents and workers in the eighteenth century. The social body was reconstituted as a moral body that was in danger because of the presence of the delinquent. A rigorous morality was enforced throughout the entire social body. The delinquent was isolated and constructed as a danger to both the rich and the poor (Foucault 1980c).

A primary function of the social worker historically has been to distinguish the deserving from the nondeserving poor. The worker makes the judgment in order to determine who is worthy of being designated as a beneficiary of charitable or public assistance. Implicit in such judgments is that the nondeserving poor are morally suspect. In fact, the lack of moral fiber characteristic of the nondeserving poor has been perceived as a threat to the moral character of the entire social body (Ehrenreich 1985; Katz 1986, 1989).

Philp (1979) has argued that a significant shift occurred in the function of the social worker during a British economic depression in the 1880s. Because the depression was prolonged, poverty could no longer be viewed as a temporary personal state associated with moral degeneracy. In a period of high unemployment, distinguishing the unemployed from the irresponsible indigent became increasingly difficult. Together, these groups represented a large and disgruntled element of the population. It became a political necessity, therefore, to distinguish the "respectable" working class from the "suspect" poor. The confidence of the respectable classes was gained with some expansion of their political and discursive rights. In addition, the "respectable" working class was engaged in moral judgment of the rest of the poor.

Social workers no longer focused exclusively on distinguishing the deserving from the nondeserving. The role shifted so that social workers helped to distinguish the legitimate demands of labor from the deviance of poor people. The social space between the legitimate working class and the deviant poor is the space in which social work has become institutionalized. Social workers mediate between the respectable and the deviant, as well as between those who have the power to exclude and the excluded. This historical social space defines the possibilities and the limits of social work discourse and knowledge. In contemporary states based on advanced capitalism, social workers continue to function between the discourse that grants legitimate claims to the right to be heard and the maintenance of the exclusion of the social deviant (Philp 1979).

The social worker in the contemporary social assistance office has the specific task of aiding in the management of the poor and helping to control the dangerous classes. This work has been divided so that the poor are the responsibility of a large network of specialists, including the police, parole officers, and social workers. Participants within the social welfare state have developed their own language, and knowledge, to explain poverty. This language is most often technical and functional. The knowledge of poverty within the welfare state is constructed through the imposition of technical categories rather than through open discourse (Ehrenreich 1985; Friedmann 1992). The creation and maintenance of knowledge in the social welfare state also aids in the exercise of distinguishing the legitimate from the deviant poor (Ehrenreich 1985; Philp 1979).

Because one function of the social worker is to mediate between the "respectable" laborer and the rest of the poor, part of the social worker's responsibility has been to explain the relationship of the poor to the "respectable" classes (Ehrenreich 1985; Friedmann 1992; Philp 1979). The social worker therefore has claimed a special knowledge devoted to human potentiality and the promotion of sociability of the excluded and deviant. Social work knowledge aids the "respectable" classes in understanding the destitute (Philp 1979). The social worker, located between those who are legitimate and those who are deviant, must also engage in the exercise of power relations to punish and discipline those who threaten the social body, that is, to punish and discipline the irresponsible poor.

The multiple functions of social work are evident in the language of the welfare workers in my study. The following workers defined their personal motivation for taking on the position of welfare worker as a desire to assist the poor. Each worker expressed surprise at the scope of the position. One worker describes the physical plant of the social assistance office and the nature of the worker's position within it as a "declaration of war" against those who sought assistance. She feels that the clients often think of the welfare worker as an enemy because of the worker's intrusive questions and categorical thinking. Another worker suggests that "ultimately what it boils down to now [is that] you're policing the poor."

Foucault might have agreed with these descriptors of the social work position—war and policing. The true nature of the interplay between knowledge and power is dynamic. Foucault warns against equating the exercise of power by the social worker with repression. If power is defined as repression, the true expression of power is veiled. Power understood as repression is too brittle a power because it is based on the notions of containment, exclusion, and censorship. The power of the social worker in fact is "positive" and technical; the exercise of power creates possibilities for both the worker and the client. The exercise of power also creates the potential for creating knowledge. The social welfare bureaucracy cannot be likened to a flat expressionless landscape in which struggle is contained; rather, it is like a battlefield (Foucault 1980a).

The war that wages within the social assistance office is part of a renewed belief in the immorality of dependence in the broader social context. In a recent poll most Americans said that they associate the increase in welfare dependency with a decline in morality within American society (National Public Radio 1996). The morality of the social body must be protected against the suspect character of the welfare recipient. Incentives to independence have been defined in terms of imposing on the welfare recipient the requirement to work and by limiting the term during which a person can collect welfare. At the same time federal governments in North America are retrenching from their commitments to the guarantee of federal assistance to the poor.

Liberalism as a defining political philosophy within Western societies explains the preoccupation with individual responsibility for dependence. The liberal philosophy seeks to define the limits of rule and to enact a vigilance over the expression of political authority. The freedom and autonomy of the individual must be respected, but at the same time it must be shaped in desired directions (Rose 1993).

Liberal philosophy in eighteenth-century England circumscribed the civil society as a realm in which natural relations occurred. Relations within such spheres of civil society as the family and the market were defined as free and therefore beyond government intrusion. At the same time, however, one responsibility of government was to nurture and shape the self-organizing activities of the civil society. The autonomy of a person's actions and relations within the civil society could not be destroyed even while the state had a role in directing relations within that sphere (Rose and Miller 1992).

Social workers play an important role in affecting change in the family and the individual. The professions of helping have developed alongside the creation of reliance on the disciplinary institutions, such as the prison or the welfare office. The professional groups, which include doctors, lawyers, psychiatrists, and psychologists, as well as social workers, claim an expertise in directing personal and family life. Those people who are incapable of respecting mutual obligations and contractual relations within the civil society are considered antisocial. Welfare recipients, for example, transgress norms of independence and autonomy by virtue of their dependence. The welfare recipient is suspect for personal, subjective defects of character that can be rectified through interrogation, leading to a heightened understanding by the social worker (Rose and Miller 1992).

Medical, psychological, and social work discourses contribute to the pathologizing of dependency. Moralizing about poverty and dependency is obscured by the neutral and medicalized language of experts in the field of human sciences. The psychological sciences also act as a moral register. Even though poverty and dependence have a racialized and gendered character, the problem of dependence is defined as an inherent flaw within groups of people or individuals (Fraser and Gordon 1994).

The person who becomes dependent must request a form of government surveillance in order to meet basic needs. These people collapse a number of contemporary myths, such as the natural character of relations within the civil society, the opportunity for complete independence for all within the marketplace, and that legal guarantees are the sole prerequisite to the expression of freedom and protection against abuse of power (Fraser and Gordon 1994). Because welfare recipients challenge these myths by their person and circumstances, they must be held accountable; they must be scrutinized in a manner that requires them to justify their selves.

These factors come together to circumscribe the location and possibilities of the practice of social work within the social assistance office. The welfare office—an office ostensibly created to deal with the security of dependent people and people in need—does not mention these functions within its mandate. The mission statement of the welfare department I studied constructs the welfare applicant as an individual active citizen who is in need of correction: "In recognition of the rights, responsibilities and dignity of each individual we . . . are committed to: promote client independence." The client must be directed toward the virtue of independence and autonomy. Furthermore, a document accompanying that mission statement instructs the worker to "create and sustain an environment . . . that will make the above philosophy a daily reality."

The mission statement of the agency does not identify a commitment to provide service to poor populations or all those citizens who are in need. Rather, the purpose of the agency is to "deliver program benefits to eligible people." Service is provided only to those who enter the panoptic mechanism of the welfare office through the exercise of eligibility requirements. The creation of knowledge about all people in need is not possible within this particular mechanism. It is possible to create knowledge about only those who are eligible.

The role of the worker is circumscribed accordingly. A welfare worker describes his role within the social assistance office: "[To] assess eligibility, interview applicants, assess their eligibility based on their income, their assets, residency requirements—determine eligibility within set guidelines, the legislated guidelines and regulations." The same worker describes the job as "a bit of investigation, a bit of social work, a bit of investigation."

The welfare worker's role involves the promulgation of techniques, exercise of power, and creation of knowledge, which is amenable but not equivalent to the political rationality of liberalism and the market economy. The social worker is an actor in government. The purpose of government in the social assistance office is the creation of the autonomous being.

Government and the Creation of the Welfare Cheat

Government is not restricted to the welfare state, state bureaucracies, or the social assistance office. Government includes the complex of knowledge and practices that seek to understand and govern particular populations. According to Rose and Miller, government is "the historically constituted matrix within which are articulated all those dreams, schemes, strategies and maneuvers of authorities that seek to shape the beliefs and conduct of others in desired directions by acting upon their will, their circumstance or their environment" (1992:175).

Within the social assistance office a particular form of political rationality and a specific knowledge base form one part of the government matrix. Of course, the population influenced by government in this case is the population of the poor and dependent. A particular set of practices is created within the social assistance office to construct a particular regime of truth about poverty and welfare (Gordon 1980).

The truth that is constructed for the purposes of government is precise and concrete. The acts of the worker and relations between the client and worker within the state are represented in ways that are measurable. The power of the state is bound up with this collection of statistics that measure the political relations. The arithmetic of these statistics represents the power relations within the state or agency. This arithmetic also is a strategy of power that increases the strength of the government body. The collection of statistics and information strengthens those who govern by controlling both the activities of individuals and communication between them (Foucault 1988b).

Within the social assistance office the exercise of government has resulted in a massive collection of information that transforms events into data. Through inquiry by welfare workers the circumstances of clients are encoded. The welfare worker asks a plethora of questions that mark the client such as birth date, income, and illnesses. The data are a form of inscription that characterizes the material conditions of the person. The inscription makes the reality of the client malleable, concrete, and stable as well as comparable and combinable with other people's realities. The collection of data in this form is not an atemporal neutral exercise. Data collection or inscription has real effects on the client in the present (Rose and Miller 1992).

Inscribing people's reality creates a trace of their life that is mobile. Other people within centers of calculation can use these mobile markers to lay claim to the knowledge of the population that they seek to govern. These people make calculations, plans, and strategies that affect the client in concrete material ways. The inscription plays a central role in the power exercised over those people who have been subjected to inquiry (Rose and Miller 1992).

Such political statistics are central to the operation and management of the social assistance office. A worker explains that one of his colleagues is considered [a member of] the quality review unit. He's doing some computer stats and stuff. He's coming up and showing me all these charts and graphs and that's like, like pretty, but what does it mean? He doesn't know what it means, and he's not even getting the correct information. So he's scanning all of these reports with all of these graphs and statistics.

According to this welfare worker, the information that the unit creates is an invention akin to "just sort of space floating around."

The type of statistical inscriptions that are collated by the quality review unit include the number of fraud hot-line allegations, how many of those allegations lead to fraud charges, how many clients receive overpayment on their checks, how many overpayments occur in each office, how much money has been recovered from clients. The worker explains that the information is seldom useful to the front-line worker because no baseline information is provided for comparison. The statistics are combined to create a preoccupation with the "welfare cheat." The welfare cheat is constructed from inscriptions collected at multiple points throughout the agency and then combined at the center of calculation, the quality review unit. The statistics create an image of fraud and a climate for its correction.

Another worker explains that the quality review unit

hands out paper all the time and I'm always getting handed documents that are statistics. It's tons of paper. It's meaningless. To most workers it's meaningless. Yet it seems to arrive. These people make decisions, and none of us is quite sure who's actually using this stuff and how they're using it.

The collation of this information suggests that decisions about welfare cheats are being made at centers of calculation separate from the dyad of welfare worker and the client. Workers feel their work is visible, yet the nature of the decisions made about the work is obscured.

In the postindustrial economy of Western societies the inscription of people is increasingly accomplished through financial mechanisms and accountancy techniques such as the audit (Gill 1995). Furthermore, financial methods of inscription have been integrated within social service agencies. These financial mechanisms increasingly are used to control human behavior and direct interactions in public sector agencies (Dominelli and Hoogvelt 1996; Rose 1993).

In the social assistance office clients are interrogated in detail about their financial well-being. The client is expected to declare income from work, pensions, disability benefits, state allowances, unemployment insurance, private sponsorship, support payments, and student loans as well as any other mechanism of income. The worker also inquires during the intake assessment about the person's assets. Assets include property, bank accounts, investments, receivables such as mortgages and loans, motor vehicles, safety deposit boxes, coins, stamps, jewelry, computers, financial interest in business, and beneficial interest in assets held in trust. Prepaid funerals and credit cards are also listed as assets. As a final act of subjection, clients are expected to show the worker the cash that they have on their person. These inscriptions are encoded on a form that is used to create a profile of the person. The profile is used to make judgments at a later date.

Instruments of normalizing judgment are used alongside the financial inscription. The instruments include the case example, the worker exercise, and the case scenario. They direct the worker in terms of making judgments with respect to the "norm" for eligible welfare recipients: these instruments aid the workers in comprehending "normality" within the rationality of the social assistance office.

The case example given to the worker is a case defined according to a variety of indicators, such as family size, income, shelter costs, and child support and child care costs. The worker is also provided with a sample of how the case is to be statistically formulated on forms in order to determine financial eligibility.

The exercise engages the worker in judgment about eligibility. For example, the "quit/fired exercise" guides the worker through a series of cases and test questions that guide the case management judgment of the worker. The following are examples of cases described within the exercises:

> Clara Smith is a 17 year old sole support parent applying for [welfare]. Clara quit her job on September 23, 1995 in order to care for her infant child.

> Janet Sumer is a single person in receipt of [welfare]. On October 24th she advised the office that she quit her job on October 20. The Social Services Administrator has determined that she had no just cause of quitting her job.

Through these cases the workers are trained how to make normalizing judgments with respect to eligibility as well as how to make the proper financial inscription. Personal circumstances and moral judgment are reconstructed in the arithmetic of the governing body.

Scenarios are similar to exercises in that the worker is engaged in making judgments about fabricated cases. For example, one scenario based on the completion of an extensive questionnaire begins by describing the case as "Sole support mother on assistance since June 1994—Living with single man and has returned questionnaire—Is she still eligible as a sole support parent?" The worker is then expected to outline an assessment and the procedures relevant to the case. The worker is expected to make judgments of similar cases and convert those judgments to financial mechanisms.

The policy guidelines and procedures manual, entitled "Customer Service Process for Employables," offers a differing set of strategies to direct the client and worker to independence. The manual reads:

> There is evidence that suggests regular and frequent contact with employable customers facilitates their transition to independence. The Service Planning Contact (SPC) is the minimum contact requirement for employable customers involved in job searching. Additional contacts need to be developed on a targeted and/or time-limited basis for customers not involved in a program option.

In order to engage the worker in this push for independence defined by market labor, the manual suggests a number of strategies, such as, "Blitzes: Increase customer contact through organized blitzes in the office, by mail or co-location; Positive Reporting System: Target caseloads for completion and return a Present Condition Report (PCR) prior to release of the following month's cheque; Automated Booth System: Increase proactive contact through planned contact with a customer on an appointment bases," and "Eligibility Review Workers: Identify high risk cases and review more frequently including the use of home visits to review eligibility requirements."

This manual describing employable recipients defines the strategic location of the client within power relations. The "role expectations" of the "customer" include:

> "Maintain [welfare] eligibility requirements including communicating any changes to the Department"
>
> "Are active participants in establishing and implementing their own plans"
>
> "Understand and meet job search and program option requirements"

"Articulate needs and goals to facilitate an assessment and their reentry to employment"

"Actively participate in a program option"

The complementary role of the worker is to communicate to the client what the client's responsibilities are for maintaining an eligible status.

Two options are open to the "employable customer," and both are intended "to provide an opportunity (for the customer) to share in the responsibility for and be an active participant in establishing and in implementing their own service plans to satisfy reasonable effort." The client can choose to engage in an "active self-directed job search." If clients choose this option, they are expected to maintain a record of job search activities for inspection by the worker. The other option involves participation in a program designed to "enhance employability and community participation" of the client. The social work knowledge base with respect to human potentiality and sociability comes into play at this point.

Overall, the mechanisms seem to be based on a rationale that market-based wage labor is the preferred outcome for all recipients, regardless of their personal circumstance. Independence is defined in this manner. At the same time eligibility seems to be equated with the clients' ability to act in an autonomous manner in terms of determining their eligibility and maintaining their status as an eligible participant within the office.

Meanwhile, a significant shift is occurring in the language used in the social assistance office. A welfare worker explains that the welfare recipient is no longer referred to as the "client of the worker" but rather as the "customer of the agency." The worker feels that the change in language reflects a broader shift of the agency from a social agency to a financial institution. At the same time the workers were once called "welfare visitors" but now are called "welfare case workers." This worker feels that the new titles of customer and caseworker are in line with the increasing automation of the work setting and a move to customer information systems. He wonders about these changes, saying, "I don't know what the ultimate goal of it is—maybe it's to get rid of the welfare visitor or caseworker and have a bank machine, welfare bank machine."

Another worker understands the shifting language in this way:

The language—we have a language we are to use. We are to call our people "customers," and often,—in brackets or in quotes—"customers" say: "Where am I, a bank?"

And, uh, I actually feel the word *client* implies there is some sense of responsibility on my part towards the individual, that it has a nurturing kind of quality to it. Whereas *customer* [pause]—the implication of the new language within social service implies there's a business transaction taking place. And I think that's what I feel is happening. It's becoming more and more a business transaction—more computerized, less worker involved.

The focus is on people doing for themselves. Of course, the meaning behind the statement is the implication that people are capable of doing for themselves. Not intending to be patronizing, I do believe that people need support. They need help and that can come in a human form. But the focus has become service in a financial form, period. And I don't know if that is necessarily successful.

The economy of power within the social assistance office is further elaborated by considering the broader social context of the social assistance office, the nature of knowledge that is created within the office, and the mechanisms of government. People are individuated as a case so that they can be reconstituted as beings who need to be directed toward independence. The clients are watched so that they become autonomous beings. Their autonomy, however, is not to be one of free action based on personal and informed judgment. Rather, the autonomy of both the worker and the client is carefully regulated within the social assistance office so that they function in reaction to specific power relations and follow specific constraints and rules of behavior. Eligible clients are self-governing people who act out the internalized consciousness of their visibility.

The economy of power within the social assistance office creates the possibility for technology and serves the needs of new technology. There is a push toward the use of a biometric identifier within the social assistance office. The biometric identifier acts directly on the body to measure some aspect of the individual that is unique. The person's body is subjected to a voice scan, a finger print, a finger scan, a palm scan, or a retina scan. The purpose of the biometric identifier is to check and verify a person's identity.

It is possible to imagine a social assistance system in the near future in which welfare customers subject themselves to technological scans. The scans would identify their being, verify their identity, and eventually link their identity with a number of inscriptions collected at a variety of locations. Customers could also update their eligibility by providing financial information and other reductive measures of their being. This would represent the ultimate victory of a system based on panopticon. The subjects of power reconstitute themselves so that they take responsibility for the external exercise of power. Discipline is acted out on the bodies of customers as they type personal information into the computer. The data they type in also represent the tracings of the meticulous exercise of power. Welfare customers choose to subject themselves to surveillance.

I suspect that such a scenario is a likely one for social assistance offices. However, it is but one strategy within a complex network of power relations. New strategies would be required elsewhere within this web. It is evident that the technology and practices that contribute to the construction of the "welfare cheat" are central to the exercise of power within social security systems. In the contemporary context the welfare recipient has to be created as a grave risk to the morality of the social body. In this manner the welfare recipient is separated from the laborer. The welfare recipient has joined the delinquent as a threat to the social body, the moral nature of work, and capitalistic enterprises. The welfare recipient shares the characterization of the criminal class as "vice ridden instigators of the gravest social perils" (Foucault 1980c:36). The social worker develops a particular rationality that aids in the judgment of welfare recipients who create a threat to the nature of social relations. The rationality is based on morality as much as empirical evidence and financial measures.

Just as delinquents served a purpose useful to the general workings of eighteenth-century society, the "welfare cheat" has a purposefulness to the contemporary postindustrial context. Foucault argues that the penal system created the delinquent so that a hostility existed toward a criminal class and toward workers. Within the economic and social structure of postindustrial capitalism is tremendous social dislocation. The vulnerability of so many people from a variety of classes makes it difficult to distinguish the morally upright poor. The life of all laborers is insecure. Hostility toward the "welfare cheat" poses the problem so that people remain divided.

It might be argued that the creation of the "welfare cheat" by the social assistance office serves political ends. The loathing of the "welfare cheat" contributes to the toleration of strategies of surveillance as they are worked out in social assistance offices and social security agencies. The panopticon is a form of laboratory in which techniques of power and control are tested. The social assistance office is a form of panopticon. The biometric scan, the examination, and the many other techniques of power within the office are part of a greater social web throughout which these mechanisms will spread (Foucault 1979).

The "welfare cheat" is part of a mechanism that links subjective personal meaning with public acts. As if to protect against the loathsome intent of some poor, the subjective beings of all who are poor are open to interrogation and reconstruction. The interrogation within the welfare office seeks to reconstruct the person—shaping their desires, reframing their sense of subjective self, and maximizing their self-consciousness. These power relations require the judgment of the expertise of human sciences that claim the authority to understand the human psyche and prescribe solutions (Rose 1990). The creation of the "welfare cheat" justifies other actions within the social assistance office. The data collection and political statistics are justified as a basis from which to reshape the welfare recipient. The subjective governance of all the recipients is also justified.

The particular matrix of power/knowledge—these strategies of power relations that exist in the social assistance office—is likely to have the perverse effect of heightening dependency and increasing marginalization. If the intent of the social security system is the optimal security of citizens, coupled with the maximization of personal autonomy, the decision-making processes and relations within the social assistance office are problematic. The problems are the obscure nature of decision making, the attempt to totalize and centralize information and decision making rather than locating decisions close to the client, and the imbalance of the dyad between worker and client so that surveillance replaces consultation work against independence (Foucault 1988c). The social assistance office seems to be creating, on one hand, self-conscious autonomous beings who are aware of and dependent on the information they must provide to stay a part of this system of power/knowledge. On the other hand, the system of power relations within the social assistance office seems to be creating "welfare cheats."

Clearly, we need to understand the economies of power that affect those who are poor or disadvantaged. The study of particular exercises of power will contribute to the understanding of how each power relationship is dangerous. At the same time more analysis is needed of those specific rationalities constructed by social workers in direct practice.

Of particular interest are those rationalities that reconstruct the client as human. The worker who chooses to walk out of the interview booth to speak to a client or the worker who puts his head down on the desk in an attempt to counter the act of surveillance is consciously seeking to subvert the relations of power. It might be argued that these acts are little more than new techniques within the innumerable strategies of power within the social assistance system. However, I feel they represent significant changes in the welfare system, for the judgments upon which the workers base these acts are not rooted in soft knowledge or irrationality. Rather, the workers have introduced a new and differing rationality within the office. The rationalities are as real as any dominant position. I contend that we know little about these type of rationalities and how they affect the economies of power within the social assistance office. The study of the specificity of relationship is vital, for it may be at this location that we may begin to understand the true complexity of relations between worker and client and the nature of social relations for the disadvantaged and poor within liberal, postindustrial, capitalist systems.

REFERENCES

Dominelli, Lena and Ankie Hoogvelt. 1996. Globalization and the technocratization of social work. *Critical Social Policy* 16: 45–62.

Ehrenreich, John. 1985. *The altruistic imagination: A history of social work and social policy in the United States.* Ithaca, N.Y.: Cornell University Press.

Foucault, Michel. 1979. *Discipline and Punish: The Birth of the Prison.* Translated by Alan Sheridan. New York: Vintage.

———. 1980a. Body/Power. In Colin Gordon, ed., *Power/Knowledge: Selected interviews and other writings,* pp. 55–62. New York: Pantheon.

———. 1980b. Power and strategies. In Colin Gordon, ed., *Power/Knowledge: Selected interviews and other writings,* pp. 134–45. New York: Pantheon.

———. 1980c. Prison talk. In Colin Gordon, ed., *Power/Knowledge: Selected interviews and other writings,* pp. 37–54. New York: Pantheon.

———. 1980d. Truth and power. In Colin Gordon, ed., *Power/Knowledge: Selected interviews and other writings,* pp. 109–33. New York: Pantheon.

———. 1988a. On power. In Lawrence D. Kritzman, ed., *Michel Foucault: Politics, philosophy, culture, interviews, and other writings, 1977–84,* pp. 96–109. New York: Routledge.

———. 1988b. Politics and reason. In Lawrence D. Kritzman, ed., *Michel Foucault: Politics, philosophy, culture, interviews, and other writings, 1977–84,* pp. 57–85. New York: Routledge.

———. 1988c. Social Security. In Lawrence D. Kritzman, ed., *Michel Foucault: Politics, philosophy, culture, interviews, and other writings, 1977–84,* pp. 159–77. New York: Routledge.

Fraser, Nancy and Linda Gordon. 1994. A genealogy of dependency: Tracing a keyword of the U.S. welfare state. *Signs: Journal of Women in Culture and Society* 19, no. 2 (Winter): 309–36.

Friedmann, John. 1992. *Empowerment: The politics of alternative development.* Cambridge, U.K.: Basil Blackwell.

Gill, Stephen. 1995. The global panopticon? The neoliberal state, economic life, and democratic surveillance. *Alternatives* 2: 1–49.

Gordon, Colin. 1980. Afterword. In Colin Gordon, ed., *Power/Knowledge: Selected interviews and other writings, 1977–84*, pp. 229–59. New York: Pantheon.

Katz, Michael. 1986. *In the shadow of the poorhouse: A social history of welfare in America*. New York: Basic Books.

——. 1989. *The undeserving poor: From the War on Poverty to the war on welfare*. New York: Pantheon.

Kritzman, Lawrence. 1988. Introduction: Foucault and the politics of experience. In Lawrence D. Kritzman, ed., *Michel Foucault: Politics, philosophy, culture, interviews, and other writings, 1977–84*, pp. ix–xxv. New York: Routledge.

National Public Radio. 1996. *All things considered*. August 14.

Philp, Mark. 1979. Notes on the form of knowledge in social work. *Sociological Review* 27 (1): 83–109.

Rose, Nikolas. 1990. *Governing the Soul: The shaping of the private self*. London: Routledge.

——. 1993. Government, authority, and expertise in advanced liberalism. *Economy and Society* 22, no. 3 (August): 283–99.

Rose, Nikolas and Peter Miller. 1992. Political power beyond the state: Problematics of government. *British Journal of Sociology* 43, no. 2 (June): 173–205.

Teeple, Gary. 1995. *Globalization and the decline of social reform*. Toronto: Garamond.

CHAPTER 10

Postmodernity, Ethnography, and Foucault

John Devine

During the late 1970s a new and sizable population of students began to emerge within the large inner-city schools of major U.S. urban areas. Unable to adapt to standard schooling and originally designated "potential dropouts," these youth soon came to be called "at-risk students," as if this latter appellation were somehow less pejorative. No one was quite sure how to categorize this assemblage of worrisome adolescents; they were deemed not quite appropriate for a "special education" diagnosis, but neither could they be considered "normal" general education students. During the early 1970s the more progressive urban school systems across the United States began to inaugurate "alternative" schools for these students who just didn't fit into, or who had been pushed out of, traditional schools. In the beginning the problem was almost always defined as one inhering in the individual student who could be separated from the regular high school and placed in an alternative center equipped to deal with the student's pathology.

However, by the early 1980s this small group of ill-equipped, often disruptive students became a sizable portion of the student population of the "regular" high schools. In New York City, for example, they had become clustered in what were known as the "lower-tier schools" (Devine 1996). These students were the chronic truants, the pregnant and parenting girls, the disciplinary problems (the euphemism for those involved in violent incidents), the hall walkers, the students who were repeating ninth grade for the third time (known as "holdovers"), the recent immigrants, youths with histories of abuse, foster children living in group homes, and teenagers who did not know how to read or write or do even the most rudimentary mathematics.

Teachers' unions began pressuring school administrators to do something to fix these problems, and the school system, by now becoming desperate, began looking for outside help. My own program—a university-based tutoring and mentoring effort originally aimed at fifty students in one high school—was one of the many initiatives organized at that time (1984–85) to respond to the crisis. As state and later federal money became available, community-based organizations (CBOs), settlement houses, youth agencies, and other universities and colleges began to work collaboratively with schools and even with one another. Outreach workers from social agencies, after a home visit, would bring "long-term absentees" (students who had been missing classes for more than thirty days) into our tutoring room in the school basement where the students would receive individualized instruction from a graduate student in an effort to reintegrate them into the school's curriculum. Similarly, when a girl would disclose to a female graduate student, in the midst of an algebra lesson, that she thought she was pregnant, the graduate student would usually refer, or accompany, the girl to a social worker or to a local clinic. As our program evolved (we are now serving almost a thousand students per year in ten New York schools), we began to make linkages with sympathetic social workers who were also located in the schools, doing "case management" of the same students with whom we were working.

Our own roles evolved simultaneously: we learned that one-on-one tutoring is far different from classroom teaching and that, as teenagers begin to depend on their "tutors" (the graduate students) for academic help, emotional bonding is not far behind. Cognitive tutoring blossomed into embodied mentoring (e.g., field trips, visits to artistic and cultural sites), into experiences of transference and countertransference, and in some instances into long-term friendships.

But if these real world experiences were going to be a valuable part of graduate education, they would have to be consolidated into a reflective praxis, a periodic meditation on how our roles were developing vis-à-vis the youth with whom we were interacting and the institutions to which they were consigned. Graduate students' logs, their spontaneous accounts and interpretations of what was happening in the daily life of these schools, became the basic text for our weekly seminars and provided an image of the social text of the school space.

Soon the resemblance between these log passages and an anthropologist's field notes became apparent and thus emerged the triple role: we began to define ourselves as tutors, mentors, and ethnographers. I have been told by a social work professor who has examined these logs that in many ways they resemble a social worker's notes. The following log, for example, comes from a white woman tutor (pseudonym: Sheila) who stayed in touch with one of our African American students (pseudonym: Lee) during the summer he spent in jail:

I had quite a surprise today—Lee came back to school today! He came down to see me during his lunch period. This was his first day back in school. We had a really good talk. He said that he got the newspapers & postcards that I sent to him. We talked about school for awhile & then finally talked about the summer. It seems he had some horrifying experiences watching people hurt other people. He said that some of the big guys had knives & when he reported them to the [jail] guards that they didn't even check up on them. He seems truly frightened & says that he doesn't want to go back. He really is on the verge of want-ing something different. We talked about high school and coming to classes and the effect it could have on your life. I really want to con-centrate on pulling him towards other things to get him away from his neighborhood & the type of crowd he hangs with. I asked him what he missed this summer. He said his friends. I said what about his fam-ily. He said that they came to visit a lot so he didn't miss them so much. I asked him if he missed home itself, its comfort, smell, & the feel of his own bed, admitting that that is probably what I would miss the most. He smiled and said that he did miss those things. He com-mented that he also missed celebrating his birthday, which turns out to have been a few days before mine, about two weeks ago. So I asked him if there was something he would like to do & he said after some thought that he would really like to go to the zoo. I thought this was an odd request after just getting out of jail but he was serious. I said, "Let's go." He said, "When?" So we are—Ted [another tutor] is going with us & possibly a few more students next Saturday. I need to con-nect with him now because if he takes the next step he might make it.

My concern here is not to press on the reader my interpretation of this particular log excerpt, which I selected more or less at random from among hundreds of passages equally suggestive of life in New York's inner-city schools. Other logs would manifest more of a concern with academic issues or with students' relationships with peers or school authorities. In the course of our seminars we consult a broad spectrum of the educational literature to attempt to gain a fuller understanding of our privileged situation in these schools, consulting everything from social reproduction theories to critical ethnography to "whole language" approaches for literacy acquisition. The question I wish to raise here is not simply what a Foucauldian reading might be of the excerpt, but what kind of a value judgment the Foucault of *Discipline and Punish* would make of our whole enterprise of collaboration. Would we not be seen, in Foucault's eyes, as colluding with an institution—the public school system—which, from its inception at the end of the nineteenth century to now, could be described as the very embodiment of the modernity, which is Foucault's central object of critical analysis? At the heart of Foucault's message is the notion that "the classical age"—the seventeenth and eighteenth centuries—had discovered the body as the object and target of power (136). The army and boarding schools of that era not only began to pay attention to the body but they began to manipulate it, control it, correct it, train it, shape it, transform it, and "improve" it so that it would respond and obey, so that it would become skillful and increase its forces for the purposes of society. This supervision was a subtle but constant coercion that exercised infinitesimal power over the active body and increased the efficiency of its movements for society's interests. Thus was born the "docile body" through what Foucault has famously called "a micro-physics of power." The minute methods of supervising the bodily processes made this meticulous management of the body's operations (e.g., the detailed timetables of schools, the minutiae of soldierly inspections) possible and guaranteed the undeviating subjection of the body's forces. These methods were what Foucault called "disciplines," which created relationships between the body's docility and its usefulness to modern society:

> A meticulous observation of detail, and at the same time a political awareness of these small things, for the control and use of men, emerged through the classical age bearing with them a whole set of techniques, a whole corpus of methods and knowledge, descriptions, plans, and data. And from such trifles, no doubt, the man of modern humanism was born.   (*141*)

And the warranty that this relationship between docility and usefulness would break out of its institutional settings and finally penetrate society as a whole was the "panoptic gaze," which was not confined to Bentham's model prison but became the metaphor for the subtle but powerful ways in which, institutionally and individually, modern humans supervise one another and, far more significantly, supervise themselves through the internalization of that gaze. For a capitalistic society of the nineteenth and twentieth centuries, slavery is no longer needed as a method of exercising power; according to Foucault, modernity is far more efficient: through schooling and other institutionalized societal practices, human bodies have been schooled and coerced, often unwittingly, for the agenda of the dominant culture. Some strains of feminist thought, further refining the insights of Foucault, have stressed how Western society's disciplinary practices have been directed against women's bodies in ways quite distinct from those of men in order to hold women in subjection (Bartky 1988:62).

Foucault's critique of modern society is so total that he would equate all recent (i.e., eighteenth-, nineteenth-, and twentieth-century) incarnations of Western institutions—the school, university, mental hospital, prison—as deceptively promising reform, progress, or freedom but in actuality delivering subjugation. For him, these establishment structures necessarily accompanied the disciplinary technology directed against the body, male or female. As for schools in particular, even before the social reproduction theorists (e.g., Bowles and Gintis 1976; Giroux 1983, 1988; McLaren 1986), Foucault saw the whole pedagogical process not as a liberating movement of upward mobility (as the conventional wisdom would have it) but as the normalization of disciplinary power subtly insinuating its intricate pattern of control throughout society. Just as he understood modern medicine and psychiatry as panoptic surveillance rather than as progressive forces in the emancipation of humanity, certainly, a fortiori, he would perceive contemporary social work and the relatively benign and friendly mentoring portrayed earlier as naive collaboration in a process that merely co-opts adolescents into an unjust system. In stating, for example, "I need to connect with him now because if he takes the next step he might make it," does not the log writer portray her collusion with the most oppressive structures of modernity? Thinking to ameliorate the human condition, in reality (a Foucauldian would argue) she is only colluding with an unjust school system, preparing this youth, fresh from a juvenile detention center, for school, graduation, and a future of essentially repressive employment in the capitalist world—for, at best, a minimum-wage job at Burger King.

It is not just Foucauldians who look with suspicion on attempts to incorporate students, especially inner-city students, into existing pedagogical systems and curricular arrangements. Most of the progressive educational literature today is saturated with calls for reconceptualizing teaching as a political activity, for empowering students, and for reshaping teachers into "transformational intellectuals" (Giroux's phrase) who would enlighten students about the injustices of the prevailing political economies. The problem with these "emancipatory" perspectives is not that they are wrong but that they totally bypass the students' desperate needs for the skills and knowledge simply to survive in today's technological economy. Academicians who have already acquired a reservoir of learning may easily decry the political hegemony that marginalizes the poor through the valuation of abstract knowledge, standardized examinations, and school credentials.

But for youths like Lee, who may have a sudden awakening through contact with a sympathetic tutor like Sheila, there often comes the realization, around age seventeen or eighteen, that they have not received a rigorous education. Influenced by television, many youngsters aspire to careers in law, medicine, and other professions but have extremely unrealistic notions of the academic requirements. Tutors like Sheila have seen many late adolescents become angry and frustrated when they become aware that they are only prepared to attain scores of 450 to 500 on the Scholastic Aptitude Tests when even mediocre colleges demand scores in the neighborhood of 1,000. They suddenly realize that high school seniors from more affluent and middle-class backgrounds may be scoring between 1,200 and 1,600. Clearly, something went wrong with their education, they feel, and it is now too late to catch up. Analyses by reproduction theorists—which would expose, for students like Lee, the hegemony of power relations and the absurdity of the standardized test-driven pedagogy present in contemporary schooling—may be astute appraisals of capitalist society, but they ignore his need to function in that same society, his need to improve his academic achievement.

I am suggesting that a critical ethnography of the most troubled secondary schools in the most marginalized neighborhoods demonstrates exactly the opposite of Foucault's central thesis. For Foucauldians *discipline* is a bad word, and a basic assumption is that our hegemonic society is heavily invested in overdisciplining adolescents, especially inside inner-city schools. This theoretical stance is unsupported by any kind of close ethnography; long-term fieldwork in fact demonstrates precisely that educators, far from excessively disciplining youth, have mostly walked away from the job and for very understandable reasons. It has become a cliché to compare the drab interiors and ambience of urban schools to prison settings, but the more precise point of comparison is the lack of regulation enforcement, which for Lee would have been a welcome relief: "It seems he had some horrifying experiences watching people hurt other people. He said that some of the big guys had knives & when he reported them to the [jail] guards that they didn't even check up on them. He seems truly frightened & says that he doesn't want to go back."

An ethnography of inner-city school corridors reveals how closely they resemble the prison setting but, ironically, not for any reasons that would be congruent with Foucault's ideas. The chief complaint we hear from the students with whom we work is that the schools provide *too little*, not *too much* discipline. Like Lee in jail, they complain that the school security guards choose not to see weapons violations and that they enforce the school rules only when they themselves are being supervised. They complain that they cannot learn because teachers who are too permissive or too inept cannot control their classrooms and they complain that teachers look the other way in the cafeterias, corridors, and public spaces of the school in order not to see student misbehavior. The teachers, they tell us, are afraid of the students, afraid to give reprimands directly. Instead, schools have inaugurated "conflict resolution" sessions that weakly—and ineffectively—deal with infractions only after the fact. What has happened to the panoptic gaze that is supposed to have permeated modernity? Or to the internalization of that gaze?

I contend that the great body of Foucauldian theory today is emanating from university milieus cut off from the real world of schooling that the poor receive. Intellectuals disapprove of the "order of things," the very order for which students in the lowest-rung schools are yearning. There is an almost total absence of ethnography, of informed reflection based on real world contact with inner-city schools in the most dangerous neighborhoods for a sustained period of time. Intellectuals and academicians imagine, perhaps, that the pedagogy being foisted upon the children of the poor is somehow similar to their own memories of middle-class schooling. They assume that today's students are being disciplined into "docile bodies" and they lament that, as a result, schooling will never become true education (see, for example, Goodson and Dowbiggin 1990:126), which seems to become defined as a state in which authorities no longer have to insist on compliance with rules.

In fact, the poor are receiving a poor education, but the most lamentable feature about it is not excessive discipline but, on the contrary, the almost total absence of a structure that cares enough to correct. American culture, and our schooling in particular, is immersed in a permissiveness that is at least as total as William Damon suggests: "Schools and teachers are shirking their responsibilities as guardians of the young if they do *not* advocate core standards such as honesty, respect, integrity, and the pursuit of excellence" (1995:208).

This permissiveness appears to become more accentuated, not less, as one moves down the socioeconomic scale. In New York City's most troubled schools, moral instruction is no longer even a topic of discussion among high school teachers. Teachers' unions have seen to it that enforcement of the disciplinary codes in the public areas of the school have now been completely delegated to the guards. More and more, teachers have been pressured by the board of education to focus only on the cognitive side of education, on the percentages of students who have passed the Regents exams and similar quantitative criteria. Granted, this in itself is a form of panopticism, but it is also one that involves an avoidance of the more demanding forms of panopticism, namely, those that concentrate on students' social forms of behavior.

This emphasis has resulted in an almost complete deemphasis of the emotional and the supervisory aspects traditionally considered an integral part of the teacher's role. New York City high school teachers no longer think of themselves as functioning in loco parentis, a development that Foucauldian theorists would no doubt applaud. The normal posture of these scholars toward any kind of pedagogy that would stress moral development is one of disdain; here is how one contributor to a volume on Foucault describes the evolution of the Victorian teacher as moral instructor:

> Subsequently, the teacher through a process of self-examination is transformed into a moral exemplar to project an ethical verity into the unknown of the Victorian city. This transformative morality pictures the teacher as an ideal father, a good and rational parent, and eventually, in an interesting reversal of gender, a good and nurturing mother. Always, however, this imagery is *in loco parentis* to remedy the inadequate parenting of the urban tenements. In this last image the teacher forms an element within a tutelary complex that exercises a bio-power to advise the urban family and examine the extent of its pathology.
>
> *(Jones 1990:75)*

This synthesis Jones establishes of Foucault's pedagogical concepts is no doubt flawless: the urban teacher is seen as the determining factor in reinforcing the bourgeois family within the framework of nineteenth- and early twentieth-century modernity. Let us grant the accuracy of this historical picture but simultaneously ask ourselves why it is no longer valid today. Although academicians do not normally like to descend to the level of discourse about the kind of school horror stories that appear almost daily in the Metro section of the *New York Times*, all these large, overcrowded inner-city schools have one feature in common: the fear of, and the actuality of, violence. One might just as easily assert the opposite proposition: that these "horror stories," far from being overemphasized, are not being sufficiently discussed. I would contend that the culture of violence now permeating schools (and, of course, societal institutions generally) has not been adequately understood or theorized.

I have tried to show (Devine 1995, 1996) that a culture of violence permeates everyday life in inner-city schools. But there also exists, side-by-side with this culture of violence, a denial of its existence, a phenomenon Allen Feldman has aptly called "cultural anesthesia" (1994). The presence of metal detectors, security guards, armed police, and the impressive array of "safety" technology that greets the visitor in the lobby of an urban school have not brought about the expected results of less alienation and a greater sense of sanctuary and community. On the contrary, the conflation of pedagogy with policing has only resulted in a distancing of teachers from interaction with the body of the student. As security comes more and more the province of the guards, the spotlight on weapons and on major crime grows stronger and stronger. Emphasis on the "minutiae" of etiquette and behavioral standards diminishes proportionately, and teachers become separated from issues of moral instruction, counseling, and even informal friendly contact with students. Despite the teachers' unions' involvement in the evolution of this process, it would be too simplistic to blame the teaching profession alone for the present state of affairs. Teachers, principals, and other school personnel have been assigned the almost impossible managerial task of administering schools of twenty-five hundred to four thousand students in an age when drugs, alcohol, and guns are available just outside—and inside—the schoolhouse door. These schools have become pressure-cookers of instability, constantly ready to explode; in such an atmosphere teachers try to focus on "teaching," which becomes synonymous with attempting to impart cognitive information (i.e., getting through the syllabus), while the "body" of the student is consigned to the guards. Everyone on the scene tries to avoid any confrontation with those manifestations of the youth culture that test the limits and the sanity of the staff.

Recent visits to ten New York City schools (during September 1997) revealed, for example, that many girls during the warm weather were wearing provocative and inappropriate clothing (e.g., tight-fitting dresses and gym shorts on the school corridors) to which boys were responding with catcalls, remarks, and physical touches. These playful interactions were certain to lead to anger, aggression, and physical fighting as the year wears on, but no staff members were willing to take on these highly sensitive and potentially explosive issues. The imparting of social skills is no longer considered part of the job description of a high school teacher. Yet we find that students expect adults to correct them, to draw limits, and to enforce the rules.

Can we, then, reconcile these apparent antinomies, this total contradiction between a Foucauldian metanarrative, which holds that a cult of discipline is all pervasive and growing through the capillary arteries of society, and what, on the other hand, ethnography clearly manifests about the daily life of inner-city schools, namely, that they are laden with an ethos of fear and violence and that discipline, moral instruction, minute surveillance, and the "micro-physics" of etiquette and character formation are now things of the past?

One response to this dilemma is to make a sharp distinction between the epoch of modernity from which we are emerging and the period of postmodernity into which we are plunging. Thus what Foucault calls panopticism would seem to have been a phenomenon inherent in modernity but now in the process of dissolution in a society no longer interested in supervising its young. This analysis also changes our understanding of postmodernism itself. The standard descriptors (such as collage, fragmentation, indeterminacy, etc.) are inadequate to express the essence of the postmodern moment, which—if the corridors of inner-city schools may be considered as one indication—can be summed up in a single word: *violence.* The paradigm of Foucault—essentially, the panopticon—served in many ways as the dominant icon to recapitulate the era of modernity. But it is essentially useless for the postmodern interval in which we find ourselves, a time when (as in postmodern architecture) it is becoming clearer and clearer that we must go back and reintegrate into the present, eclectically and without nostalgia, some of the elements of the classical age that Foucault would have totally discarded: discipline, surveillance, caring, and other aspects of a humanism. This is not to deny, of course, that that same humanism must be thoroughly demythologized and depatriarchalized.

REFERENCES

Bartky, Sandra Lee. 1988. Foucault, femininity, and the modernization of patriarchal power. In Irene Diamond and Lee Quinby, eds., *Feminism and Foucault: Reflections on resistance.* Boston: Northeastern University Press.

Bowles, Samuel and Herbert Gintis. 1976. *Schooling in capitalist America.* New York: Basic Books.

Damon, William. 1995. *Greater expectations: Overcoming the culture of indulgence in America's homes and schools.* New York: Free Press.

Devine, John. 1995. Can metal detectors replace the panopticon? *Cultural Anthropology* 10 (2): 171–95.

———. 1996. *Maximum security: The culture of violence in inner-city schools*. Chicago: University of Chicago Press.

Feldman, Allen. 1994. On cultural anesthesia: From Desert Storm to Rodney King. *American Ethnologist* 21 (2): 404–18.

Foucault, Michel. 1977. *Discipline and punish: The birth of the prison*. New York: Vintage.

Giroux, Henry A. 1983. *Theory and resistance in education*. South Hadley, Mass.: Bergin and Garvey.

———. 1988. *Schooling and the struggle for public life: Critical pedagogy in the modern age*. Minneapolis: University of Minnesota Press.

Goodson, Ivor and Ian Dowbiggin. 1990. Docile bodies: Commonalities in the history of psychiatry and schooling. In Stephen J. Ball, ed., *Foucault and education: Disciplines and knowledge*. London: Routledge.

Jones, Dave. 1990. The genealogy of the urban schoolteacher. In Stephen J. Ball, ed., *Foucault and education: Disciplines and knowledge*. London: Routledge.

McLaren, Peter. 1986. *Schooling as a ritual performance: Toward a political economy of educational symbols and gestures*. London: Routledge and Kegan Paul.

Issues to Look Forward to

Adrienne S. Chambon and Allan Irving

Writing a conclusion is often an act of authority couched in words of humility. Are we proposing the true, final interpretation of Foucault for social work? There is no need for such a definitive claim. Can we garner support and establish our credibility? Can we conclusively state what lessons we have learned or which echoes have been created? We can, at least, reflect on some ways we could read this text. The ultimate reading is that of the reader.

A number of threads run through these essays. Arguments taken up by Foucault and his contemporaries in the Roundtable flicker persistently through the remaining chapters. A conversation takes place between the authors through the juxtaposition of their contributions—at times reinforcing and complementing, and at other times, it might seem, contradicting one another.

For all the contributors Foucault problematizes what we take for granted—our tools, practices, and assumptions of knowing. This basic questioning characterizes his work. Such an approach can be stimulating or perplexing, if not downright vexing. Most often it induces all those responses at once. It can be exhilarating to recognize aspects of experience, knowledge, or habit not generally attended to and to follow a process of defamiliarization and redefinition—such that what is familiar first becomes unfamiliar through problematization and then ends up refocused, newly shaped. At that point there is often a joyful sense of recognition. This combination of blurring and focus, muddle and recognition generally happens in reading Foucault.

The process of undoing is no doubt disquieting. It stirs up large pools of certainty and opens them up for scrutiny. Facts in themselves are no longer treated as solid (cf. chap. 2). They do not in themselves demonstrate adequacy or veracity. Solidity is an artifact of the structure of habit that takes on the appearance of common sense and self-evidence. Facts tell stories. Events and circumstances can be grouped together to illuminate certain logics. The reader may feel uneasy because of this unending probing and wonder where all this will end. What if it all unravels? What can be saved that is valued? Will it all be denigrated or destroyed? Will this immobilize or inhibit movement?

Chapters 5 and 7 provide parallel arguments in response. The authors similarly conclude that far from dissolving the relevance of policy or practice, a Foucauldian approach broadens the scope of both and gives them a sturdier ground, with the consequences leading to different decisions.

Foucault shows us not only the unnaturalness but also the contested nature of our activities and our assumptions. The canon of a time is the result of contestation and the product of disputations. It is not the outcome of progressive enlightenment. Such are the arenas of child welfare as demonstrated by Nigel Parton (chap. 5), sexuality as shown by Carol-Anne O'Brien (chap. 6), age group identity as shown by Frank Wang (chap. 8). There is a constant struggle for positions, which mobilizes the self existentially and organizationally—a horizon present in the chapters by Irving (chap. 2) and by Wang (chap. 8). Critically, as argued by the participants in the Roundtable in chapter 4, professions as a whole are subject to the periodic redrawing of domains of competency and to changing relations of influence between allied disciplines. For social work the concern is its changing relation to the fields of law, health, and mental health.

Even when no tensions are apparent, the appearance of consensus requires that we go beneath the smooth surface of things. That is the constant objective in Laura Epstein's work, the stirring of the pot, to make visible the tissue, the battle scars, the sewing of a seemingly seamless fabric, and the unveiling of the familiar environment, in the words of Adrienne Chambon.

Things are not simply as they are, they come to be; we come to be who we are along with them, as argued by Irving. Foucault brings in a historical viewpoint more as a window for locating our present than for explicating the past. History is no longer the restricted domain of historians. We are invited to conduct "histories of the present," starting from our own field (chaps. 1, 3, and 5). The contributions with historical content in this book rely mostly on secondary sources, unlike Foucault who worked extensively with archives. There lies an enormous potential for social workers to do archival work about the many turns of our profession and not to leave this exclusively in the hands of historians. This was the conclusion that Laura Epstein was moving toward as she worked her way deeper into her own Foucauldian project; this is what she was starting to do. Clearly, there is a trend in this direction. Howard Goldstein (1996) has examined the archives of a children's institution as a way of connecting personal testimony and institutional history. Within a Foucauldian perspective Vivienne Cree (1995) examined the historical transformation of British social work through an agency's archives. Patrick Selmi is working from the social welfare archives in Minnesota to understand the gap between the claims made by social work about its community mission and the positions taken historically by the discipline.

Foucault's fundamental suspiciousness of taken-for-granted realities is particularly applicable to the foundational logic of our discipline—itself, a product of history. As presented by Irving, Foucault centrally objects to the Enlightenment model of rational thought as the royal road to knowledge or action. In the history of social work, as argued by Epstein, "the human or social sciences are the backbone of the technologies that have emerged as instruments by which the state can govern with minimal coercion; or when coercion is employed . . . human science offers ways to support, ameliorate, disguise, and justify the state's carceral machinery" (chap. 1). The scientific dogma and its combination with other paradigms, such as psychologism or therapeutism (chaps. 1 and 4), the science of sexuality (chap. 6), rational accounts for the processing of emotions (chap. 7), the elaborate calculations of "risk" (chap. 5), and procedural mechanisms implemented between clients and workers (chap. 9) are all "rational" modalities that, through their exercise, create subjectivities in particular ways and not in others. There are no indifferent structures of knowledge. Various attempts to attain the most "neutral" knowledge or modality of practice hide the functions and effects of these very attempts (chap. 3). Each structure creates a worldview, and dominant forms dominate other subjugated forms.

Along this line, our "models" and technology mold the participation of clients and workers. Technology is not only know-how; it is also knowledge presented as truth, or prescriptive knowledge. It is important to recognize that seeking to do something well according to the norm may not leave much room for examining the nature of those assumptions. This is not to say that there is "good" knowledge as opposed to "bad" knowledge but that knowledge and, similarly, practice always have a prescriptive side. There is no "neutral" choice; instead, we make choices of a particular kind. The issue is to be able to see what our decisions entail and to consider alternatives.

Paying close attention to the language of our knowledge claims and of our practices provides clues for reading into the logics of meaning and action that we are advocating. Again, language is not neutral. It is a form of action that commits the source and the speakers (see chaps. 1, 3, 5, and 6; see also Chambon 1994), and this includes how we teach and how we write about social work.

In an observation that could have come straight from Foucault, Laura Epstein reminds us that social work, as it is conventionally practiced, "must produce an effect without force, without command, indirectly. It must not be authoritative. It must enable its clients to be transformed, to adopt normative ways and thoughts, voluntarily." Her argument echoes the Roundtable participants.' They see a continuity between overt forms of sanction or exclusion and gentler forms of normalization that extend broadly into the general public.

As Epstein astutely points out, social work has been imbricated with liberalism's view of poverty in individualistic terms and has been instrumental in turning therapy into social policy. For their part, Roundtable participants decried social work's contribution to clinical reductionism and to the process of "dismemberment and atomization of the social fabric." Within this logic even community interventions can become an intrusive involvement in the everyday life of individual community members. These contributors alert us to the consequences of targeting categories of people. They argue that differentiation among groups of all kinds goes hand in hand with processes of exclusion and stifles the emergence of potential movements of solidarity among clients and workers.

In these essays the authors do not share a unitary usage of the questions of power and the subject from Foucault's work, and at first this may be confusing. What did Foucault say? Which understanding is the right one? Can't the authors agree? The diversity of this project is most manifest in this broad issue of power and self—we can read "multiple entries" into a source and not only diverse applications—with the caveat that, given the space, only a few views are presented. Do the authors really disagree with one another? It seemed to us that the emphasis of each overlaps with that of the others, for power and the subject are multifaceted.

Ken Moffatt shows us the multiplicity of obvious and subtle mechanisms (architectural, body posture, interactional speech, bureaucratic forms, use of time) that together create a "regime" of authority, control, and knowledge. Foote and Frank discuss the pervasiveness of expanding circles of influence (individualizing, universalizing, normalizing). Broader macromechanisms are present in Parton and in Wang, who show how wider societal conditions facilitate certain modalities.

Power is external and internal. Its repressive quality is more obvious in the first instance (see chaps. 5 and 9); in the second it is an apparently "positive" shaping and claiming of a particular normative self (chap. 7); it can even be enhancing (i.e., empowering) at the individual, group, and societal levels (chap. 8). That is when power is productive. This does not mean to say that it is one *or* the other but that it is both. Power is not encompassed solely by the stern figure of authority but also through intriguing forms of incitement and self-recruitment, through expectations about emotions and relations. Power is regulation and self-governance. We can read the chapters and see that each contains the other facets as well but in a fainter manner.

Is power everywhere? It is certainly not contained by the acts of overt domination. The power exercised by social workers over others and over themselves can take on many forms and serve many functions simultaneously. Can we hold onto the many sides of power and making of the self as positive and negative all at once? From such a vantage point the notion of "effective" practice is no longer straightforward but becomes multifaceted. Resistance itself, as discussed by Foote and Frank, Wang, and Moffatt (chaps. 7, 8, and 9), is a form of power and that also alerts us to the mechanisms of normally hidden power (chap. 3). Empowering practices can have a down side; they can impose and exclude. Conversely, certain apparently disempowering practices may contain kernels of productivity, as Devine suggests about the positive effect of structuring practices (chap. 10).

Does this mean that all is "relative"? Relative is the opposite of what the authors are saying. *Relative* means that everything is equally good in a given circumstance, that it does not matter. In a Foucauldian approach it very much matters—indeed, it matters more than before. As emphasized by Wang, Foucault calls for "local" intellectuals to do the difficult work of examining particular grounded conditions. Indeed, in their case examples the authors show us the production of power and the constitution of self in very specific constellations. These are not haphazard.

What are the limits of applicability of a Foucauldian analysis? There is the limit to our willingness to attempt to conduct such work and to stand on uncertain ground. Irving discusses the uncomfortable, if not downright painful, position we come to occupy when we choose to reexamine it all. The tone of Epstein's chapter points to the acrimonious quality that goes along with reexamining our own practices, our fiefdom, cleaning up our house. Freedom is the unknown; the quest is also an unknown. There is no predetermined grid that will reveal the sunken structure. It is up to us to do the work.

Examining the "local" necessarily raises the question of the limits of applicability. Whereas Wang raises the question of the "local" (cultural and historical) in positive terms, Devine questions the applicability of Foucauldian notions across historical periods, particularly their relevance to the current times, pointing as he does to the split between modernist and postmodern conditions. Should Foucault be confined, he asks, to the study of modernist (or more traditional) forms of power? McBeath and Webb's 1991 inquiry does not sustain this position; they apply a Foucauldian analysis to the contemporary fragmentation in administration and the expansion of managerial logic.

Yet Devine's chapter raises a critical question: How do we import theoretical concepts into local practices? (See also John [1994] on this issue.) Devine provides one set of answers. A different option can be argued along the following line: that Foucault developed the figure of the panopticon at the endpoint of his analysis (see chap. 3), as an outcome of his examination of the historical figure of modernity. To be consistent with Foucault's approach would require that we start from the empirical examination of the small facts, the ethnography that Devine speaks of, and then derive from it the name of the construction, the figure that represents this particular type of relations of power. If we do this, we come to the conclusion that the type of rationality that Devine speaks of is a vacuum of structure, the relinquishing of traditional moral identity, and the recomposing of areas of expertise and involvement, whereby teachers no longer educate. This historical reshuffling necessarily entails new figures of practice, and new figures of understanding, so that we develop this "figure" and we name it differently. The figure of the inner-city schools may strike us as the stark opposite, or "counterfigure," of the panopticon. Those schools (and similar situations) are no longer characterized by a surplus of involvement but instead by its absence; this invisibility is achieved in relinquishing intrusion through underinvolvement. It is the panopticon turned inside out. Indeed, Devine's example illustrates well the limits of applicability of concepts but does not, in our minds, restrict the applicability of a Foucauldian approach, which is then to be taken heuristically.

Substantively, Devine's and Moffatt's chapters may appear to be in contradiction with one another, with Moffatt's description of intrusive mechanisms at play in the welfare office. This may not be a conflict but may instead show that diverse rationalities can operate side by side in society and within a professional field at a given historical point—an argument made by Foucault and taken up in the Roundtable. In social work today we find the archaic, the modern, and the postmodern side by side. How this takes place, either as distinct spheres of influence or as competing ones, remains to be examined.

Saying this, we relate to Foucault as a reader of signs. Can we entertain the thought that the current signs might point to the end of social work or the end of social work as we know it? This is historically a transition point, and there is a need to read the cultural symbols. Are we equipped? As this book shows, bringing Foucault into the discussion enhances our ability to decipher the times.

Is Foucault a pessimist? Is he a negativist in elegant clothing who can only critique, deconstruct, demystify, and leave us holding the bag as he moves on? Or is he also the author who claims that this is done to encourage new "possibles," as Parton, Irving, and Chambon underscore; one who strives for freedom—for a freedom that can never be achieved. Neither a bird of gloom nor a prophet (Foote and Frank), Foucault opens up new thinking and imagery without being a visionary. This book does not address pedagogy directly, but the essays individually and collectively have a lot to say about teaching social work. One reading of these essays begins to move us away from what seems to be increasingly at times a technology in our pedagogical practices.

If pedagogy is a system of redress, as argued in the Roundtable, redress itself can be read differently. Rather than getting the story "straight," we might want to get the story crooked.

This book does not exhaust the interpretations of Foucault or potential fields of application (see, for instance, Katz 1996 or Lupton 1995) but offers a particular range of interpretations of his work. Rather than seek exhaustiveness, we can try to put closure to this volume by highlighting several arguments.

Through his continuous search Foucault shows us that philosophy can be reconciled with empirical evidence. Practices are institutional, and a critical understanding comes by examining the details of small facts. Equally important is the other side of the equation: the social arena benefits from the theoretical as well as from the poetic. The humanities can become a safety net.

Substantively, his writings challenge our readiness and our ability to examine the functions served by our discipline and the consequences of our services. While social workers focus on the values of self-determination and empowerment, we need to allow ourselves to ask the question of the profession as whole: Does social work have enough autonomy as a discipline? Do social workers exercise autonomy in their practice? This troubling issue is central to the discussion held between Foucault and the others at the Roundtable. Indeed, what is the degree of autonomy of our profession? What kind of a power does it exercise? What alliances does it entertain? Where does the knowledge that we develop truly come from and what aims does it accomplish? What kind of a world is sustained by the professional activities of social workers? Do we not automatically adopt a number of ways that function to control, to contain, to render us subservient to the logic of power relations established elsewhere, outside the discipline? What margin exists for developing knowledge and action of a different kind?

There are grave concerns today about the nature of social work and of its future, how we position ourselves, and which side we are on. With the undoing of the rationality of the welfare states, it is now urgent to develop strategies of response. Foucault is not to be our guide in this venture, but he can be a concrete source of inspiration through the profound questions he poses of professionals' involvement in the constitution of self and society. Foucault harps at a grating challenge when he suggests that our unexamined assumptions block our view and our situation; they inhibit our ability to fight for alternative arrangements. We can pick up and adapt some of the tools that Foucault crafted to gaze into, and actively shape, the nature of our commitments. For social work cannot simply roll along in the present storm of dislocating change. We need to act—contemplating, in doing so, alternative possibilities.

REFERENCES

Chambon, Adrienne S. 1994. Postmodernity and social work discourses: Notes on the changing language of a profession. In Adrienne S. Chambon and Allan Irving, eds., *Essays on postmodernism and social work*, pp. 61–75. Toronto: Canadian Scholars' Press.

Cree, V. E. 1995. *From public streets to private lives: The changing task of social work.* Aldershot, U.K.: Avebury.

Goldstein, Howard. 1996. *The home on Gorham street and the voices of its children.* Tuscaloosa: University of Alabama Press.

John, L. H. 1994. Borrowed knowledge in social work: An introduction to poststructuralism and postmodernity. In A. S. Chambon and Allan Irving, eds., *Essays on postmodernism and social work*, pp. 47–60. Toronto: Canadian Scholars' Press.

Katz, Stephen. 1996. *Disciplining old age: The formation of gerontological knowledge.* Charlottesville and London: University Press of Virginia.

Lupton, Deborah. 1995. *The imperative of health: Public health and the regulated body.* Thousand Oaks, Calif.: Sage.

McBeath, G. B. and S. A. Webb. 1991. Social work, modernity, and postmodernity. *Sociological Review* 39 (4): 745–62.

Foucault did not rely on a standard use of concepts. In keeping with his theory, he developed appropriate tools, created new conceptual definitions and usages, and when needed, coined new terms.

This glossary is to be approached as a set of keys that gives access to Foucault's work, as a tool for understanding. It is not to be taken as the definitive list of key terms, nor the definitions as prescriptive standards. These concepts were not fixed once and for all in Foucault's writings. They changed as his thinking evolved, through phases of his work and concurrently with the development of contemporary ideas. Various formulations were also responsive to the diverse audiences he was addressing. The glossary is here to prompt reflection about what concepts can do, how they can be seen for their heuristic value as generators of new knowledge. In brief, a glossary is another form of commentary (on this point, see the *Concise Oxford Dictionary*, 7th ed., 1982).

The glossary includes quotes from Foucault's work. It directs readers to some of his key writings and to a few compendia of original Foucauldian material complemented by discussions. A list of these sources appears at the end of the glossary.

Archaeology

Archaeology is a concept used by Foucault in the earlier phase of his work to explore the origins of contemporary ideas in the field of health and more

---

[1]*Developed by Adrienne S. Chambon and Frank Wang.*

generally in the human sciences. It points to a type of reconstructive work that uncovers the historical layers of implicit rules and assumptions that have come to sustain today's commonly accepted knowledge. It is in no way predictive or deterministic. He later revised archeology into the concept of *genealogy.*

"The word archaeology is not supposed to carry any suggestion of anticipation; it simply indicates a possible line of attachment for the analysis of verbal performances: the specification of a structural level . . . the regularities of statements, or 'enunciations,' the 'positivities,' or, constitution of domains; [it enables] the application of such concepts as rules of formation, archaeological derivation, and historical a priori" (translation adapted from 1972:206).
    References: 1972, 1973b, 1975.

Bio-power

Bio-power is a conceptual tool that makes it possible to analyze historically how power has come to work in relation to the human body. The concept refers to the mechanism that takes the body and life as objects of intervention. Power operates on the individual body to optimize its capabilities, efficiency, usefulness, and docility. On a macroscale it also manages the biological processes of a population—births, mortality, and probabilities of life. Bio-power relies on associated forms of knowledge, such as surveys, demographic studies, and public health campaigns.
    Sexuality is located at a privileged intersection between the individual and the population. It is a target of self-knowledge and the essential means to regulate the reproduction of a population.

"The old power of death that symbolized sovereign power was now carefully supplanted by the administration of bodies and the calculated management of life" (1990:139–40).
    "One would have to speak of bio-power to designate what brought life and its mechanisms into the realm of explicit calculations and made knowledge-power an agent of transformation of human life" (1990:143).
    "Sex as a political issue . . . was at the pivot of the two axes along which developed the entire political technology of life. On the one hand, it was tied to the disciplines of the body: the harnessing, intensification, and distribution of forces, the adjustment and economy of energies. On the other hand,

it was applied to the regulation of populations, through all the far-reaching effects of its activity. It fitted in both categories at once, giving rise to infinitesimal surveillances, permanent controls, extremely meticulous orderings of space, indeterminate medical or psychological examinations, to an entire micropower concerned with the body. But it gave rise as well to comprehensive measures, statistical assessments, and interventions aimed at the entire social body or at groups taken as a whole" (1984:267).

"As the rise of bio-power is seen as indispensable to the development of capitalism which compels the state to manage its population without coercive action, the political response to this new form of power on life is the right to life and to one's body, and the right to discover what one is and all that one can be" (1990:145).

References: 1973b, 1984, 1990, 1991.

Discipline

Foucault used the concept of *discipline* to describe how power operates in very small ways to guide behavior through clusters of means and diverse technologies. The use of the word plays on its multiple meanings. Discipline refers equally to acts of punishment and correction and to fields of knowledge that diagnose deviance from the norm and intervene to remove it. Foucault argues that disciplines emerged historically with the rise of the human sciences. Disciplines turn human beings into an object of study and within each domain produce a "specific individual," such that health disciplines create a "medicalized self."

Disciplines invite individuals to willingly participate in the process of self-construction. We become at once our own object of study and the instrument for disciplining ourselves. The *panopticon* is an example that Foucault used to illustrate the ideal form of disciplinary technology.

"'Discipline' may be identified neither with an institution nor with an apparatus; it is a type of power, a modality for its exercise, comprising a whole set of instruments, techniques, procedures, levels of application, targets; it is a 'physics' or an 'anatomy' of power, a technology" (1995:215).

"Discipline 'makes' individuals; it is the specific technique of power that regards individuals both as objects and as instruments of its exercise" (1995:170).

"Disciplines constitute a system of control in the production of discourse, fixing its limits through the action of an identity taking the form of a permanent reactivation of the rules" (1972:224).

References: 1972, 1986, 1990, 1991, 1995.

Discourse

Foucault frequently uses the term *discourse*, and it has taken on a range of meanings. Discourses are structures of knowledge and systematic ways of carving out reality that characterize particular historical moments. The embodied acts of discourse, or *discursive practices*, provide parameters for what can be known, said, and thought. How we think about things is what constitutes them. Even the self is constituted through discourse.

A discourse can be empirically traced to a group of statements, produced and structured through clusters of signs that appear consistently together. These statements follow a family of rules and are characterized by a certain type of rationality. Discourses emerge across diverse institutions and in the context of (nondiscursive) sociopolitical mechanisms. New *discursive formations* accompany historical changes.

"Discursive practices are characterized by the delimitation of a field of objects, the definition of a legitimate perspective for the agent of knowledge, and the fixing of norms for the elaboration of concepts and theories. Thus, each discursive practice implies a play of prescriptions that designate its exclusions and choices" (1977:199).

"Treat discourse . . . as practices that systematically form the objects of which they speak" (1972:49).

"The transformation of a discursive practice is linked to a whole range of usually complex modifications that can occur outside of its domain (in the forms of production, in social relationships, in political institutions), inside it (in its techniques for determining its object, in its accumulation of facts), or to the side of it (in other discursive practices)" (1977:200).

"We must make allowance for the complex and unstable process whereby discourse can be both an instrument and an effect of power, but also a hindrance, a stumbling-block, a point of resistance and a starting point for an opposing strategy. Discourse transmits and produces power; it reinforces it, but also undermines and exposes it, renders it fragile and makes it possible to thwart it" (1990:101).

References: 1972, 1973b, 1995, 1977, 1990, 1991.

Dividing Practices

Dividing practices lie at the heart of the techniques of power by establishing partitions and creating categories. They differentiate between the normal and the abnormal, or the pathological. Dividing practices are implemented through procedures that distinguish, separate, and categorize populations—as deviant, criminal, vagabond, or nonproductive in the prison system (1995), healthy/sick in medicine (1973a), sane/mad in psychiatry (1973b), and heterosexual/homosexual in sexuality (1990). The logic of differentiation and exclusion tends to locate individuals within expanding systems of classifications.

Dividing practices also occur at the level of the self. When individuals apply to themselves the same criteria of judgment and self-evaluation, they engage in dividing the self between an observer, or knowing, self and an observed and managed self.

"'Dividing practices' . . . constitute polarities between self and other, good versus bad, normal versus pathological. They create classes of features, and categories of people: If the science of man [social sciences] appeared as an extension of the science of life, . . . the very subjects it devoted itself to (man, his behaviour, his individual and social realizations) therefore opened up a field that was divided up according to the principles of the normal and the pathological" (1975:36).

"In the second part of my work, I have studied the objectivizing of the subject which I shall call 'dividing practices.' The subject is either divided inside himself or divided from others. This process objectivizes him. Examples are the mad and the sane, the sick and the healthy, the criminals and the 'good boys'" (1982:208).

References: 1973a, 1975, 1982, 1995.

Episteme

By the *episteme of an age* Foucault meant an encompassing notion, not quite a worldview or ideology but a system of discourses that underpins bodies of knowledge. An episteme is a system of references against which statements are "measured." It allows some statements to be seen as true and others as false. In a given historical period its episteme assumes the active role of defining the conditions of possibility of thought, of legislating and establishing the limits of understanding.

"In any given culture and at any given moment, there is always only one episteme that defines the conditions of possibility of all knowledge, whether expressed in a theory or silently invested in a practice" (1973a:168).

References: 1973a, 1973b.

Genealogy

The genealogical approach is a refinement of the earlier concept of archaeology. *Genealogy* refers to a "history of the present" that traces the existence of practices and knowledge from the present to the past. It provides a new understanding of historical development and makes room for complex circumstances. Attention is given to those events that mark local struggles and discontinuities, that act as turning points in the emergence of new forms of reasoning, assumptions about normality, and the constitution of the self. Genealogies equally reveal continuities in ways of doing and thinking that are commonly masked by distinctions that are only apparent.

"What I would call genealogy . . . [is] a form of history which can account for the constitution of knowledges, discourses, domains of objects, etc., without having to make reference to a subject which is either transcendental in relation to the field of events or runs in its empty sameness throughout the course of history" (1980:117)

"Genealogical work makes no sweeping generalizations. Selecting particular practices and statements, it traces back the 'conditions of their existence,' or how they came to be what they are, and not other. In this manner, it identifies new continuities and discontinuities among the ideas and practices of a field. It highlights critical moments, breaks and departures" (1977:146).

"An examination of descent permits the discovery, under the unique aspect of a trait or concept, of the myriad events through which—thanks to which, against which—they were formed. . . . Where the soul pretends unification or the self fabricates a coherent identity, the genealogist sets out to study the beginning—numberless beginnings whose faint traces and hints of color are readily seen by an historical eye" (1977:146).

References: 1973b, 1977, 1980,1991.

Governmentality

With the concept of *governmentality* Foucault expands the realm of what is seen as political, or state power, to encompass a wide range of everyday practices that are generally not thought of in this manner. This concept underscores the historical emergence of an *art of government* organized to enhance and maximize the capacities of populations. The concept of governmentality draws attention to the diversity of techniques through which a population enters into calculations of rule.

In later formulations, governmentality is also defined as a point of contact between institutional technologies of regulation and modalities of self-regulation.

"This word must be allowed the very broad meaning which it had in the sixteenth century. *Government* did not refer only to political structures or to the management of states; rather it designated the way in which the conduct of individuals or of groups might be directed: the government of children, of souls, of communities, of families, of the sick. It did not only cover the legitimately constituted forms of political or economic subjection, but also modes of action, more or less considered and calculated which were destined to act upon the possibilities of action of other people. To govern, in this sense, is to structure the possible field of action of others" (1982:221).

Governmentality is an "ensemble formed by the institutions, procedures, analyses and reflections, the calculations and tactics, that allow the exercise of this specific albeit complex form of power which has as its target population, as its principal form of knowledge political economy, and as its essential technical means apparatuses of security" (1991:102).

References: 1982, 1991.

Knowledge

Knowledge is a partial and selective representation of reality. Through his studies of the psychiatric ward, the clinic, the prison, and sexuality, Foucault traced the *history of ideas*, and concomitant practices, in different disciplines.

Knowledge and power are inevitably and inextricably connected, not in the abstract but through specific and contextual relations. Every development of knowledge fosters an increase in specific forms of power, and conversely, any expansion of specific power required an increase in specific forms of knowledge.

"My aim is to uncover the principles and consequences of an autochthonous transformation that is taking place in the field of historical knowledge" (1972:15).

References: 1972, 1973b, 1995.

Normalization

Normalization refers to establishing the normal as a standard for judgment and against which to distinguish the pathological. Normalization implies the development of forms of knowledge that set standards and ideals for human thought and human conduct and against which individuals are assessed, measured, and judged. It implies processes by which society (specifically, the human sciences and the helping professions) acts upon individuals and groups to regulate, shape, or make them conform to a norm. Normalization also requires that one render one's self normal. Individuals being transformed should desire and participate in the process of their own free will.

"It introduces through this 'value-giving measure' the constraint of a conformity that must be achieved" (1984:196).

"Normalization becomes one of the great instruments of power at the end of the classical age. For the marks that once indicated status, privilege, and affiliation were increasingly replaced—or at least supplemented—by a whole range of degrees of normality indicating membership of a homogeneous social body, but also playing a part in classification, hierarchization, and the distribution of rank" (1984:196).

"In a sense, the power of normalization imposes homogeneity; but it individualizes by making it possible to measure gaps, to determine levels, to fix specialties, and to render the differences useful by fitting them one to another" (1984:197).

References: 1984, 1990, 1995.

Panopticon

Foucault drew on the architectural design of Jeremy Bentham's *panopticon* as the prototype of a mode of surveillance and monitoring—"a prison so radially that a guard at a central position can see all the prisoners" (*Merriam Webster's Collegiate Dictionary*, 10th ed.)—that can be applied to different institutions. The panopticon imposes on the subjects a continuous and compulsory visibility, which makes them visible to the guardian of authority without the possibility of returning the gaze. It stands for a mechanism that monitors the effects of interventions to train or correct people. Self-discipline can replace coercion as the method of social control, when, having internalized the gaze, individuals come to monitor themselves.

"The exercise of discipline presupposes a mechanism that coerces by means of observation; an apparatus in which the techniques that make it possible to see induced effects of power and in which, conversely, the means of coercion make those on whom they are applied clearly visible" (1995:170–71).

"In the peripheric ring, one is totally seen without ever seeing; in the central tower one sees everything without ever being seen" (1995:202).

"The panoptic schema . . . was destined to spread throughout the social body; its vocation was to become a generalized function" (1995:207).

Panopticon, as "an architecture transparent to the administration of power, made it possible to substitute for force or other violent constraints the gentle efficiency of total surveillance" (1984:217).

References: 1984, 1995.

Power

The concept of *power* is central to Foucault's thinking. Foucault does not locate power in macrostructures, whether economic or political, but instead sees power as diffused throughout the social system—dispersed, typically disguised through covert means—and manifested at a microlevel through local forms. Power is not an essence. It exists only in relationships, as *relations of power*.

The concept of power is not all negative for Foucault. Unlike *force*, which is purely repressive and stifles individual autonomy, power has a productive aspect, for it promotes particular subjectivities. Power regulates and shapes fields of possibility through actions and knowledge.

"Power is everywhere; not because it embraces everything, but because it comes from everywhere. . . . Power is not an institution, and not a structure; neither is it a certain strength we are endowed with; it is the name that one attributes to a complex strategical situation in a particular society" (1990:93).

"Power is not something that is acquired, seized, or shared. . . . Power is exercised from innumerable points, in the interplay of nonegalitarian and mobile relations. . . . Power comes from below. . . . Power relations are both intentional and nonsubjective. . . . Where there is power, there is resistance" (1990:94–95).

References: 1980, 1990, 1995.

Resistance

For Foucault *resistance* is an aspect of relations of power. Like power, it takes on local forms. Resistance often is a reverse form of power. It is sometimes easier to identify power through the manifestations of forms of resistance. In his later work on the formation of personhood through "technologies of the self" Foucault started to explore how people develop everyday strategies of resistance to such techniques.

"Where there is power, there is resistance, and yet, or rather consequently, this resistance is never in a position of exteriority in relation to power. Should it be said that one is always 'inside' power, there is no 'escaping' it, there is no absolute outside where it is concerned, because one is subject to the law in any case? . . . This would be to misunderstand the strictly relational character of power relationships. Their existence depends on a multiplicity of points of resistance" (1990:95).

"And it is doubtless the strategic codification of these points of resistance that makes a revolution possible, somewhat similar to the way in which the state relies on the institutional integration of power relationships" (1990:96).

References: 1990.

Self/Subjectivity

Self is an outcome of historical developments. It is not an essence. Self does not exist outside established forms of knowledge and institutionalized practices. Foucault examines the multiple forms of knowledge that constitute self as "object" for analysis and understanding and constitute particular identities or subjectivities, whether as "medicalized self," "sexual self," or psychiatrically defined self. He included the model of "rational self" that is invoked in scientific knowledge. In later phases of his work Foucault expanded on concepts of self-knowledge and self-government, how individuals take upon themselves to direct the self through *technologies of the self.* He sought a new understanding of modes of "care of the self" as an "ethics of self."

"My work has dealt with three modes of objectification which transform human beings into subjects. The first is the modes of inquiry which try to give themselves the status of sciences. . . . In the second part of my work, I have studied the objectivizing of the subject in what I shall call 'dividing practices.' . . . Finally, I have sought to study . . . the way a human being turns him- or herself into a subject. For example, I have chosen the domain of sexuality—how men have learned to recognize themselves as subjects of 'sexuality'" (1982:208).

"This form of power applies itself to immediate everyday life which categorizes the individual, marks him by his own individuality, attaches him to his own identity, imposes a law of truth on him which he must recognize and which others have to recognize in him. It is a form of power which makes individuals subjects. There are two meanings of the word subject: subject to someone else by control and dependence, and tied to his own identity by a conscience or self-knowledge. Both meanings suggest a form of power which subjugates and makes subject to" (1982:212).

"The subject constitutes himself in an active fashion, by the practices of self, these practices are nevertheless not something that the individual invents by himself. They are patterns that he finds in his culture and which are proposed, suggested and imposed on him by his culture, his society and his social group" (1988a:11).

"Technologies of the self . . . permit individuals to effect by their own means or with the help of others a certain number of operations on their own bodies and souls, thoughts, conduct, and way of being, so as to transform themselves in order to attain a certain state of happiness, purity, wisdom, perfection, or immortality" (1988a:18).

References: 1982, 1985, 1986, 1988a.

WORKS BY MICHEL FOUCAULT

1972. *The archaeology of knowledge*, and *The discourse on language*, Translated by A. M. Sheridan Smith. New York: Pantheon.

1973a. *Madness and civilization: A history of insanity in the age of reason*, Translated by Richard Howard. New York: Vintage/Random House.

1973b. *The order of things: An archaeology of the human sciences.* New York: Vintage/Random House.

1975. *The birth of the clinic: An archaeology of medical perception.* Translated by A. M. Sheridan Smith. New York: Vintage.

1977. History of systems of thought: Course description of Foucault's first year at Collège de France. In D. F. Bouchard, ed., and D. F. Bouchard and Sherry Simon, trans., *Michel Foucault: Language, countermemory, practice: Selected essays and interviews*, pp. 199–204. Ithaca, N.Y.: Cornell University Press.

1980. *Power/knowledge: Selected interviews and other writings, 1972–77*. Edited by Colin Gordon. New York: Pantheon.

1982. The subject and power. In H. L. Dreyfus and Paul Rabinow, eds., *Michel Foucault: Beyond structuralism and hermeneutics*, pp. 208–26. Chicago: University of Chicago Press.

1984. *The Foucault reader*. Edited by Paul Rabinow. New York: Pantheon.

1985. *The use of pleasure*, vol. 2 of *The history of sexuality*. New York: Random House.

1986. *The care of the self*, vol. 3 of *The history of sexuality*. New York: Random House.

1988a. *Technologies of the self: A seminar with Michel Foucault*. Edited by Luther H. Martin, Huck Gutman, and Patrick H. Hutton. Amherst: University of Massachusetts Press.

1988b. *Michel Foucault: Politics, philosophy: Interviews and other writings, 1977–84*. Edited by Lawrence D. Kritzman. London: Routledge.

1990. *Introduction*, vol. 1 of *The history of sexuality*. 1978. Reprint, New York: Random House.

1991. *The Foucault effect: Studies in governmentality*. Edited by Graham Burchell, Colin Gordon, and Peter Miller. Chicago: University of Chicago Press.

1995. *Discipline and punish: The birth of the prison*. 2d ed. Edited and translated Alan sSheridan. 1977. Translation, New York: Vintage.

ADRIENNE S. CHAMBON is associate professor at the University of Toronto, Faculty of Social Work, where she teaches theory, clinical practice, and research methodology. She is developing a critical reflexive understanding of the social work profession. Expanding on *Essays on Postmodernism and Social Work* (1994, coedited with Allan Irving), she has examined micropractices at the intersection of clinical acts and institutional arrangements. She is also involved in two projects, one on the therapeutic dialogue, the other on the bridging of communities and the meaning of social ties for refugees who are survivors of torture.

JOHN DEVINE is director of the School Partnership Program at the Metropolitan Center for Urban Education and adjunct professor at New York University's School of Education. He is the author of *Maximum Security: The Culture of Violence in Inner-City Schools* (1996) and of several articles dealing with the phenomenon of violence in American schools. He has collaborated on a volume entitled *Staying in School: Partnerships for Educational Change* (1995), which describes his efforts and those of other universities throughout New York State to motivate and encourage "at-risk" students to remain in school, complete their studies, and seek their highest potential.

For the past fourteen years he has directed and trained teams of NYU graduate students who provide individualized instruction and mentoring for students in some of the most troubled schools in New York City. He was the recipient of an award from the Harry Frank Guggenheim Foundation that enabled him to continue and expand his research into a broader spectrum of schools. A former Jesuit priest, he holds degrees in theology, anthropology, and international education and is investigating effective approaches to preventing school violence through a grant from the U.S. Department of Education.

LAURA EPSTEIN, who died in September 1996, was professor emeritus at the University of Chicago School of Social Service Administration where she had taught since 1973. She became known as a leader in social work for the approach she developed with William Reid, *Task Centered Casework* (1972) and *Task-Centered Practice* (1977). She expanded this work into brief treatment models (*Helping People: The Task-Centered Approach*, 1980, 1988, and *Brief Treatment and a New Look at the Task-Centered Approach*, 1992). She had been immersed since the late 1980s in a major critical history project to reexamine the foundations of the social work profession, entitled Origins/The Therapeutic Idea. She lectured and wrote extensively in this area.

CATHERINE E. FOOTE, who holds master's degrees in sociology and social work, is a therapist and researcher who has been studying grief since 1987, primarily at the Alberta Children's Hospital in Calgary, Alberta, Canada. She is now a doctoral candidate in the Faculty of Social Work at the University of Toronto; her dissertation develops a Foucauldian analysis of bereaved parents. Using a feminist perspective, she also publishes on the topic of adult women whose mothers have died.

ARTHUR W. FRANK is professor of sociology at the University of Calgary in Calgary, Alberta, Canada. He is the author of *At the Will of the Body: Reflections on Illness* (1991) and *The Wounded Storyteller: Body, Illness, and Ethics* (1995). His recent writings on Foucault have appeared in the journals *Body and Society* and *Health*.

During the 1998-99 academic year, ALLAN IRVING was a professor at the Center for Social Work Education at Widener University in Pennsylvania. He has been an associate professor at the Faculty of Social Work at the University of Toronto for the past fifteen years. His main research and teaching interests are the history and philosophy of social work and social welfare, social policy, and the influence of contemporary and pop culture on social work. He is the editor with Adrienne Chambon of *Essays on Postmodernism and Social Work* (1994), coauthor with Donald Bellamy and Harriet Parsons of *Neighbors: Three Social Settlements in Downtown Toronto* (1995), and author of *Doctor to the World: A Biography of Brock Chishom* (1998).

KEN MOFFAT is an assistant professor in the School of Social Work, Atkinson College, York University, Toronto. His research interests include the microanalysis of knowledge, power, and subjectivity in direct practice, and the historical constitution of social work and social welfare knowledge.

CAROL-ANNE O'BRIEN teaches community work in the Faculty of Social Work, Wilfrid Laurier University, Waterloo, Ontario. Her research interests are sexuality in social work and social policy, community action for equity in social services, and community development in Ireland and the European Union. She is active in lesbian and gay community groups in Dublin and Toronto.

NIGEL PARTON is professor of child care and director of the Centre for Applied Childhood Studies at the University of Huddersfield, Huddersfield, England. He is the author of numerous articles, chapters, and books in the areas of social work, social theory, and child welfare. His books include *The Politics of Child Abuse* (1985); *Governing the Family* (1991); (as editor) *Social Theory, Social Change, and Social Work* (1996); and (with David Thorpe and Corinne Wattam) *Child Protection: Risk and the Moral Order* (1997). He is editing a book with Corinne Wattam on child sexual abuse, and another with Patrick O'Byrne, *Constructive Social Work*, which develops and applies narrative and social constructionist approaches to social work practice.

FRANK T. Y. WANG obtained his master's degree in social work from Columbia University and his Ph.D. from the University of Toronto, Faculty of Social Work. His thesis, "Disciplining Taiwanese Families," explores the everyday operation of family ideology in the context of home care in Taiwan, where Western-style professionalism dominates. He teaches on aging in National Yang Ming University Institute of Health and Welfare Policy.